PATRIOT OR TRAITOR

Sir Walter Ralegh in 1588 (artist unknown)

Patriot or Traitor

The Life and Death of Sir Walter Ralegh

ANNA BEER

ONEWORLD

A Oneworld Book

First published by Oneworld Publications, 2018

ISBN 978-1-78607-434-8
eISBN 978-1-78607-435-5

Illustrations: 1588 portrait © Hi-Story/Alamy; Ralegh Cadiz portrait © GL Archive/Alamy; Earl of Essex Cadiz portrait © ART Collection/Alamy; Hilliard miniature © World History Archive/Alamy; Ralegh and son © Granger Historical Picture Archive/Alamy; Ralegh at the head of the Queen's Guard, courtesy of South West Heritage Trust (held at Somerset Archives and Local Studies, ref. DD/SAS/C1193/28); Tower of London © Antiqua Print Gallery/Alamy; letter to Queen Anne, courtesy of the National Archives (Public Record Office, Kew, Surrey, SP14/67); *The Way the Indians Fished* by John White © North Wind Picture Archives/Alamy; John White's 'The Towne of Pomeiock…' and map © Photo 12/Alamy; Elizabeth I miniature © Victoria & Albert Museum/ Bridgeman; James I © National Galleries of Scotland/Bridgeman; Henry, Prince of Wales © Royal Collection Trust, Her Majesty Queen Elizabeth II, 2018/ Bridgeman; Lady Ralegh © Granger Historical Picture Archive/Alamy

Typeset by Tetragon, London
Printed and bound in Great Britain by Clays Ltd, Elcograf S.p.A.

Oneworld Publications
10 Bloomsbury Street
London WC1B 3SR
England

For Becca and Elise

Contents

Note on spelling, orthography and pronunciation

All spelling and orthography have been modernised, except for the occasional moment when the difficulties of understanding the original text are outweighed by the insight – and pleasure – to be gained from a direct encounter with the remarkable language of Ralegh's own time. Readers who wish to enjoy the letters and other documents in their original form should turn to *Sir Walter Ralegh in his own words*, where works such as Youings' and Latham's 1999 edition of the *Letters* are listed.

Sir Walter's contemporaries wrote his surname as Raleigh, Raliegh, Ralegh, Raghley, Rawley, Rawly, Rawlic, Rawlcigh, Raulighe, Raughlie and Rayly. This is hardly a surprise. A well-known playwright never signed his name Shakespeare, preferring (usually, but not always) Shakspere. I have chosen Ralegh because that, more often than not, was Sir Walter's own spelling, and he used it consistently in later life.

As for how to pronounce Ralegh, I spent many years calling him 'Raw–lee' (the evidence being the punning attacks of his hostile contemporaries) but now prefer his name to rhyme with barley. We are slightly clearer about Ralegh's own pronunciation of his first name: a deep, Devonian 'Water'.

The scaffold: Winchester

A SCAFFOLD IS BEING built beneath his window, 'twelve feet square and railed about'. He knows what is coming, because he has been told.

Since you have been found guilty of these horrible treasons, the judgement of the court is that you shall be had from hence to the place whence you came, there to remain until the day of execution. And from thence you shall be drawn upon a hurdle through the open streets to the place of execution, there to be hanged and cut down alive, and your body shall be opened, your heart and bowels plucked out, and your privy members cut off, and thrown into the fire before your eyes; then your head to be stricken off from your body, and your body shall be divided into four quarters, to be disposed of at the king's pleasure.

And God have mercy on your soul.

He knows what is coming, because he has watched two other traitors, Catholic priests William Watson and William Clarke, being hung, drawn and quartered just days before. It was 'very bloodily handled for they were both cut down alive', tutted one spectator. Then again, for most, that was the whole point of the exercise – to force the guilty to confront their own corruption through witnessing their own disembowelling and dismemberment. Despite the bloody handling both men die 'boldly', Clarke seeing himself as a martyr, Watson aggressively unrepentant and delighting in his treason or, as he saw it, his perfectly reasonable demand for religious toleration for his fellow Catholics. Their quarters are now 'set on Winchester gates and their heads on the first tower of the castle' as a lesson to all, their traitors' hearts already displayed on the scaffold, the public proof of their hidden treachery.

As the priests' carcasses begin rotting, another traitor, George Brooke, is beheaded in the castle yard. Brooke is of the nobility, his brother a lord, so he avoids being hung, drawn and quartered; he will merely be decapitated. His is a better death than that of the priests, at least from the point of view of the authorities. Not 'bold'; Brooke meets 'a patient and constant end', according to the King's chief minister, Robert Cecil, who is taking notes. And yet, even at the last, Brooke only admits to 'errors' not 'crimes', and at the holding up of the traitor's head, when the executioner cries 'God save the King', he is 'not seconded by the voice of any one man but the sheriff'. Is it revulsion or apathy on the part of the crowd? It is hard to tell. Few people come to watch, and only a couple of 'men of quality'.

The Bishop of Winchester, who has prepared George Brooke well for his 'constant end', does his rounds of the remaining traitors, including Brooke's older brother Henry, Lord Cobham, and Sir Walter Ralegh. The Bishop has instructions from King James – to 'prepare them for their ends as likewise to bring them to liberal confessions and by that means reconcile the contradictions'.

The Crown, troubled by the refusal of their two high-profile prisoners to admit their treason, is haunted by the 'contradictions' in the testimonies of Ralegh and Cobham. King James desires not merely that justice be done, but that justice is seen to be done. The Bishop finds Ralegh 'well-settled and resolved to die a Christian and a good Protestant', which is all very well, but 'for the point of confession he found him so strait-laced that he would yield to no part of Cobham's accusation'.

Dealing with Watson and Clarke had been straightforward in comparison. The priests had planned to launch a surprise attack on the royal court at Greenwich on Midsummer's Night. The King would be kidnapped and then held hostage in the Tower of London, until he granted the prize of religious tolerance: a Utopian ideal for those, both Catholics and evangelical Protestants, whose beliefs took them beyond the bounds set by the Church of England. To that end, any royal ministers who stood in the way of toleration would be removed. In their more fanciful moments, the conspirators saw themselves in the ministers' places. In their even more fanciful moments, they believed this could be achieved without violence. Ideally, the King himself would convert to Catholicism. Watson even looked forward to discussing the finer points of religion with the theologically minded James I.

The attack never happened.

The priests' plot had been doomed from the beginning. Robert Cecil knew of it in early June, only a few months after the death of Queen Elizabeth and the peaceful succession of the Stuarts to the throne of England, in the shape of James VI of Scotland. Cecil's personal loyalties would be sorely tested by the revelation that one of the conspirators was his brother-in-law: Robert's beloved wife, until her early death in childbirth some eight years earlier, had been Elizabeth Brooke. Cecil's political loyalty was, however, never in doubt. He had the situation under control. For years during the late Queen's reign he and his fellow Privy Councillors had carefully fostered divisions amongst Catholics. While one man talked treason, another turned informer. By July the leaders, if that is the right word for such a shambolic and fractured conspiracy, were being rounded up. Sir George Brooke was the highest-placed gentleman to be questioned, drawn to the conspiracy, as was another knight, Sir Griffin Markham, because of political rather than religious frustration: neither had received the advancement under the new King that he had hoped or expected. Interrogated on 15 July, Sir George gave the Crown everything they needed to know, and more. Not only were Watson and Clarke now marked men, but Brooke revealed a second strand of treachery, one involving his brother, Lord Cobham, and his brother's close friend, Sir Walter Ralegh. Bankrolled by Spain, Cobham and Ralegh sought nothing less than the death of the King and had their own monarch-in-waiting to take his place. These were indeed 'horrible treasons'.

The following day, the Crown issued a proclamation for the arrest of William Watson ('a man of the lowest sort', about thirty-six years of age, 'his hair betwixt abram [auburn] and flaxen, he looketh asquint, and is very purblind'). It took less than three weeks to find the short-sighted priest, in a field near Hay-on-Wye on the Anglo-Welsh border. By 10 August he too had confessed all. Three days later, William Clark was arrested in Worcester. It was the end of the line for the priests, who had been ordained in France some twenty years earlier, and sent almost immediately and in secret ('brought of the sea in mariner's apparel') to do the Catholic God's work in Protestant England. Years of imprisonments, escapes and further imprisonments had followed for both men, a familiar dance between the Protestant state and the Catholic insurgents, all conducted in the great houses of England and their rather useful priest holes. Marshalsea, Bridewell, the Gatehouse; whipping, grinding in the mill, racking: Watson even had the nerve to complain Her Majesty Queen Elizabeth didn't know what went on in her own prisons.

Her ministers certainly knew. Twenty years earlier, in 1583, Francis Walsingham, the late Queen's minister for national security, was dealing with a Catholic who would not talk: Francis Throckmorton. Spymaster Walsingham simply sent him back for more, this time to Mr Norton, the notorious 'rackmaster'. He was quite sure the prisoner would not hold out again: 'I have seen as resolute men as Throckmorton stoop, notwithstanding the great show he hath made of Roman resolution. I suppose the grief of the last torture will suffice without any extremity of racking to make him more conformable than he hath hitherto shown himself'. Walsingham was right. When Throckmorton was placed on the rack again on 19 November and 'before he was strained to any purpose', he confessed. No wonder George Brooke, new to this world of sedition and torture, was 'conformable', swiftly giving up Ralegh and Cobham, his own brother, as traitors.

It was now their turn to die. To the last, Sir Walter Ralegh continues to hope. When, on Sunday 4 December, the Bishop of Winchester, attending now to Sir Walter's soul rather than seeking a 'liberal' confession, visits the prisoner, he finds in him a 'lingering expectation of life'. There is still just over a week until the date set for his execution, Monday the twelfth, and Ralegh attempts one last appeal to the King's mercy, throwing in an assertion of his own innocence: 'I never invented treason, consented to treason, performed treason'. He begs James for just one year of respite, Faustus-like in his attempt to bargain at the last for just a little more time.

Any expectation of life dies with George Brooke's execution. In its place, a furious energy overtakes the prisoner. Ralegh's keeper writes he has been 'very importunate with me twice or thrice'. He simply must see his wife, Bess, and some others of his closest friends. Sir Walter is still trying to salvage something from the wreckage, with the keeper noting, in awe but also with some scepticism, that there's '£50,000 (as he saith)' that Ralegh wants to pass to his survivors 'in trust'.

While Ralegh's loyal friends, John Shelbury and Thomas Harriot, liaise with the Privy Council about his estate, the prisoner writes to Bess, his 'dear wife'. Husband and wife have been separated for weeks. A letter is all he can offer, but it is a controlled, intense expression of love. The message is simple and passionate: Walter sends his love to Bess, and he asks her to keep it for him, for ever.

> You shall now receive (my dear wife) my last words in these my last lines. My love I send you, that you may keep it when I am dead, and my counsel, that you may remember it when I am no more.

He asks his 'dear Bess' to face her grief with her customary strength: to 'bear it patiently and with a heart like your self'. He offers her 'all the thanks which my heart can conceive or my words can express' for her tireless work, her 'travails', on his behalf. He cannot repay her, at least not in this world.

He also looks to the future, her future. She will be on her own and must work to save herself and her 'miserable fortunes' and, crucially, the 'right' of their child, young Walter, still only ten years old. She should not grieve: 'thy mourning cannot avail me: I am but dust'. He doesn't ask for much, only that she and their son should live 'free from want' – this from the man who had once owned, it was said, shoes encrusted with jewels worth more than six thousand six hundred gold pieces – for 'the rest is but vanity'. And he offers her God as her new husband and father, a husband and father 'which cannot be taken from you', although in the same breath, he acknowledges a second marriage would 'be best for you, both in respect of the world and of God'. As if to convince her she is now free, he insists that:

> as for me, I am no more yours, nor you mine. Death has cast us asunder and God hath divided me from the world and you from me. Remember your poor child for his father's sake, who chose you and loved you in his happiest times.

In the midst of his agony, Ralegh transports himself and his 'dear Bess' back in imagination some twelve or thirteen years, to their 'happiest' time when anything seemed possible.

The letter oscillates uneasily but honestly between words of intense emotional and psychological import and practical, mundane concerns: 'Bayley owes me £200 and Adrian Gilbert £600', or 'Get those letters (if it be possible) which I writ to the lords wherein I sued for my life. God is my witness, it was for you and yours I desired life. But it is true that I disdain my self for begging it'. Walter goes on to assure Bess he is a 'true man, and one who, in his own respect, despises death, and all his misshapen and ugly shapes'. Is this a reference to hanging, drawing and quartering, the death he faced?

The defiance and courage can only be sustained so far. His farewell is heartrending:

> I cannot write much. God knows how hardly I steal this time while others sleep, and it is also high time that I should separate my thoughts from the world. Beg my dead body which living was denied thee, and either lay it at Sherborne (if the land continue)

or in Exeter church by my father and mother. I can say no more, time and death call me away.

The everlasting, powerful, infinite and omnipotent God, that Almighty God who is goodness itself, the true life and true light, keep thee and thine. Have mercy on me and teach me to forgive my persecutors and accusers, and send us to meet in his glorious kingdom.

My dear wife farewell. Bless my poor boy. Pray for me and let my good God hold you both in his arms. Written with the dying hand of sometime thy husband but now (alas) overthrown.

Yours that was, but now not my own

WR

This would be one of the iconic letters of its century, copied and copied and copied again, but that would come later. At the time, most people thought they knew what they were seeing: a once-great man, the late Queen Elizabeth's favourite, now brought low. Ralegh had been 'deciphered' as the 'ugliest traitor that ever was heard of in England'. His 'overweening wit' had, at last, been exposed. He was, he always had been, too clever by half.

> Now may you see the sudden fall
> Of him that thought to climb full high
> A man well known unto you all
> Whose state you see doth stand Rawlie.

Hated, despised, wings burnt, Sir Walter was falling, although being Sir Walter, his compelling voice could still be heard even in its 'dying moan'.

> I pity that the summer's nightingale
> Immortal Cynthia's sometimes dear delight
> That used to sing so sweet a madrigal
> Should like an owl go wander in the night

Hated of all, and pitied of none
Though swan-like now he makes his dying moan.

Most did not bother with the pity. Cheap print pamphlets, or 'libels', the tabloids of their time, accused him of atheism, Machiavellianism, unspeakable vices, but above all, of complicity in the fall of the Earl of Essex, the late Queen's other great favourite in the final decade or so of her rule. No matter that the 'hellish verses' being circulated by the 'atheist and traitor' in which Ralegh says 'what god I do not know, nor greatly care' were in fact lifted from an anonymous play printed in 1594. Those who were reaping the benefit of Sir Walter's fall were enjoying this riot of fake news. Robert Cecil kept a few choice items in his papers. You could throw anything at Ralegh that winter and it would stick.

The clock ticks down. Now it is time for Henry, Lord Cobham to take the final sacrament. To the last, he asserts his one-time friend Ralegh's guilt, but only in the lesser charges against him. It is not much, but perhaps he hopes to save Ralegh from his own fate, to offer a final, if lukewarm, gesture of friendship. On the scaffold, Cobham is composed and dignified: a wit noted 'we might see by him it is an easier matter to die well then live well'.

How had it come to this?

PART ONE

I

Soldier

How does Ralegh, a man whose year of birth we do not even know for sure, the fifth son of a Devonshire gentleman, 'climb full high' in the England of Elizabeth? He begins by going to the wars. In young Walter's case, the year was 1569, and the battleground was France. Earlier in the decade, a massacre of French Protestants, Huguenots, had triggered the country's wars of religion. The young Queen Elizabeth, only three years into her own Protestant reign, made a secret treaty with her co-religionists and, over the following years, a steady stream of Englishmen travelled across the Channel to offer their military support to the Huguenots. The teenaged Walter Ralegh was one, under the command of Count Lodewijk van Nassau, brother of William the Silent, the Netherlands' Prince of Orange. The details are hazy: Walter rode 'as a very young man' with his cousin Henry Champernowne's troop; another source claims his early years were full of 'wars and martial services'. It is possible he was recruited by a Huguenot ship sent out from La Rochelle, or a 'sea-beggar' from Holland, with their 'letters of marque' (of extremely dubious authority) from William of Orange or Gaspard de Coligny, the French Huguenot leader. The boats descended on English ports to find young men just like Walter. Once in France, he found himself in the midst of a protracted, and sometimes vicious, civil war.

Ralegh's future brother-in-law, Arthur Throckmorton, made a similar expedition, ten years later, but to the Low Countries. He was impelled by the same reason, to support the beleaguered Protestants, and his diary is a reminder of the quotidian nature of violence in wartime. He writes, with neither comment nor horror, that the English have captured the enemy's 'kine [cattle], mares and horses' and that some spies 'are taken and put to death in our camp'.

There is no diary for Walter. The only detail of his experience is provided by him, many years later. He writes he was at Moncontour near Poitiers in October 1569 (he would have been in his mid-teens) when Lodowick of Nassau's competent retreat had 'saved the one half of the Protestant army, then broken and disbanded; of which my self was an eye-witness, and was one of them that had cause to thank him for it'. A strategic retreat is valued much more than empty heroics. The foundation had been laid for Ralegh's fascination with realpolitik and the art of war.

The Peace of St Germain of August 1570, which marked the end of the third phase of wars of religion in France, probably meant a return home for young Walter. England was facing its own religious crisis. On 25 February 1570, Pope Pius V had declared Elizabeth illegitimate, a mere usurper, a Prince due no obedience from her subjects. By doing so, he was explicitly giving sanction to Roman Catholics to assassinate her. They would even gain merit by doing so. If that was not enough to stiffen the sinews of a true Protestant Englishman, then the 1572 St Bartholomew's Day massacre of French Huguenots in Paris raised the stakes still further.

But there is no indication the teenaged Walter went to the wars out of religious zeal. It was more that this was simply what young men did, particularly young men without titles or prospects and in search of both. For Arthur Throckmorton ten years later, a return from the wars meant one thing and one thing only: a chance to gain access to the Queen. Although he sent news to his mother Anne, and his sister Bess, that he was safely landed in Margate, his primary destination was Richmond Palace, where the Queen was based for the Christmas season that year. Arthur partied, celebrating Twelfth Night at the palace, and only in the new year did he return home. He had been seen.

It helped that Arthur was a Throckmorton, with family in high places. Ralegh was not only a fifth son but the product of a third marriage on the part of his father, Walter Ralegh, who had three other sons, and a second marriage on the part of his mother, Katherine Gilbert, née Champernoun, who had four other sons. Yes, he would be helped, and occasionally hindered, by a vast network of brothers and half-brothers and cousins in a world in which kinship ties could be the difference between success and failure; sometimes between life and death. But in the late 1560s and early 1570s, Walter was just one of hundreds of young men who went to the wars and then disappeared without trace. In 1577, long after he'd gone to be a soldier, he was living in Islington which, by any Elizabethan measure, is a long way from Richmond Palace.

Three years later, however, we can tell his prospects were improving. Not because he was on the receiving end of three charges of brawling but because one of them was 'besides the tennis court in Westminster', a popular location for the settling of scores with other young men. No more Islington: it was around this time that Walter Ralegh was appointed Extraordinary Esquire of the Body to the Queen, personally attendant upon his monarch.

Ireland effected the transformation. In the summer of 1579, with Elizabeth's court preoccupied by the possibility of a marriage between the Queen and the Duke of Anjou, and with both parties apparently considering the marriage as a serious proposition for serious political reasons, not least the increasing power of Spain, rebellion broke out in Ireland. This was hardly a new phenomenon. Ever since the Anglo-Norman invasion of the island in the twelfth century there had been conflict, whether simmering or outright, between the native Irish and the feudal lords who pledged their loyalty to the King of England. The 1560s had been a decade of on-off warfare in Ireland, although well into the seventies there were those who still hoped that the English could reduce the island to 'civility' by peaceful means: 'Can the sword teach them to speak English, to use English apparel, to restrain them?'

In 1579, the threat level rose. Under the banner of the Pope, the Irish leader James Fitzmaurice Fitzgerald gathered an expedition-ary force from Catholic Europe. His goal was nothing less than the removal of the Protestant 'she-tyrant', Elizabeth. The she-tyrant asked one of Walter Ralegh's half-brothers, Humphrey Gilbert, to patrol the south coast of Ireland. It was not his finest hour. Gilbert failed to pay his sailors, who promptly disappeared with two of the ships. Gilbert himself lost £2,000. Another rebellion followed in August, this time led by the Earl of Desmond. But then the military tide turned. Fewer than a thousand English troops engaged twelve hundred Irish, at Monasternenagh near Limerick, and won. Desmond was proclaimed a traitor, and the suppression of the rebellion became 'an exercise in reducing the Earl's strongholds one by one, ravaging his lands and forcing the submission of his suspected allies, while a naval task force prevented any foreign reinforcements arriving from abroad', in the words of the historian Paul Hammer, in his book on Elizabeth's wars. The Queen chose Arthur, 14th Lord Grey of Wilton (the recently appointed Lord Deputy of Ireland) to complete this 'exercise' in the summer of 1580, and he duly brought more than two thousand new men. Amongst them was one Captain Ralegh, with his hundred men, levied in London in July. As the summer faded, the younger brother of the Earl of Desmond was hung, drawn and quartered for his part in the rebellion. It was reported Captain Ralegh's men played a part in cutting up the body into small pieces, an act praised by a contemporary historian, who noted, happily, that 'thus the pestilent hydra hath lost another of his heads'. Lord Grey set the tone for the campaign, being a man fuelled by a hatred of Catholicism and a desire to crush the Irish, ironically through the use of the same methods as the notorious Duke of Alba, the Spanish scourge of the Low Countries.

Despite these successes, Irish submission proved hard to achieve. An unexpected uprising in Leinster was swiftly followed by the arrival of six hundred new Spanish and Italian troops in the south west of Ireland at Smerwick (now Ard na Caithne) in September. They took the opportunity to land when Elizabeth's ships were forced to sail for

supply and maintenance. A forceful response was needed and by mid-
October 1580 the Queen had committed 6,500 Englishmen to Ireland,
with another thirteen hundred on their way. Their strategic goal was
the reclaiming of the small earth fort at Smerwick, which was duly
surrounded from the sea by royal warships, which could join in the
land bombardment. Smerwick surrendered to Lord Grey within days
despite his offering no terms to those inside the fort. At the surrender, the Spanish officers were spared, but all the other defenders were
killed, the majority by troops under the command of Captain Ralegh.

There have been attempts to justify the massacre at Smerwick.
Those killed were mercenaries; the Spanish commander, more fool he,
surrendered knowing no assurances had been given; those surrender-
ing could expect nothing better; by the standards of sixteenth-century
warfare, it really wasn't too bad. Even if one puts aside the horror,
however, Smerwick proved about as successful as other English wartime massacres. Over the next two years some fifteen hundred 'chief
men and gentlemen' were executed in an attempt to enforce English
rule, a number that does not include the uncounted 'meaner sort'. But
still the Irish forces grew.

Ralegh's letters from this time do not dwell on these aspects of
war, in part because he has to write about everyday matters (such as
paying his men) and in part because he *wants* to write about high-
level policy. His correspondent is Francis Walsingham, the Queen's
Principal Secretary and master of 'intelligence'. With each letter Walter
shows increasing confidence, sometimes writing again within a couple
of days, certain Walsingham will listen. He supplies up-to-date news
from the front line ('Davy Barrey has broken and burnt all his castles
and entered publicly into the action of rebellion') but also begins to
offer political advice. Elizabeth, having spent a further £100,000 on the
war, has made a mistake by appointing an Irish 'president' of Munster,
the Earl of Ormond. He'd been in post for two years, but 'there are a
thousand traitors more than there were the first day'. (Ironically, the
placatory Earl of Ormond had been appointed in a conciliatory move
because all-out war was proving both expensive and futile.) Ralegh

recommends his own half-brother, Humphrey Gilbert, for the post, despite or because of his reputation for savagery and violence, reminding Walsingham that Gilbert suppressed a rebellion in two months with only a third of the men, and is the most 'feared' among the Irish nation. 'The end shall prove this to be true'. In another sign of his growing confidence, and in a move which would become characteristic of the mature man, Ralegh offers to serve the Queen privately, with 'a dozen or ten horse'. He knows he's pushing the envelope, and asks Walsingham to 'take my bold writing in good part'. Walsingham did nothing, at least not in 1581. But the fact this letter was written on the day his father was buried in faraway Exeter shows Captain Ralegh's priorities. Family was important: political preferment, through soldiering, was more important.

Ralegh's experiences in Ireland were a world away from those of the man who would become his most significant political rival in later years. Robert Devereux, the young Earl of Essex, gained his first taste of war when he joined his stepfather, Robert Dudley Earl of Leicester's, expedition to the Low Countries in 1585. This was the first official English army for a generation to be sent abroad; the military follow-up to Queen Elizabeth's proclamation on 14 August of that year that she was, at last, taking the Netherlands under her protection. This proclamation of 1585 precipitated war with Spain and would dominate Ralegh's life and inform his politics for years to come.

The Queen appointed the Earl of Essex as colonel general of the cavalry (no captain, let alone foot soldier, he) and he was present at the battle at Zutphen in September 1586, where the great English hero Sir Philip Sidney was killed. The dying Sidney bequeathed the young Earl his best sword (some say he bequeathed his *two* best swords) and the Earl of Leicester made his stepson a knight. No matter the expedition's military aims remained unachieved and fighting was sporadic. Essex saw himself as a 'second Sidney', a martial hero, and took every opportunity to live the military dream. In 1589 he would join Sir Francis Drake and Sir John Norris's expedition to Portugal, without the Queen's permission. Two years later, this time with Elizabeth's blessing, he led English troops in Normandy, although he could not resist conferring twenty-four knighthoods during the campaign, twenty-four more than he was authorised to do. Both ventures were military failures, but Essex, if only by right of birth, remained England's 'senior aristocratic soldier', in the words of one biographer.

Back in 1581, mere Captain Ralegh, approaching his thirties, was becoming frustrated with the attritional reality of the guerrilla warfare he was being forced to wage against the Irish. He'd come to accept he had to supply his men with victuals from his own pocket and then plead for repayment (with some success, receiving £43, 14 shillings and 8 pence from the English authorities in Dublin for the wages of himself and his company for thirty-two days). But now, writing to Lord Grey from Cork, he complains he and his company have made 'two journeys', 'one in horrible weather and the other utterly bootless being done without draught [plan] or espiall [information from spying], and beside enforced to walk such unreasonable march'. The only result has been the laming of their own soldiers. There's bitterness (about a property he believed he should have had), and there's need: he wants another hundred soldiers to counter the enemy's 'galligass' (tall, strong men who carried battleaxes) and 'kerne' (lightly-armed foot-soldiers). This particular letter would be used by Grey as ammunition when he challenged the Queen's conciliatory policy. The zealous Protestant Grey was outraged that 'God's cause is made a second or nothing at all'.

Captain Ralegh, in contrast, is far more pragmatic, and far more self-serving, as demonstrated in a letter from this time recounting 'a hard escape' he'd achieved when set upon by fourteen horsemen and 'three score footmen'. He was hugely outnumbered, having only three horsemen and a couple of Irish footmen.

> I coveted to recover a little old castle and in that retire [retreat] I lost three men and three horses. The manner of mine own behaviour I leave to the report of others but the escape was strong to all men. The castle was a long mile off from the place where he first set on us.

Immediately, Ralegh moves into a request for more support from London and Dublin, a request authorised by his own heroism but also by his on-the-ground experience. He's straight-talking and hard-headed:

> There is great need of a supply in Munster for the bands are all much decayed…Beside the men are such poor and miserable creatures as their captains dare not lead them to serve. If your honours beheld them when they arrive here you would think them far unfit to fight for Her Majesty's crown.

Later, the story of the escape would get even better, and in interesting ways, in the hands of a sympathetic (to Ralegh), patriotic and imperialist historian, John Hooker. He lowers the number of horsemen attacking but adds Ralegh crossing the ford alone and going back to rescue his servant, Henry Moile, whose horse had foundered. It is one of the earliest stories to be attached to Ralegh's name, and shows him as a selfless leader, looking out for the ordinary man. Hooker is, of course, out to flatter his patron, but that so many of his contemporaries remember similar moments of generosity and even egalitarianism suggests Ralegh did indeed have these qualities.

Hooker's text, written later and with an eye to the New World and its 'savages', contains an element missing from Ralegh's own writings:

> For what can be more pleasant to God, than to gain and reduce in all Christianlike manner, a lost people to the knowledge of the gospel, and a true Christian religion, than which cannot be a more pleasant and a sweet sacrifice, and a more acceptable service before God?

For Hooker, as for Lord Grey, the priority in Ireland was the imposition of religion. That was the fundamental reason to establish English government. There were of course other compelling reasons, social, political and economic. The control of Ireland would enlarge 'the bounds of the English kingdom', and transfer 'the superfluous multitude of fruitless and idle people (here at home daily increasing) to travel, conquer, and manure another land', all of which would 'yield infinite commodities'. With or without the religiosity, it was a powerful, if profoundly flawed, vision; one that would run like a seam through the English imperial project over the coming centuries.

How to achieve the enlargement of the 'bounds of the English kingdom' when the Irish were still in Ireland was another question. Ralegh's half-brother, Humphrey Gilbert, colonel of Munster between 1569 and 1571, thought he knew, ordering the decapitation of entire villages in order to have the path to his tent decorated with 'a lane of heads' prior to inviting the submission of local chiefs and leaders. As Thomas Churchyard, propagandist for Gilbert's approach, expressed it, the sight of 'the heads of their dead fathers, brothers, children, kinsfolk and friends' brought 'great terror to the people' and made them seek peace under the new regime. Nearly thirty years later (and still no peace in Ireland), Edmund Spenser, the poet, to whom Ralegh would give his patronage in the late 1580s and early 1590s, proposed an approach possibly even more horrific than Gilbert's, even by the standards of English colonial policy at the time. Justifying his stance, spelt out in his *A View of the Present State of Ireland* (probably written in 1596, but unpublished in his lifetime), by insisting that the Irish are degenerate barbarians, Spenser advocates the use of martial law. This is controversial enough, but Spenser goes on to insist that famine is the best and quickest way to pacify the Irish. His words remain shocking more than four hundred years later. (Some would argue that Spenser intended the reader to question the extreme 'solution' offered by one of the participants in what is, after all, a fictional dialogue but, for me, this is a view born of modern discomfort with the work's viciousness.)

> The end will, I assure me, be very short, and much sooner than can be in so great a trouble, as it seemeth, hoped for. Although there should none of them fall by the sword nor be slain by the soldier, yet thus being kept from manurance and their cattle from running

abroad, by this hard restraint they would quickly consume themselves and devour one another. The proof whereof I saw sufficiently exampled in these late wars of Munster, for, notwithstanding that the same was a most rich and plentiful country, full of corn and cattle, that you would have thought they should have been able to stand long, yet ere one year and a half they were brought to such wretchedness as that any stony heart would have rued the same. Out of every corner of the woods and glens they came creeping forth upon their hands, for their legs could not bear them. They looked like anatomies of death; they spake like ghosts crying out of their graves; they did eat the dead carrions, happy where they could find them; yea, and one another soon after, insomuch as the very carcasses they spared not to scrape out of their graves. And if they found a plot of watercresses or shamrocks, there they flocked as to a feast for the time, yet not able long to continue there withal; that in short space there were none almost left, and a most populous and plentiful country suddenly left void of man and beast. Yet sure, in all that war there perished not many by the sword, but all by the extremity of famine which they themselves had wrought.

Ralegh never wrote anything as appalling as this, and he rarely offered religious justifications for violence, but that does not mean he somehow stands apart from men such as Hooker, Grey and Spenser, not to mention his half-brother, Humphrey Gilbert. As he would say, again and again, the end justified the means.

At the same time he never lost sight, because he never could, of the reality of military life. In Ireland, in the late 1570s and early 1580s, that reality was sick, hungry English soldiers and a daily diet of often futile violence. Later, he would write that he was running low on men 'because the new come men die so fast'. Others, understandably, attempted to escape. They were caught and hanged. Either way, the numbers went down. From the first, Captain Ralegh learned that, as much as anything else, war is about paying your soldiers. Day by day, he made his priority the feeding and payment (of eight pence a day) of his 'footband of one hundred men', writing back to base in pedantic detail about dates, times and costs.

Ralegh presents himself in his letters as the experienced military man but the truth was that he hated life in Ireland. He knew where he wanted to be: at court. On 26 August 1581, he wrote from Lismore to the Queen's favourite, Robert Dudley, the Earl of Leicester, making an abject offer of his service. He explains that he is in Ireland, serving Lord Grey, something he only does because he knows Grey 'to be one of yours'. It is only loyalty to Leicester that keeps him there. Without that, 'I would disdain it as much as to keep sheep'. Ireland is not a commonwealth, it's a 'common woe'.

A few months later, he escaped the 'common woe'; he was sent back to England with dispatches. It was a golden opportunity for the man whose ability to write powerfully in defence of himself and in support of policies, whose ability not just to create a good story but to embellish it, was never in doubt. Without getting his Irish commission, Captain Ralegh would not have come to Elizabeth's attention but without writing about it, he would not have stuck.

Ralegh knew how to get things done. He could justify the unjustifiable, while in the same breath standing up for the underdog. He knew how to cover his back and the backs of those more powerful than he. And he knew, or at least he said he knew, for whom he was doing everything he did. In one letter he can be outraged that five hundred 'milk kine' [cows] have been taken 'from the poor people. Some had but two, and some three, to relieve their poor wives and children, and in a strange country newly set down to build and plant' and, having expressed his outrage, in the same letter offer himself as the answer to the problem he has identified. The poor people will be protected. At three days' notice, Ralegh will 'raise her a better band, and arm it better tenfold, and better men, whensoever she shall need it'.

She is Elizabeth. And at the heart of what would become a most remarkable political intimacy was Ralegh's ability to make his Queen believe that he could deliver, or more cynically, that if he did not, he would be able to make it look as if he (and his monarch) had delivered.

That was all ahead of him. Returned to England in December of 1581, he caught the attention of the Queen herself, now in her late forties. She insisted that he remain. Apparently, he needed further training. Captain Ralegh, a soldier and sailor for thirteen years, needed no further training, but his Queen needed him near her, and Ralegh, ever the opportunist, needed no further encouragement. He'd made it to court.

Courtier

E VERYONE KNEW, and everyone said, that the court, any court, was dangerous, from the poet courtier Thomas Wyatt, who warned of the 'slipper top/Of court's estates' (and was charged with treason) to John Webster's remarkable, fascinating character Vittoria, the 'white devil' created by the playwright in 1612, whose last words are:

> O happy they that never saw the court,
> Nor ever knew great man but by report.

Everyone knew, and some complained, that success meant scrambling over the bodies (metaphorically in most but not all cases) of your rivals, or as John Webster's equally remarkable villain Bosola puts it in *The Duchess of Malfi*: 'places in the court are but like beds in the hospital, where this man's head lies at that man's foot, and so lower, and lower'.

Everyone knew, but took great care *not* to say, that Kings and Princes were often only one step away from losing their crown. Take Ralegh's own Queen. When Walter was born, in the early to mid-1550s, Protestant Princess Elizabeth, daughter of adulterous, executed Anne Boleyn, was still a prisoner of her older sister, the Catholic Mary Tudor. Few would have expected that, by the time Walter came of age, his Queen would have successfully consolidated her rule after the most precarious of starts. Her reign would be thirteen years old before a nobleman (Thomas Howard, Duke of Norfolk) was executed, for his part in a treasonous plot to oust Elizabeth. Thirteen years without a noble execution was a long time in Tudor politics, a measure of the Queen's strong and stable leadership.

The threats to Elizabeth remained, not least Mary, Queen of Scots's claim to the English throne. Mary had married her first husband Francis, the French *dauphin*, just before Elizabeth's accession in 1559, and boldly declared herself Queen of England just months into her cousin Elizabeth's reign. Mary continued to create problems, not least by producing a male heir in 1566. No matter that in the same year, Mary's husband, the eight-month-old baby James's father, was murdered, that Mary was abducted by Bothwell, who she then married and that when her son was just one year old, Mary was forced to abdicate, making her baby the King. Now there was King James VI of Scotland to consider, in addition to his provocative mother.

The traumatic and violent events of Mary Queen of Scots's life offered a stark warning to the young Elizabeth, who presented herself as being, and indeed was, a much more cautious, canny operator when it came to sexual politics. She had her moments, however. In the early months of her reign, Elizabeth's closest adviser was Robert Dudley, the man who had supported her through the years of imprisonment and uncertainty – her sweet Robin. Then, on 8 September 1560, Amy Robsart, Dudley's wife, was found with her neck broken at the foot of the stairs in her house (*her* house, because she and Dudley had lived apart for at least a year, Robert with his Queen, Amy in faraway Cumnor, just outside Oxford). Questions were, understandably, asked. Did she fall or was she pushed? Dudley himself wanted to have her death investigated, although perhaps 'more with an eye to the damage it might do to him than from grief at her loss' according to a biographer. The most damning evidence comes from the Spanish ambassador, reporting on Dudley's dangerous influence over the Queen (whom he persuaded to spend all her time hunting): he writes that the two were plotting the death of Dudley's wife. The ambassador is writing after the event, however, and although there was smoke, no one could find, or maybe no one wanted to find, a fire. And Elizabeth did not marry the newly-single Dudley. She did, however, make him Earl of Leicester some four years later and he remained the most powerful man at court.

The Queen's choice of husband was, predictably, the hottest topic in the early decades of her reign, but sanctioned or unsanctioned marriages amongst her courtiers ran it a close second. Among the elite, marriages were not personal but dynastic matters, with each alliance reconfiguring the political landscape in small or large ways. This was why they needed to be approved by the Queen. Elizabeth was full of praise for 'honest or honorable' marriages, 'without scandal and infamy'. These were pleasing to her, so long as they were 'orderly broken unto her'. And that was the issue: she wanted and needed to be in control and have full knowledge of these alliances to ensure her political security.

Eighteen years after the death of Amy Robsart, Leicester risked his position with a secret, unsanctioned marriage to Lettice Knollys, a cousin of the Queen. The Queen was certainly dismayed by the political disloyalty, perhaps dismayed by the emotional disloyalty, but probably unconcerned by the sexual disloyalty. Nevertheless, she forgave Leicester, as she would, again and again when her courtiers behaved badly, as long as there was no direct threat to her power, and as long as some form of public apology or punishment took place. Some, such as the historian Paul Hammer, see her as less forgiving of the women involved: Elizabeth 'continued to nurse a grudge against her cousin Lettice…for marrying the man she could not'.

It was a slippery, dangerous, exciting, glamorous world and Ralegh wanted nothing more than to be at its heart. He had not been born to it. Ralegh's father, Walter, was certainly of the gentry but not of the elite. His mother, Katherine, provided something of a link to the court, as her older sister was governess to the Princess and then Queen Elizabeth. As with soldiering, the Earl of Essex provides a stark contrast. Lettice Knollys was Essex's mother: that helped. Robert Devereux succeeded to his title when he was not yet eleven years of age. He was immediately placed in wardship under William Cecil, Lord Burghley, master of the Court of Wards and the Queen's most trusted minister from the earliest days of her reign and spent a brief period in Burghley's household in 1577, before going up to Trinity College, Cambridge. That also helped. Ralegh may have attended Oriel College earlier in the 1570s, but no great household was going to take him in, bring him up and position him for success at court, although he did make some very good friends while at Oxford. Nor for Ralegh the grand tour; he had no family to bankroll a leisurely journey through the capital cities of Europe. No wonder that, in his mid-twenties, Captain Ralegh remained unrecognised, except for his propensity for fighting. Even that was hardly exceptional: the prisons were full of young men with too much energy, easy access to weapons and not enough money or opportunity, at least in their own minds.

All this had changed by 1583. Walter writes to his half-brother Humphrey Gilbert (although, as was usual at the time, Humphrey is addressed simply as his 'loving brother') on 15 March, from the court at 'Richmond this Friday morning', utterly revelling in his intimacy with the Queen. Ralegh is now a trusted intermediary; he sends his brother a jewel from Elizabeth herself, for Humphrey is off on another transatlantic voyage. It is 'a token from Her Majesty, an anchor guided by a Lady as you see'. Three days later, Gilbert received the 'very excellent Jewel – an anchor of gold set with 29 diamonds with the portraiture of a Queen…on the back side of the anchor is written *Tuemur sub sacra ancora*'. Just as important as this economically and politically valuable piece of jewellery, Walter passes on the Queen's wishes for 'good hap' on the voyage, and 'farther she commands that you leave your picture with me'. There were worse places to be than at Richmond Palace, passing on personal messages from your monarch. (One of those worse places would be the Atlantic during Gilbert's return journey, where he would die.)

Ralegh was operating in a political culture based on access to the body of the absolute monarch, and he was making it work for him. In a centralised court, the transmission of power, favour and information was dependent on physical presence, partly so that one could pick up important information, but also because it was vital for courtiers to understand Elizabeth's personal preferences. And Elizabeth liked Captain Ralegh. He was hard to dislike, at least in terms of his physical attractiveness. The 'outward man', in the words of a contemporary, had 'a good presence, in a handsome and well-compacted person'. Around six feet tall (very tall for his time), he had thick dark hair and his beard even 'turned up naturally'.

Then there's the famous anecdote involving a cloak and a puddle:

> Coming to the English court, Ralegh found the queen walking, till meeting with a plashy place, she seemed to scruple going thereon. Presently, Ralegh cast and spread his new plush cloak on the ground, whereon the queen trod gently, rewarding him afterwards with many suits, for his so free and seasonable tender of so fair a footcloth.

Ralegh's more recent biographers, Nicholls and Williams, point out sternly that this story was penned by a man not born until 1608 and that, worse still, it doesn't quite fit with the ways a Queen 'went about her business'. Elizabeth did not just go walking amongst her people: 'with the threat of assassination so potent in the 1580s, royal walkabouts in the uncontrolled press of a crowd were deemed too risky'. And yet there is a Ralegh-esque showmanship and chutzpah quality to the action, which suggests that something like it might well have happened.

Cloak or no cloak, the months passed and Ralegh became more and more powerful. April, and he writes to the Solicitor General Thomas Egerton about leases from All Souls College. In May, even more tellingly, he writes to Lord Secretary William Cecil, Lord Burghley (now in Greenwich) about his son-in-law. Lord Burghley was not only the Queen's chief minister but also her most trusted counsellor. Elizabeth believed that he was both incorruptible and faithful and, crucially, a genuinely honest adviser who would put aside all personal considerations to give 'that counsel that you think best'. Few in this century questioned the political validity of absolute, divinely-sanctioned monarchy but even fewer questioned the necessity of good counsel to the success of any monarchy. It was essential that the all-powerful monarch had the best advisers, people willing to tell truth to power. Burghley was one such adviser.

But even the wisest of counsellors can have errant relatives who are hard to handle. In Burghley's case, it was his oldest daughter's husband, the Earl of Oxford. The Earl had been in serious trouble in recent years, confessing, together with Lord Henry Howard, Charles Arundel and Francis Southwell, all closet Catholics, to participating in a conspiracy against Elizabeth, a conspiracy that had only been thwarted because the group had fallen out among themselves. Lord Burghley turned to Captain Ralegh to intercede on behalf of his son-in-law, now under house arrest. Walter Ralegh can reassure the highest statesman in the land that her Majesty 'confessed that she meant it only thereby to give the earl warning', and that all he himself wants is his lordship's 'health and quiet'. Ralegh had things under control by the first of June. After 'some bitter words and speeches in the end all sins are forgiven' and Oxford was allowed to return to court 'at his pleasure. Master Ralley was a great mean herein'.

This was all the more remarkable given his lack of a political network. The true elite always had their retainers in place at court to feed back news and to create and counter rumours, even if they could not be present themselves. Ralegh had to do it all himself, and did so ruthlessly. It did not make him popular with those who were born to power. As Lord Burghley said, 'seek not to be E[ssex] and shun to be R[alegh]'. Ralegh was never going to be 'one of us', but he was doing surprisingly well. No one felt safe. When the Earl of Leicester spent time away from court, his man became seriously worried because there were 'some rumours given out here in court' suggesting that Ralegh was 'an ill instrument towards her [the Queen] against your lordship'.

On 13 November 1584, a courtier, Sir Edward Hoby, approached 'Mr Ralegh to be a dealer in his domestic and private troubles, rather than Mr Secretary'. Mr Secretary is Lord Burghley: in this matter at least, for this week at least, Ralegh takes precedence over the Queen's most senior minister. Four days later, he stars in the Accession Day tilt, one of the most lavish spectacles in the courtly calendar. Held every year on 17 November to celebrate the day on which Elizabeth had become Queen, the increasingly significant tilts were 'annual exercises in arms begun and occasioned' by the 'great zeal and earnest desire to eternise the glory of her Majesty's Court'. Held in the Whitehall Tiltyard, it was only one part of the extensive celebrations surrounding this extremely popular national holiday. Throughout England there were sermons and bell-ringings, bonfires and gun salutes. The poor were given bread, prisoners given alms, and the great houses of the land opened their doors to their community, who could feast, for once, at the expense of their landlords. Particularly virulent anti-papal and anti-Spanish propaganda accompanied the celebrations. No one was allowed to forget that Elizabeth was a Protestant Queen, denounced and excommunicated by the Pope of Rome, the prospective target of a Catholic holy war at any time. It was the kind of spectacle for which Ralegh was made, if not born.

But even performing in the Accession Day tilt did not mark his zenith. In 1585, his Queen knighted him. Sir Walter was appointed steward of the Duchy of Cornwall and Lord Warden of the Stannaries. The execution of Mary Queen of Scots, on 8 February 1587, enhanced his position still further, with Ralegh the beneficiary of the Babington traitors' money and land. The same year he received forty-two thousand acres of prime Irish land.

There would be more. The Queen gave him Durham House on the Strand, a splendid palace with two large courtyards, built in the time of Henry III. Five hundred feet square, with a hall 'stately and high, supported with lofty marble pillars', the palace 'standeth on the Thames very pleasantly', wrote one traveller. You can still see the stones of the slipway if you visit the Royal Society of Arts in John Adam Street in London, although it is hard to imagine the surrounding extensive orchards and vegetable gardens, or the fresh water coming from a spring in nearby Covent Garden.

By 1586, Ralegh is even in a position to patronise, in both senses, the Earl of Leicester, although his patronage is offered in a post-script. He is writing to the Earl in response to Leicester's request for a thousand 'pioneers', one hundred of whom should be miners, to be sent to the Low Countries from the West Country. Ralegh takes the opportunity to defend himself, since there has been a 'very pestilent' report of his 'suspect doubleness'. He reassures Leicester that he is his true servant, and that he is no lover of Spain. So far, so obsequious and predictable, but the postscript has Ralegh reassuring the Earl in another way: 'The Queen is in very good terms with you and, thank be to God, well pacified and you are again her sweet Robin'.

Yet there was always something more to Ralegh than merely being a courtly power player, although he was certainly that. He understood, or more accurately, could articulate, better than most the wheelings and dealings of patronage, exposing the lies of a 'smooth knave' (Walter himself is of course even smoother), but just as quickly getting back on good terms with him. He understood, and perhaps foolishly spelt out in his letters, how to manage the Queen. To his kinsman George Carew, he wrote 'The Queen thinks that George Carew longs to see her, and therefore see her'. He understood, and perhaps dangerously spelt out in his letters, that money talks. He writes to Robert Cecil, Lord Burghley's up and coming son, to say he has given the Queen a jewel worth £250 'to make [persuade] the bishop'. And typically, he always follows up: how did the Queen like the jewel? Ralegh was never going to sell himself short. As the same man who noted Ralegh's handsomeness put it, he had 'a bold and plausible tongue, whereby he could set out his parts to the best advantage'.

Then again, Ralegh is never straightforward, for his letters also show him to be a generous and concerned supporter of courtly aspirants, usually ready to help them up the greasy pole. As his power grew, he became the go-to man for countless people who were in exactly the same position as he had been a few years earlier. Moreover, despite the granting of the splendid Durham House, Ralegh made moves to buy a modest farmhouse in Devon. It was, however, not just any farmhouse, but 'Hayes, a farm sometime in my father's possession' and crucially, the house in which he had been born. Ralegh offers to pay whatever it takes and assures the seller that he won't be a bad neighbour, because of his 'natural disposition' towards the place. Sir Walter, drawn as much to the West Country as to the court, handled the politics of access with tact and, it seems, some generosity.

On the other hand, he hardly held back when it came to furnishing Durham House. His new-found wealth meant that his palace on the Strand was dressed in different ways in different seasons, and for different occasions. Wall paintings and wall hangings set off the rare and beautiful things acquired through his increasing connoisseurship. Quite how legitimately these items came to be in Durham House was questionable. One October, for example, Ralegh wrote to his nephew John Gilbert, who was down in the West Country, at Plymouth. Gilbert's privateering ship, the *Refusal*, had recently taken a Brazilian vessel laden with porcelain and silks. Gilbert was suspected of having removed part of the cargo and allowing it to be 'stolen'. Sir Walter was not backward in coming forward in his requests for some of the booty: his wife, Bess, wanted porcelain and he wanted 'pied silks for curtains'. Indeed, Ralegh makes a half-joke about his request (Gilbert should get hold of these things 'if you mean to bribe me'), acknowledging the reality of political and social life. This letter, written by Ralegh to a trusted family member, and lacking his often over-played rhetorical flourishes, offers a further glimpse of the man's attractions. When confident and relaxed, he is direct, persuasive and utterly charming. His life at court meant, of course, that he was invariably on the defensive or anxious. A couple of weeks later he was still trying to get nice things from Gilbert, reminding him about the porcelain and adding a request for a certain fine saddle and some luxurious wall hangings. And, in a surprise move, he asks for some 'silk stockings' for himself.

Clothes always mattered to Sir Walter. They mattered to everyone, of course. During Elizabeth's reign all portraits, particularly those of the Queen, show the sitters in their most uncomfortable, most formal clothes. As the historian of clothing Anna Reynolds writes, in 'their rich fabrics, shimmering jewellery and complex hairstyles, monarchs and those surrounding them were moving displays of expensive finery from head to toe'. It was a time when men dressed to be noticed. As one stern commentator thundered: 'What should I say of their doublets with pendant codpieces, or the breast full of jags and cuts, and sleeves of sundry colours?' This all offered an opportunity for the fifth son of a Devonshire gentleman to punch considerably above his weight, at least in terms of his fashion statements. Clothing was all about status: if you could afford the most complex, highly-decorated silks, and had the time to get dressed in them, then you would wear them as 'a legitimate and admirable proclamation of an individual's worth'. Thus the importance of silk stockings. It was a life of strategic display, and Ralegh displayed himself well, to the disgust of those who despised his shameless proclamations of his own worth.

He was always concerned to look the part, even if it meant toning down the 'bling'. When charged with hosting a French delegation he notes, with urgency, that the 'French wear all black and no kind of bravery at all, so as I have only made me a black taffeta suit to be in and leave all my other suits'. There's more: 'I am even now going all night to London to provide me a plain taffeta suit and a plain black saddle'. It wasn't always all about him (although it usually was). As Captain of the Guard he wanted his men to look good as well. One letter urgently requests that the 'spangles of the coats of the guards' should be on their way.

Not only in London or at the court did Ralegh reveal his ambitions and aesthetics. Although he failed to buy his humble birthplace, Hayes Barton, Sir Walter was rewarded with the estate of Sherborne by his Queen, yet another example of his successful courtiership. The twelfth-century Sherborne Castle was, at first glance, not perhaps the most enticing of country residences, being cold, crumbling, damp and neglected. Ralegh had, nevertheless, coveted the location for years: the courtier John Harington recounted that on passing by for the first time, riding from London to Plymouth, Ralegh was so excited that he fell off his horse. Even today, it is easy to understand what attracted him:

the rich farmland, the superb hunting grounds and the ideal location for a man whose political and adventuring life regularly took him from London to the far west of England and back again. Ralegh saw that beneath the walls of the castle ran the river Yeo (which flooded at mid-winter) and that beyond the river, across some water meadows, lay a small hunting lodge, built in the time of Henry II.

In the years after 1592, Sir Walter and his lady, prompted by a couple of uncomfortable seasons in the old castle, created a new style of living, one to be admired and imitated by their contemporaries, in that old hunting lodge beyond the water meadows. It became the site of Sherborne Lodge, a beautifully designed country house, constructed to the latest French specifications. Sir Walter's new home was one of the earliest (some would argue the earliest) English houses to use plaster on the exterior walls, while further lightness and elegance were created by the unusually large number of windows and the beautifully worked plaster ceilings, complete with Ralegh's symbol of the Buck (a deer) in the Great Bed Room. The Buck is still to be seen today, in what is now Lady Bristol's Bedroom, as is the 'romantic' ruin of the medieval castle, last occupied in Ralegh's own century. The lodge was functional as well as refined: fresh water was pumped directly into the house from springs on a nearby hill, while the spacious kitchen and bakehouse, in the basement, had generous fireplaces. A fan-vaulted wine cellar and a barrel-roofed beer cellar ensured the household was well-provided for. Ralegh's very design of the lodge embodied a rejection of the court and its values, for he abandoned the communal long gallery and the great hall, the defining features of a traditional courtier's house. The servants' quarters were also separated from the family's rooms, further removing Sherborne from the spatially and socially enmeshed old ways.

Meanwhile at Durham House, Ralegh, in silk stockings, his table laid with the finest porcelain, patronising rather than seeking patronage, played host to some of London's most interesting and cosmopolitan gatherings. There were foreigners, or 'strangers' as the Elizabethans called them; men such as Cayaworaco (son of a South American King).

Although not a slave, Cayaworaco was not an equal; he may well have hovered somewhere between the two, gazed upon as a curiosity until he returned to become leader of his faraway homeland, Arromaia.

It was not just the presence of exotic strangers that made Durham House exceptional; it was the intellectual coterie that Ralegh gathered around him. Writers, scientists and thinkers were reliant on positions in the great households, where they would not only receive food and shelter but also access to books, something almost as important as financial reward. The quality of the men that Ralegh gathered around him was remarkable. Quality did not only mean rank but also ability. Ralegh cared little for lineage. Nothing is known, for example, about Thomas Harriot's life before he matriculated at the University of Oxford, while another good friend and servant, in the broadest sense, was John Shelbury, the son of a London grocer. Shelbury, who studied at Oxford and Lincoln's Inn, was elected MP for West Looe in Cornwall, most probably through Ralegh's influence. Shelbury would be Ralegh's trusted fixer of business and financial affairs for many, many years, and Harriot and Shelbury would liaise with the Privy Council in the dark days of 1603.

It is Thomas Harriot who stands out at Durham House. He was involved in the design and construction of ships and the hiring of sailors, and often acted as Ralegh's accountant. But he was far, far more than this; he was one of the great scientists of his time. In Ralegh's service, he achieved some of his most significant mathematical breakthroughs, prompted by his investigations into 'the navigator's art', 'the chief ornament of an island kingdom' and an art that would reach its greatest heights if 'the aid of the mathematical sciences were enlisted'.

Ralegh, for example, wanted Harriot to solve certain problems regarding the stacking of cannonballs. The scientist promptly provided a mathematical table to answer his patron's initial question regarding the shape of the base of the stack. Further calculations followed, demonstrating how to compute the number of cannon balls in the pile. Harriot, in the words of an historian of science 'was too much the mathematician to stop there' and moved inexorably on to examine the implications of his calculations for the atomic theory of matter, in which he was a believer. Later, he would correspond with Johannes Kepler about atomic theory and mention the packing problem. Kepler offered an intuitive solution, which was finally proved in 1998 by Thomas Hales of the University of Michigan, with the help of reams of computer-generated data.

Harriot's mathematical and scientific achievements are truly impressive, from breakthroughs in optics and chemistry to solving the problem of 'reconciling the sun and pole star observations for determining latitude' and other navigational achievements. But for Sir Walter Ralegh, Harriot offered a chance to learn. He not only paid his in-house scientist to do the maths (and the physics and the accounts) but also to instruct him, so that by Harriot's aid Ralegh 'might acquire those noble sciences' in his 'leisure hours'. Others saw the lessons going on at Durham House as sinister rather than noble, in part because any discussion of cosmology, an essential element in navigation, was dangerous in Ralegh's time. About ten years before Ralegh's birth, in 1543, Nicolaus Copernicus had published his scientific theory of heliocentrism, removing the Earth from the centre of the universe. Others followed in his path, including Giordano Bruno and Galileo Galilei. Bruno was burned to death and Galileo imprisoned for their scientific enquiry. Harriot and Ralegh were asking dangerous questions of the universe. Whether Harriot was a servant, friend or (dangerous) teacher, or all three, he was certainly loyal to Sir Walter, not always an easy task with a man who attracted controversy and danger like moths to a flame.

The high water mark for the attacks on Durham House came in 1593. Ralegh's enemies labelled the house a 'school of atheism' where the 'scholars' are 'taught, among other things, to spell God backwards' by a 'conjurer that is master thereof'. The master conjuror was probably Thomas Harriot, or possibly John Dee, but both feared he was the one meant. These claims were all part of the witch-hunt (or more precisely, atheist hunt) of 1593, whose most celebrated, if possibly tangential, victim was Christopher Marlowe. The Privy Council was investigating the playwright's activities, calling Marlowe before them in mid-May and ordering him to report daily until 'licensed to the contrary'. A couple of weeks later, the informer Richard Baines accused Marlowe of atheism, in 'A note containing the opinion of one Christopher Marley [*sic*] concerning his damnable judgment of religion and scorn of God's word': 'that the first beginning of Religion was only to keep men in awe', 'that Christ was a bastard and his mother dishonest' and 'that the sacrament…would have been much better being administered in a tobacco pipe'. And Baines explicitly linked Marlowe to Ralegh and to Harriot.

A couple of days later, Marlowe was dead, stabbed in a house in Deptford Strand in an argument over the bill, 'the sum of pence, that is, *le recknynge*'. The links, if any, between Marlowe's supposed atheism and the circumstances of his death on 30 May 1593 remain a matter of intense debate. Conspiracy theorists have suggested that Ralegh had him killed to stop his mouth, but there is no evidence. Then again, there wouldn't be.

A year later, Marlowe's death came back to haunt Ralegh, in the form of an inquiry by the Court of High Commission into his religious beliefs. The evidence brought before the court came from the summer of 1593. The court heard that, shortly after the mysterious death of Christopher Marlowe, Sir Walter and his lady went out to dine with friends and family near Sherborne. Over the meal, they discussed religion. Sir Walter kept pushing the argument further and further, challenging every definition ('neither could I learn hitherto what God is…') and appealing to what he called 'our mathematics' for certainty, rather than to the Bible. There was no stopping him and there were those present who remembered the conversation and months later used it to attempt to destroy him.

The Court of High Commission's task was to establish whether Ralegh had indeed 'called the godhead into question and the whole course of Scriptures'. Throughout March 1594 those who had been present at the dinner party the previous summer were questioned intensively. Harriot was dragged into the enquiry. It was pointed out that he had been cited before the Privy Council for denying the resurrection of the body of Christ. It was a close-run thing, but Sir Walter convinced the court that he was no atheist, and that hearsay was no evidence. It was an argument that wasn't going to work again in 1603. In 1594 Ralegh lived to fight another day, but the enquiry resulted in his spending the next few months travelling restlessly around the West Country, attending to the political and military business conferred on him, more and more the provincial outcast. His curiosity remained undiminished but was now tempered by an acute awareness of the perils of enquiry, and a new (if short-lived) caution.

That caution may have been fuelled by the fact that he now had even more to lose, for Sir Walter had become a father the previous year. It was at Sherborne, in a suitably darkened room (light and air were thought to harm the new-born baby), attended by the women of her household and a professional midwife, that his wife Bess gave birth to a baby boy in the autumn of 1593. In precisely this year, a doctor, John Jones, when questioned as to who should be present at a birth, replied that there should ideally be a few 'godly, expert and learned women', rather than 'a rude multitude given either to folly, banqueting or bravery, as in the towns of the West Country is too much used'. Whether there was 'banqueting and bravery' in Dorset is unknown, but mother and baby survived, and on 1 November 1593, little Walter (to be known as Wat) was christened in the small country church of Lillington, close to Sherborne. The records for the following few months are scanty, which may indicate that they were relatively peaceful. Bess would have had her churching, a ceremony of thanksgiving for the safe delivery of the mother, which took place about four weeks after a baby's birth. Women were churched even if their baby were stillborn or had died in the first weeks of infancy, and the ritual could be a crucial part of coming to terms with the loss. The ceremony signalled the woman's status as a mother, her community's recognition of her experience and her own thanksgiving for survival. Soon after came the Christmas festivities, the twelve days of holidays filled with feasting and entertainments.

Sir Walter's son thrived at Sherborne and would become the centre of his father's dreams of a dynasty. His competitors had other ideas, however. In the years when Ralegh consolidated his wealth and power, the Earl of Essex rapidly emerged as a force to be reckoned with. Essex was younger than Ralegh, as handsome as Ralegh (at least to contemporaries), and crucially, was backed by his stepfather, the Earl of Leicester. In the summer of 1587, the Queen made Essex her master of the horse (a position Leicester had given up allow his stepson to take it). After Leicester's unexpected death in September 1588, the rivalry between Sir Walter and the Earl became ever more intense. It was said the Queen had to intervene to prevent a duel between the two men, travelling all the way from Greenwich to Richmond to do so.

The tensions between Ralegh and Essex had been simmering since the mid-1580s, when the latter had begun to rival, and then usurp, the former as the Queen's most intimate favourite. As the gossips noted, the Queen was often 'abroad, nobody near her but the Earl of Essex and, at night, my Lord is at cards, or one game or another with her, that he cometh not to his own lodging till birds sing in the morning'. The relationship between Queen and courtier was stormy; Essex's pride and impetuosity both attracting and infuriating Elizabeth. He understood, only too well, the workings of the court and, in particular, how vital it was to have access to the body of the monarch. He fantasised, dangerously, that he could always freely declare his mind in the presence of the Queen, that she would always forgive him and then move swiftly to destroy his enemies. It was when Elizabeth denied the Earl access that problems arose, because Essex foolishly demanded to see his Queen, bursting in upon her, invading her personal and political space. This was in 1589, and Elizabeth forgave her Essex. This time.

Nor was 1589 a good year for Ralegh. In the summer, he was in Ireland, busy telling anyone who would listen that he had not been pushed out by a triumphant Essex ('For my retreat from the Court it was upon good cause, to take order for my prize', referring to his privateering success) and insisting that he still maintained his crucial 'nearness to her Majesty'. The court gossips told a different story: he had been 'chased' away by Essex. Ralegh had never been popular, and now there was some downright pleasure in his apparent disfavour.

Chased into Ireland or Cornwall; put on trial for atheism; the lies and the cabals: whatever the rewards of the courtier's life for Ralegh, he was always acutely aware of the dark side. He was, of course, well able to live up to the ideal of the courtier: humanist discussion, courtesy and chivalry, the occasional poem; all in a day's work. He writes about, while also demonstrating, the skills of the perfect courtier in his elegy for Sir Philip Sidney, a poem that ends by saying, with fitting modesty:

> That day their Hannibal died, our Scipio fell:
> Scipio, Cicero, and Petrarch of our time,
> Whose virtues, wounded by my worthless rhyme,
> Let angels speak, and heaven thy praises tell.

These qualities (which Ralegh must have known, or hoped, he had, although modesty forbad him to declare them, and his lineage suggested he should not have them) needed to be delivered with panache, or more precisely, *sprezzatura*. No effort should be seen. In Elizabeth's court, as one scholar has pointed out:

> To perform with skill that which is difficult requires grace, but to perform successively, uninterruptedly, and without apparent contradiction roles that are in continual tension if not in conflict requires dexterity, aplomb, self-mastery, and wit; in a word – Castiglione's word – *sprezzatura*. Such a performance, in an arena of fierce competition for material advancement and status reward, could not be rendered indefinitely without cost.

Elizabeth herself was always performing, and there are sometimes glimpses of that cost. Late in her reign, the French ambassador described his meeting with the Queen, revealing a woman of both anxiety and confidence, frailty and power, whose life was one of great freedom but at the same time frighteningly constricted, lived always in the public gaze. He writes:

> She looked at me kindly, and began to excuse herself that she had not sooner given me audience, saying that the day before she had been very ill with a gathering on the right side of her face, which I should never have thought seeing her eyes and face: but she did not remember ever to have been so ill before. She excused herself because I found her attired in her nightgown, and began to rebuke those of her Council who were present, saying, 'What will these gentlemen say' – speaking of those who accompanied me – 'to see me so attired? I am much disturbed that they should see me in this state.'

The entire interview involved a dance of etiquette, played out before the nightgowned Elizabeth: the taking off and putting on of headwear, the standing or sitting of Queen and ambassador, all conducted in front of the assembled gentlemen. Admittedly, the Queen's was a rather special nightgown: its lining was 'adorned with little pendants of rubies and pearls, very many, but quite small', while the exterior was of 'silver cloth, white and crimson, or silver "gauze", as they call it'. Her 'dress had slashed sleeves lined with red taffeta, and was girt about with other little sleeves that hung down to the ground', with which Elizabeth constantly played. 'She would complain that the fire was hurting her eyes, though there was a great screen before it and she six or seven feet away; yet did she give orders to have it extinguished, making them bring water to pour upon it.' The Queen's nervous tension is palpable: it was the price she paid for sustaining her public image.

For Ralegh, the cost was a kind of disgust at the fictions of the court, and perhaps at himself for perpetuating them. It seeps into his writing from this period, in particular into his poetry, most notably his magnificent tirade, *The Lie*. Although it remains uncertain exactly when

Sir Walter wrote the poem, its message is clear. His soul (merely the body's guest) is instructed to go on a 'thankless errand' since 'I needs must die'. The soul, soon to be parted from the body, must 'give the world the lie'. The truths told by the soul are hardly comfortable ones for the court, the church, for potentates and leaders; the 'best', as the poet writes with bitter irony:

> Say to the court it glows
> And shines like rotten wood;
> Say to the church it shows
> What's good, and doth no good:
> If court and church reply,
> Then give them both the lie.

> Tell potentates they live
> Acting by others' action,
> Not loved unless they give,
> Not strong but by a faction.
> If potentates reply,
> Give potentates the lie.

> Tell men of high condition
> That manage the estate,
> Their purpose is ambition,
> Their practice only hate:
> And if they make reply,
> Then give them all the lie.

And that's just the start.

The court might shine like 'rotten wood' but, during the second half of the 1580s, it provided Ralegh with unimagined wealth, in the first instance through his monopoly on wine licences. He had money to burn and he burned it. Indeed, he was sometimes forced to burn it: Accession Day tilts didn't come cheap. Nor did two pearls the size of quail's eggs, to be worn in one ear only. There were many ways to spend one's fortune, some more necessary than others.

And yet it was still not enough for Walter Ralegh. He was much more than a mere courtier, at least in his own mind. Ralegh's thoughts turned to Ireland. His service there – however violent, grim and frustrating – had provided him with a route to the Queen's attention, a sufficient prize for most men. Now he wanted to go back, his goal the establishment of his own successful colony ('plantation'), a fitting reward for Captain Ralegh's years of military service.

The timing was right. At the very moment of his new-found political intimacy with the Queen the Irish rebellion had been, in theory, defeated. In January 1584 Sir John Perrott, the newly-appointed governor, was commissioned by Lord Burghley, still grateful to Captain Ralegh for helping with his errant son-in-law, 'to repeople' the 'dispeopled' province of Munster so that 'the lands escheated should be inhabited with obedient people'. English appropriation of Irish lands for settlement had been going on for centuries, but in Ralegh's lifetime, and then most notably in the 1580s, the pace and purpose of the colonial project changed, with mass confiscations of land and large-scale importation of English settlers. The commissioners surveying Munster in 1584 welcomed the interest of those English 'undertakers'; well-placed, wealthy, loyal subjects of Elizabeth who 'undertook' to populate the new lands. So began the plantation of Munster, and Ralegh was at the front of the queue. This would be his true legacy.

But in the same year Queen Elizabeth conferred an even greater prize, an even more visionary opportunity, upon her favourite; one which made the prospect of an estate in the south of Ireland pale into insignificance. Elizabeth granted Ralegh the patent to discover unknown lands, to take possession of them in the Queen's name, and to hold them for six years. This was the first, and most vital, step towards establishing a colony in 'Virginia', named for Ralegh's Virgin Queen, a brave new (English) world across the ocean. It was a vision that would absorb much of Ralegh's money and energy – and channel his powerful ambition – over the following years.

3

Coloniser

THE PLAN WAS to establish England's own Protestant colony in the New World, Virginia, 'the first English colony that ever was there planted, to the no little derogation of the glory of the Spaniards'. To bring down Spain: Ralegh figures so prominently in our deeply contested stories of empire that it can be hard to remember that his colonial efforts were only a tiny part of a larger geopolitical struggle; Protestant England's war with Catholic Spain. It was a struggle over which Ralegh had little control, but one which had dominated his life since he was a boy. While the teenaged Walter was cutting his teeth as a soldier and Queen Elizabeth was beginning to feel (almost) secure on the throne of England – despite the best efforts of the Pope, religious extremists at both ends of the spectrum, disgruntled nobles and regional rebels – Spain had already established a Catholic empire in the New World. Any challenge to the might of Spain in 1584 therefore had to be not merely a political and military operation but also a religious and ideological one. The English attempted to assert moral superiority, always a good strategy when your firepower is never going to win the war. Not cruel *conquistadores*, they were the true evangelist liberators, bringing savages to the light of truth. The English were doing God's work, following God's providential divine plan for the reform of the church. The English might grudgingly acknowledge that Queen Isabella of Spain had begun with pious intentions, but her understandable and proper support of colonial imperial

Christianity had become tarnished by the innate corruption of the Catholic Church. Who better then to continue the task of converting the heathen than the virtuous Protestant Queen Elizabeth of England?

For Ralegh, these religious justifications for the colonisation of indigenous people in the Americas always came a poor second to his desire simply to go up against Spain, England's European enemy. Thomas Harriot, Ralegh's fellow traveller, literally and ideologically, summed up his patron's position. Philip II of Spain should be made equal to the 'princes his neighbors'. The aim is to attack him where he is weakest: the West Indies. There, the Spaniard was 'planted very thinly and slenderly without having the Indian multitude in subjection'. To attack Philip, to attack Spain, in the Indies is to 'touch the apple of his eye', because to 'take away his treasure which is his *nervus belli* [the sinews of war]' is to defeat him: his 'bands of soldiers will soon be dissolved, his purposes defeated, his power and strength diminished, his pride abated, and his tyranny utterly suppressed'.

Ralegh could have written these lines, so clearly do they articulate his particular brand of patriotism. For there is no doubt, at least in the 1580s, of his loyalty to Queen and country and to the state religion. The Acts of Supremacy and Uniformity, passed in May 1559, marking the beginnings of the Elizabethan Religious Settlement, determined that if Walter was going to be a patriot, he would be a Protestant patriot. But his was a resolutely *political* Protestantism in an era of religious zeal. As has been seen, Ralegh's scepticism created some serious problems for him during his life, not to mention some notable lacunae in his writings: he hardly ever refers to Christ, and even when writing about 'savages' does not concern himself with their conversion to true religion. In many ways, he was that rare thing, a cultural relativist in a century of religious absolutism. Through his reading, his meetings with 'strangers' and his travels beyond England, he would develop an understanding of religious belief and practice as a product of particular times and places. This is not to sanitise either Ralegh's ruthless pragmatism or his equally powerful self-interest. In Ireland, the end, the subjugation of Ireland to the English Crown, for that was his commission, had justified the means. So it would be with his attempt to achieve the 'utter suppression' of the Spanish tyranny.

To this end, Ralegh used his new-found wealth and power to sponsor a reconnoitring expedition to Roanoke Island off the coast of North Carolina. Captains Barlowe and Amadas, its leaders, reported back positively to their master and, thrillingly, brought home to him 'two men of the country'. In the October of Ralegh's *annus mirabilis* of 1584, a German visitor to London wrote that Amadas and Barlowe had 'found a land or an island which is said to be larger than England, and which had as yet been untrodden by Christians'. Ralegh (the German is uncertain whether he is Master or Captain Ralegh) had two strangers 'about his person':

[They] were in countenance and stature like white Moors. Their usual habit was a mantle of rudely tanned skins of wild animals, no shirts, and a pelt before their privy parts. Now, they were clad in brown taffeta. No one was able to understand them, and they made a most childish and silly figure.

The men's names were Manteo and Wanchese. The former was a commander of the Croatoan tribe, while Wanchese was a Roanoke. Both were far from home.

These two men, savages in taffeta, would serve Ralegh's purposes well. Parliament confirmed his patent to his American claims, in part motivated because 'some of the people born in those parts brought home into this our realm of England' had been conveyed to the Houses of Parliament, so that 'the singular great commodities of that land are revealed and made known to us'. Were Manteo and Wanchese people, commodities, or both? No matter: the imperial project had officially begun, and the Queen and her parliament had placed Ralegh at its head.

The imperial project had made a stuttering start the previous year, guided by Ralegh's half-brother, Humphrey Gilbert. He had been an early propogandist for colonisation, setting out lofty arguments for its benefits in reducing vagrancy and poverty in the mother country. The more tangible benefit to Humphrey himself was the letters patent granted to him by Queen Elizabeth, which authorised him to search out 'remote heathen and barbarous lands' not 'actually possessed of any Christian prince'. Lands which, when found, he and his heirs could 'have, hold, occupy, and enjoy forever'. Newfoundland was the first English possession in the New World, had, held and occupied (for two weeks) by Gilbert in 1583, although not enjoyed forever, because he died on the voyage home. Perfect timing for his half-brother Captain Ralegh, to whom the Queen passed the letters patent the following year.

Less ideal for Ralegh was the Queen's uncertain support for his vision of English empire to be seized despite the power and wealth of Spain. It was not only that, as ever, Spanish tyranny needed to be 'utterly suppressed' on the cheap. Just as the use of private forces fuelled the naval war with Spain; just as Elizabeth was reliant on her great nobles both to finance and to lead military engagements, so it would have to be for England's colonial endeavour. In fact, the two strands were interlinked. John Watts, called the 'greatest privateering promoter of his time' (and rewarded with the Lord Mayorship of London), would happily sign a bond of five thousand pounds to support the founding of an English colony and/or trading post, knowing there was money to be made in the New World through mercantile and commercial initiatives. But there was also money to be burned, particularly if the aim was plantation and empire rather simply trade.

For the Queen the cost of imperialism was a pressing concern, but even more important was her commitment to maintaining political stability, and her fear of over-taxing, literally and politically, the English nation. Over the years, therefore, the Elizabethan state adopted a policy of limited war, a pragmatic response to the Queen's sense of her nation's tolerance for military action, and a reflection of her belief that war was at best a necessary evil. Her courtiers often had very different priorities, whether their militarism was fuelled by political or religious ardour. For Essex 'the war against Spain was a crusade which involved religion and a sense of national destiny', according to Paul Hammer, in his study of the Earl of Essex, *The Polarisation of Elizabethan Politics*. No wonder the Earl, and those who thought like him, were constantly frustrated because, ultimately, Elizabeth's primary concern was to protect and defend national honour, 'avoiding defeat and expense, not achieving victory'. How could Ralegh take the Indies, 'the apple' of the Spanish King's eye? How could England cut off the source of Spain's wealth – for that was the dream of Virginia – unless Elizabeth committed wholeheartedly to the imperial project?

Early in 1585 there were signs that things were moving in the right direction. The military hawks in the English court were in the ascendant because, when the French refused to stand against Spain (Henri III rejecting the Dutch offer of sovereignty), Elizabeth and her Council were forced into discussing England's response. During the spring, the Queen pondered the wisdom of letting Sir Francis Drake raid the East Indies, a venture that inspired almost all her male courtiers (from Sidney and Ralegh to Leicester and Walsingham) to reach into their pockets, if not for their swords. Yet Drake's twenty ships remained in port.

Then, in a sign not only of her increasing trust in Sir Walter – she had knighted him in January 1585 – but also of her desire to move cautiously, the Queen permitted a small expedition to sail for 'Virginia'. It would be less provocative than Drake's raid, but its purpose no less incendiary: to establish a launching pad for attacks on Spanish power in the West Indies. Any potential English settlement was part of a larger war strategy. The planting of 'sufficient Colonies, under discreet governors in the aptest places of Terra Virginea' was important for the shipping opportunities. The English would be poised to seize Spanish prizes. Colonies would be 'the sure way to ruin at one instant' the power of Spain.

On 9 April 1585, the first official expedition, masterminded and largely financed by Ralegh and led by one of Sir Walter's cousins, Sir Richard Grenville, set off. The aim was a permanent English garrison and settlement in the New World. The 'two tall Indians' were going home.

The Spanish, noting every move made, recorded that both men 'spoke English' and were 'treated well'. Some modern scholars, reviewing these early years of imperial expansion, suggest that these native Americans were not simply victims but protagonists with their own political agendas. For example, Wanchese, late of Durham House, may well have been sent by his tribe to find out more about England. His people had been learning quickly about Europeans since the 1560s' incursions of the French and Spanish in the lower Carolinas and the activities of Jesuit missionaries in the Chesapeake area in the early 1570s. Did Wanchese realise that the English would (consciously or unconsciously) achieve the complete destruction of the life to which he had been born?

Other travellers on this first expedition included Thomas Harriot, Ralegh's erstwhile science tutor, who sailed on the *Tiger* and was thrilled to observe a solar eclipse on 19 April. Sir Walter instructed Harriot to establish which of the many indigenous communities the English should deal with, since the situation was far from simple, comprising a complex network of *weroances* (district leaders). No fewer than eighteen towns owed the weroance Menatonon allegiance, while his rival Wingina constantly sought new alliances and opportunities for exchange with communities – both familiar and as-yet unknown – across the interior of the continent.

The English found they were in the land of Ossomocomuck. The name cannot be translated with certainty but may mean, according to the historian Michael Oberg, something as straightforward as 'the land we inhabit', 'the dwelling house' or 'the house site'. This was no *tabula rasa*. As Oberg is keen to point out, the Algonquin peoples of Ossomocomuck 'practised politics before Europeans arrived. They fought wars and engaged in trade. They forged alliances and betrayed their enemies. They competed for control of access to valuable items and cooperated when it served their communities' interest'.

Indeed, as Harriot realised – while trying to master the language – the English needed to learn from the Algonquin peoples of Ossomocomuck. It was easy to make mistakes. At first, the visitors believed that the land was called Wingandacon and used this word in patents, documents and proclamations. Unfortunately, the word did not refer to a place at all. Ralegh was amused when he found out the truth: 'when some of my people asked the name of that country, one of the savages answered "Wingandacon", which is to say, as you wear good clothes or gay clothes'.

The English did indeed wear clothes but they did not know how to eat well all year, as did the inhabitants of Ossomocomuck. In late winter and early spring, there was fish aplenty (sturgeon, and herring, some two feet in length 'and better'), caught in weirs or speared in the shallows from one's dugout canoe. The herring could be preserved by smoking for the leaner months, but there were also turkeys, squirrels, rabbits and 'land tortoises' to be had, along with crabs and shellfish, not to mention 'strawberries, mulberries, and such like'. In May and June the fields were planted. There was no need, noted Harriot, to fertilise the soil with 'muck, dung, or any other thing' and nor did the people 'plow nor dig it as we in England'. Instead, men and women broke 'the upper part of the ground to raise up the weeds, grass, & old stubs of cornstalks with their roots'. Once the fields were cleared, the women set the corn, planting four grains in a series of holes, around which they planted beans, squash and sunflowers. And so it had been since the first woman had emerged from the waters of Ossomocomuck.

This apparent Eden for the Algonquins would become a form of hell for the English settlers. The first wave of colonists managed to stay for almost an entire year, aided by the indigenous people. With hopes high, the plan was to send a second cohort of Englishmen – and women. An expedition of 1587, led by Governor John White, included fourteen families. Two of the women were pregnant, including the governor's daughter, Eleanor. In the interim, fifteen men were left in the area by Richard Grenville to maintain English claims of continuous occupation.

The new Virginia would include 'the Cittie of Ralegh', to be built near a deep-water anchorage. It would be a safe harbour for English ships, which could be reprovisioned from the bounty provided by the settlers, if only they could work out how to produce food in the first place. It was with this vision in mind that the second group of settlers was sent out. Not merely soldiers, they had the skills to grow crops and build cities, while also being adept with their weapons. They were, after all, going amongst savages.

Governor John White's expedition sailed towards Roanoke Island, intending to confer with 'those fifteen Englishmen' who Sir Richard Grenville had left there the year before 'concerning the state of the Country, and Savages, meaning after he had so done, to return again to the fleet, and pass along the coast, to the Bay of Chesepiok, where we intended to make our seat and fort'. The plan was that Fort Roanoke would remain in English hands as a base for raiding the Spanish treasure fleets, but that the 'City of Ralegh in Virginia' would be the foundation of the colony.

'Our seat and fort.' 'The City of Ralegh in Virginia.' 'Fifteen Englishmen.' It was not to be. The fifteen men could not be found.

Over the coming months, this first serious attempt at colonisation unravelled. The English made heavy demands on the Algonquins for food. Unsurprisingly, when they headed inland in desperation, the local people either melted away or shot arrows at them. The English went hungry and found nothing. As the fault lines widened into chasms, as a baby girl (Virginia, a granddaughter for John White) was born on 18 August 1587, the colonists decided that White should 'return himself to England, for the better and sooner obtaining of supplies, and other necessaries for them'. It was a terrible journey home. Fresh water supplies ran out and food levels went dangerously low, but somehow White made it to Ireland in mid-October 1587. Ralegh received White's 'letters and other advertisements concerning his last voyage and state of the planters' some six weeks later.

The colonists might still have received the aid they so urgently needed, but at precisely this time the Queen gave the command that no ships were to leave English ports because of the real threat of a Spanish invasion. When White at last succeeded in returning to Roanoke, he 'found the bones and carcasses of divers men, who had perished (as we thought) by famine in those woods, being either stragglers from their company, or landed by some men of war'. More hopefully, they also saw 'a great smoke rise in the Ile of Roanoke near the place where I left our Colony', which 'smoke put us in good hope that some of the Colony were there expecting my return out of England'. The English fired their guns, so that 'our people' might know of their coming. No answer came. A final attempt: seeing the letters C R O A T O A N carved into a tree, they hurried to the island of Croatoan, only to find no evidence that their fellows had ever been there.

Those carved letters have inspired generations of conspiracy theorists to speculate as to the colonists' fate: cannibalised, killed, assimilated or possessed by the indigenous spirit of the wild, the *wendigo*. No one knew then. No one knows now. But it was the end for Roanoke, the end of the attempt to cut off Spain's treasure at its source and the end of Ralegh's dreams of a Virginian empire.

Many commentators over the years have admired Ralegh's colonial vision, if only because it was less bloodthirsty and evangelical than most of his contemporaries'. They are impressed by Ralegh's employment of Thomas Harriot to learn the Algonquin dialect, renamed, of course, 'the *Virginian* language', and by Harriot's creation of a 'universal alphabet' of thirty-six symbols to express the 'Virginian speech'. They appreciate his sending of the limner John White to provide portraits of the indigenous peoples. These acts, they argue, showed that Ralegh respected the culture and people he was intruding on, and sought to understand it and them.

Others argue that the softer imperialism practised by Ralegh (the quest for hearts and minds, the drive towards education and employment rather than enslavement or genocide) was a far more sophisticated and long-lasting way of subjugating a 'savage' race. Softer imperialism it might have been, but it remains difficult to swallow the view of the most sentimental of modern-day historians, such as Alden T. Vaughan, that the lost English colonists merged with the 'natives', in a fairy tale of multiculturalism, to produce 'an ethnically and culturally mixed society', the precursor of today's United States of America.

The dark underbelly of the English colonial project is only too visible in Roanoke. The New World proved to be not so very different to the old one. The violence of England's efforts to impose its rule on, and establish its plantations in, Ireland is echoed in the Outer Banks on the other side of the Atlantic. It is telling that several expedition leaders were old Ireland hands; men such as Richard Grenville, for whom violence was the default setting. Grenville was delayed in bringing help to the first wave of colonists because he preferred the short-term (and bloody) gains of privateering rather than the long-term (and ideally peaceful) benefits of colonialism.

Ralegh may have supported, in every sense, the attempt to understand the culture with which the colonists were engaging, but the English presence would first transform and then obliterate that culture. However, that was all to come. For the moment, the colonisation of Virginia was an imperial dead-end, at least in Queen Elizabeth's time.

Ralegh himself never quite gave up on the 'lost colonists'. He sent expeditions to seek for any traces of the English men, women and children who were the first and last citizens of the putative city of Ralegh, Virginia. There were reports of 'Crosses & Letters, the Characters and assured Testimonies of Christians newly cut in the barks of trees'. Oberg argues that these were carved by English people who had 'accepted the roles native peoples offered them'. Perhaps. The region would suffer in the following years, become overgrown and depopulated. When, in 1602, Ralegh sent Samuel Mace to seek, yet once more, for the lost colonists, Mace neither met nor spoke with the people of Ossomocomuck.

Mace was more concerned to bring home samples of the medicinal plants abundant there. John Gilbert, Ralegh's half-brother, also in the area at the time, came back with a ship laden with sassafras wood. When Ralegh writes to Robert Cecil – now fully established as his father's successor in government – about Gilbert, some twenty years after the first expeditions to Virginia had set sail, the letter reveals his changed priorities. Writing from Weymouth, where he has come to 'speak with a pinnace [a small boat] of mine arrived from Virginia', he admits that both voyages went to the wrong place but asks that Gilbert's ships' cargoes are seized when they come to London 'because I have a patent that all ships and goods are confiscate that shall trade there without my leave'. To Ralegh's horror, Gilbert has been foolishly selling his sassafras cheaply. This 'cloying of the market will overthrow all mine, and his own also'. Ralegh insists that Gilbert is happy for him to have his share, primarily because Gilbert intends to head to 'Virginia' again and wants prices to stay up. The real problem is that a 'man of the lord Admiral's' has taken his cut, which Ralegh says should be his.

Ralegh's focus is now simply trade. His letters patent of 1584 authorised colonisation and plantation, but these goals are now almost forgotten. In the midst of Sir Walter's extended economic complaint, there is but one mention of the imperial dream: 'It were a pity to overthrow the enterprise for I shall yet live to see it an English nation'.

With Virginia yet to become an English nation, Ralegh turned his attention, albeit at the bidding of his Queen, back to the plantations in Ireland, and specifically to his own plantation of three-and-a-half seignories in the vicinity of Youghal and Lismore. While he had been pouring his money and energy into the Roanoke colony, the Elizabethan state had continued its attempts to consolidate its hold on Ireland through plantation. As the historian Nicholas Canny puts it, officials assured eager investors that 'all was in place for what would be a glorious experiment at colonization justified by universally accepted principles'. English planters or 'undertakers' had been active since the mid-1580s but unfortunately for the Crown the Irish colonial project was stuttering by the end of the decade, just as it had in Virginia.

Unlike Virginia, there was still a sense that it could be put right. Robert Payne's 1589 *A Briefe Description of Ireland* attempted to dispel the fears of prospective planters. It was hardly a good year to make the journey to Ireland, with anti-Catholic hysteria in England at its height in the wake of the Armada of 1588. But having got the small matter of the journey out of the way, Payne is adamant that, not only are there some decent Irish people (they are not all rebels, although they do remain attached to popery) but they are as fully anti-Spanish as any true-born Englishman. Their patriotism was fuelled by the recently-translated writings of the Dominican missionary Bartolomé de Las Casas, which had revealed the Spaniard's 'monstrous cruelties in the West Indies' and, Payne notes happily, the way in which the Irish treated Spaniards shipwrecked on the west coast of Ireland. The Irish slew the Spanish 'like dogs in such plentiful numbers that their garments went about the country to be sold as cheap as beasts' skins'. These were people the English could work with.

Payne goes on to set out the economic benefits for people of all ranks in Munster. The abundant natural resources and the low cost of living mean that a landowner 'may keep better house in Ireland for £50 a year, than in England for £200 a year'. Tenants would be just as happy, able to enjoy 'either three hundred acres of land in fee farm or four hundred acres by lease for one hundred years for 6 pence the acre without any [entry] fine'.

Payne's propaganda made it sound so plausible, but Munster, as historian Nicholas Canny writes, 'quickly began to assume an appearance and function very different from anything envisaged by its planners'. There were some attempts at model settlements, English enclaves, but the parcels of lands were scattered, and became more so as Irish proprietors 'recovered substantial parcels of confiscated land through the law courts'. At the same time, English settlers without resources sought to undermine or provoke 'those Irish lords who still retained property and influence in the province'.

As Canny also points out, Ralegh fell into both camps. He was, once again, attempting to create a model settlement, planting some of his best servants and friends there, such as John White and Thomas Harriot, both veterans of Roanoke. In 1589, the latter was commissioned to carry out surveys of the Lismore estate; he continued to advise Ralegh on Ireland for the next decade and beyond. But Sir Walter was not averse to supporting the aggressive claims of less well-placed English planters, who were targeting the surviving Irish lords for dispossession; nor to supporting the claims of an Irish lord if it suited his purposes. Early in 1590, Ralegh took the part of Teig Onorsi, who had travelled with him to England in 1587 to surrender his lands. Ralegh supported the regranting of the lands, and 'on the consideration of the favourable report made of him to Her Majesty' by Sir Walter Ralegh, the Queen leased the land to Teig at a low rent. Ralegh's argument in January 1590 was that the 'contenting of this man will be to great purpose, for no man is better followed of those dangerous men of the west parts [of Ireland] than himself'.

Ralegh had no such concerns when it came to some of his English plantation owner rivals. He knew he needed good people to make the plantation work and didn't care where he got them from, even drawing tenants from other estates. Most undertakers failed, he said, 'not even able to perform what they have undertaken nor the hundreth part thereof'. Ralegh was determined to succeed, and if some disgruntled Englishman were the price to pay for success, then so be it.

The longed-for control of Ireland and Virginia was predicated on the belief that if English towns and settlements could be established then all would be well. There was much talk of the Romans in Britain and the Anglo-Normans in Ireland, talk that would resonate with the historians and imperialists of the nineteenth century, not to mention the English far-right leaders of our own time, obsessed with finding a connection with the 'Saxon' freemen of pre-Norman England. We 'mustn't let Anglo-Saxon British culture die' pronounced the UKIP leader in October 2017.

Roanoke and Munster show the reality behind the rhetoric. In both cases, financial and human resources were limited. In hindsight, the most effective English tactic in Ireland was the moderate policies of a governor such as Sir Henry Sidney or, as Lord Burghley put it in 1580, the winning of hearts and minds. To 'avoid the stirring up of rebellion in Ireland' the Queen should seek 'to recover the minds of all the nobility of late greatly grieved by very hard dealings, and to permit them to continue their ancient greatness, strength, honour and surety'. The best approach in Virginia would have been to follow up the first expedition swiftly and effectively and to have continued to learn far more, far more quickly, from the indigenous people on whom the colonists found themselves dependent.

Nevertheless, Ireland, for all its problems, offered Sir Walter a substantial estate, although hardly a city of Ralegh in a brave new world. He was still there in 1601, passing on news about Spanish plans: thirty-six ships, supported by three Irish ships, an Irish bishop with many priests and other Irish men. The Spanish were intending to land at Cork or Limerick with eight thousand men, six thousand of them soldiers. The other two thousand were to bring back the ships. The ships were well furnished with victuals, munition and money 'and had also with them many women'. In other words, the report suggests that Spain intended a settlement. Ireland remains not only a strategic military prize but a prospective colony for the Spanish, so Ralegh thinks. A later report from a Captain Morgan downgraded the invasion force to a mere four thousand soldiers, many of them ill. Yet another report has even fewer men: a thousand have been put ashore, another thousand are heading back to Spain with the ships. The women turned out to be returning Irish refugees.

No matter. Spain remained the enemy. They had been the enemy in 1593, when Ralegh wrote to Robert Cecil that 'the king of Spain seeketh not Ireland for Ireland but having raised up troops of beggars in our backs shall be able to enforce us to cast our eyes over our shoulders while those before us strike us on the brains'. Indeed, they had been the enemy since war was declared in 1585 and – despite or because of all his efforts at plantation in the old and new worlds – Ralegh believed that true victory over Spain could be achieved only one way: at sea.

4

Sailor

RALEGH, BY HIS own admission, was an unlikely naval hero. He even found it hard to sleep on board ship: 'I shall never sleep night if I be here till Christmas', he complains, or jokes that he is 'an excellent watchman at sea', since his eyes do not close. The sea was, however, if not in his blood, then in his family and environment. His parents' multiple marriages tied Walter to both the Drake and Gilbert families, and as a West Country man and boy, he had grown up on the water.

Yet Ralegh is not a key figure in our histories of the most celebrated naval encounter of these years, the Spanish Armada of 1588. He's there in the small print, but his absence from the headlines is a signal, if one were needed, that his achievements were often made against the social and political grain of his era. It also confirms that, if and when we do remember Ralegh, it is often due to his talent for self-publicity.

It was not that Queen Elizabeth did not value Sir Walter the sailor just as much as she appreciated him as a courtier. She used him to further England's imperial ambitions and what is more she needed him, because as a woman, Elizabeth was unable to lead her men into battle. She could, however, choose her military leaders and advisers. In 1587, with England facing a mighty 'heaven-threatening Armado', the loyal and battle-hardened Ralegh was the answer to her prayers. She entrusted him with the defence of Cornwall, which with Devon formed the front line against Spain's attack. Ralegh positioned men and weapons (receiving ordnance and ammunition from her Majesty's own store) along the southern Cornish coast from Cape Cornwall to the Tamar estuary. Guns of cast iron 'well mounted upon carriages with wheels, shod with iron, with ladles, sponges and rammers, with all other accessories' and plenty of powder and shot: Ralegh's Cornwall would be ready for the Spaniards. Promoted to Lieutenant of Cornwall in the same year, he joined one of the small, select group of men chosen to carry out especially sensitive tasks, an elite stratum of trusted Protestant gentry with which the Queen and the Council could work, as the historian Neil Younger argues.

Every Tudor monarch was utterly reliant on the loyalty – and political administration – of the elite families who governed the provinces of England. Absolute monarchs they might be but they were also absolutely dependent on their great subjects to maintain their rule. Obedience and social order were the watchwords, preached again and again in the religious homilies written to be read in every parish in the country.

The message was simple and relentless: almighty God has created and appointed all things in heaven in a most excellent and perfect order. This heavenly order is replicated on Earth: God has assigned and appointed Kings and Princes, with other governors under them in all good and necessary order. Each person's degree in society is appointed:

> Some are in high degree, some in low, some Kings and Princes, some inferiors and subjects, priests and layfolk, masters and servants, fathers and children, husbands and wives, rich and poor, and everyone needs the other, so that in all things God, in good order, is lauded and praised, without which no house, city or commonwealth can continue, endure or last.

The alternative is nightmarish: 'For where there is no right order, there reigns abuse, carnal liberty, enormity, sin and Babylonian confusion'. There will be robbery and murder; wives, children and possessions will be 'in common' and 'there must needs follow all kinds of mischief, and utter destruction of souls, bodies, goods and social well being'.

With the threat of invasion, of mischief and utter destruction from outside, Elizabeth more than ever needed the support of the great families within England. Her problem was that, at least in the west, so many of those great families had been implicated in rebellion and disorder; so many had Catholic sympathies. Ralegh was the only lieutenant appointed by Queen Elizabeth who was neither peer nor counsellor, an indication of her concern about her wild west. It was quite an achievement for Sir Walter, a sign of his Queen's belief in his loyalty, but also a reminder of just how complete was his dependence on her. For Ralegh, patronage came from the Queen, and the Queen alone.

His appointment did not make him any more popular with the nobles who were being circumvented. Ralegh himself fans these flames in a letter of 21 December 1587, when he makes clear the virtues of his own kinfolk (loyal, capable and optimistic) and points the finger at others who are far from trustworthy: 'infected in religion and vehemently malcontent', they 'are secretly great hindrance of all the actions tending to the good of Her Majesty or safety of the present state', offering a 'thousand dilatory cavelations'. Ralegh is angry because, earlier in the month, he had been instructed to hold musters 'against any sudden invasion' and to repair defences. A few days later, two thousand foot and two hundred horse were put on hold, with no reason given. Ralegh's letter reached Westminster three days later (good going), but little was done. It was simply too expensive and too onerous to assemble forces at this stage. Sixteen years on, it was Ireland all over again: being asked to do something but not given the means to do it.

And so Ralegh was back sorting out the land defences of the south-west, writing the typically detailed, logistically-focused letters that were his *métier*. In one letter, he says that Cornwall is long and thin four times: 'Cornwall is stretched out all in length, and hath little breadth...the river Tamar not fordable in any place within 12 miles of Plymouth...four thousand men need to march over at Newbridge above Calstock'. Therefore, writes Sir Walter, the chosen defensive strategy is just not going to work.

This was the reality of Ralegh's Armada year. No wonder he does not make the headlines. Look beyond 1588, however, and a more complex picture of naval endeavour and achievement emerges, one revelatory of both the man and his era. Ten years earlier, and only in his mid-twenties, Ralegh had taken command of his first ship, the hundred-ton *Falcon*, crewed by seven gentlemen and about sixty mariners and soldiers. At the head of the expedition was his half-brother, Humphrey Gilbert. Typically, Walter found a good motto for himself: *Nec mortem peto, nec finem fugio* (I neither seek out death, nor flee from the end). Equally typically, he made sure he had the services of Simon Fernandes, an experienced Portuguese navigator, as master mariner. Yet more characteristically, not only did he do well in the venture despite his half-brother's bad luck with both storms and politics but – somehow – ensured the story of his adventures made it into the history books. Captain Ralegh, it was written years later, was 'desirous to do somewhat worthy of honour' and therefore 'took his course for the West Indies'. 'In this voyage he passed many dangerous adventures, as well by tempests as fights on the sea'. The voyage became a symbol of Ralegh's determination to conquer the Atlantic and the New World, a clear sign that he would not 'give over'.

What Hooker, the historian in question, fails to mention is that Ralegh's ship had run out of food by the time he reached the Cape Verde islands. He would not make the same mistake again. He will always make sure, as he does in a letter of 1586 to John Gilbert, another half-brother, that his men have bread and cider. His pragmatism, his readiness to consider a 'plan B', is equally evident. The bread and cider are needed for an expedition to seize some Spanish ships off Newfoundland, but – failing that – they will catch pilchards.

These qualities are equally visible in the June 1583 expedition to Newfoundland, from which Humphrey Gilbert would not return. The newly wealthy soldier-courtier Captain Ralegh had invested thousands of pounds in a ship that bore his name, the two hundred-ton *Bark Raleigh*. The entire expedition returned to port after only two days out at sea. Gilbert regrouped and set out again with five vessels, the *Golden Hind* among them. The Queen herself tried to persuade Gilbert to stay on land, pointing out that he was a man 'of not good hap by sea'. Only the *Bark Raleigh* eventually turned back, the other four continuing to Newfoundland where Gilbert, with his letters patent from the Queen, formally took possession of the island. They were there for only a fortnight before embarking on the return voyage. On the evening of 9 September, it was said (by the captain of the *Golden Hind*, the only ship to make it home) that, in the midst of terrifying seas, Gilbert sat astern of his ship crying: 'We are as near to Heaven by sea as by land'. He was indeed near heaven, or the other place. Close to midnight, Ralegh's half-brother and his ship were 'devoured and swallowed up of the Sea'. Ralegh's caution was vindicated and he lived to sail another day.

He knew there was little that was glamorous and much that was dangerous, not to mention expensive, about Elizabethan sea voyages, whether for economic, colonial or military gain. He knew it because, according to one naval historian, he racked up more sea miles than any other man in a similarly exalted position.

The Spanish knew what all those sea miles made Ralegh: a pirate. In some ways, it is a fair assessment, given the nature of naval warfare in the 1580s and 1590s. What was piracy, after all? Ralegh's father had been an investor in the seizure of foreign ships, something known as 'piracy' by those who did not understand the political and economic life of the 'audaciously lawless' (in the words of one historian) south-west coastal regions. All attempts to stamp out so-called piracy foundered, partly because the local officials were so enmeshed in the business, but mainly because the Elizabethan state, with its limited resources, needed it to achieve its military goals. State-sanctioned piracy, it turned out, was often an effective way to fight a war against a much more powerful enemy; something Ralegh understood early. He contributed his own ship, the *Job*, to a fleet led by his cousin Bernard Drake and his brother Carew in June 1585. The fleet took several Spanish ships off Newfoundland and its private backers kept most of the money. This June raid is seen by most historians as one of the first overt English acts in the war with Spain. If so, it was war conducted on the basis of piracy.

'Deniable' forms of war, conducted by English 'volunteer' soldiers in France and the Low Countries and by English privateers at sea, were part and parcel of Ralegh's era. Having fought in France as a teenager, having grown up in the West Country and seen the letters of reprisal issued by French and later Dutch Protestants – described by one historian as a 'legal fig-leaf for otherwise naked piracy' – he knew all about 'deniable' forms of war.

Until the mid-1580s, these forms of war supported Protestant dissidents in states with which England was formally at peace, but in 1585 they were harnessed to the official struggle against Spain. For some historians, this is not playing by the rules. K.R. Andrews describes the era as one of 'criminal and indiscriminate piracy on a disturbing scale [...] Godliness, manliness and patriotism had very little to do with it. It was simply the maritime version of robbery with violence, which in that context often meant killing some of the victims and torturing others'. The state sometimes had need of robbery with violence, however, and as the years went by, 'piracy' became subsumed within, and indeed partially legitimised by, what is known as the 'privateering war'.

It was a breeding ground for conflicting loyalties. One month, all ships and mariners throughout the kingdom were stayed from going to sea because the Queen needed those resources against Spain. The same month, in one of his characteristic postscripts, Ralegh tells his half-brother John Gilbert that it's fine to let a couple of ships steal away. In this instance, Ralegh's motives were not piratical (he was sending aid to the stranded colonists in Virginia) but he was still undermining the Crown's cause.

By October 1591, Ralegh could speak openly to Lord Burghley about the progress of this 'privateering war'. His concern is what happens to the prizes. As he says, 'We might have got more to have sent them afishing, I assure your lordship'. Ralegh offers a financial breakdown. Half the prize goes 'away from the adventurers' (that is, the investors in the fleet) and to the mariners, the Lord Admiral and the Queen. That leaves only the small amount of £14,000, which when divided amongst twelve investors, is (and Ralegh insists that this is the truth) a small matter. The result is that investors will 'never our men of war put out, and so all our ships may rot, our mariners run away and Her Majesty lose the best part of her custom, and besides the sum not worth the looking after'. It's Ralegh at his straight-talking best. No wonder Lord Burghley, and even Elizabeth herself, never quite understood him.

They did know, however, how to use this restless, pragmatic man. Ralegh's energy in these years is almost tiring to witness, as he moves from place to place with a remarkable intensity of purpose. One September he travels from Cornwall to the court in London and on to Ireland. These were not insubstantial journeys in Elizabethan times, nor was Sir Walter a young man. But, for all his visionary qualities, for all his rhetoric, Ralegh was also profoundly practical, thinking through the logistics of the situation, frustrated by empty talk or emptier rank, always impatient to get the job done. In the letter in which he effortlessly dissects the world of the court; the bribes, the politicking, the delays, he is also utterly focused on the sailing conditions (if the winds blow at south, south-west, or south-south-west there will be problems; it will be 'perilous'). Sir Walter writes he is forced to 'leave it to your wisdoms' as to when they sail, revealing he is as dependent on those with real power in court as he is on the capricious winds. Both are perilous.

In 1594, Ralegh was granted 'letters of marque' to prey on Spanish shipping, writing on 20 July to Cecil, itching for a chance to get out into the Channel. The Spanish are establishing themselves in Brittany and he knows he can do some serious damage if only he can get to sea. Instead, in a reprise of the Armada year, his orders are to muster men first in Devon and Cornwall, and then only in Cornwall. Worse and worse, in Ralegh's view, because 'Devon may better spare men than Cornwall'. Ralegh is, as ever, frustrated. He knows the West Country, knows about mustering, knows that what's really needed are some naval attacks on Spanish ships and ports.

He was to get his wish two years later. For years, Ralegh had regularly warned his Queen and her Council about the threat from Spain, but in November 1595 they appeared to listen to him. Spain was gathering a significant armada to support the claims of the Earl of Tyrone in Ireland, and Elizabeth decided that attack was the best form of defence. She authorised a full-scale assault on the port of Cadiz in the far south-west of Spain, to be launched in the spring of 1596.

Cadiz, one of the oldest cities in Europe, was an obvious target. It was the home port of the Spanish treasure fleet, a 'city at once rich, vulnerable and strategic'. Those riches mattered: it always helped motivate reluctant English soldiers and sailors if looting was a possibility. It would be 1587 all over again; the time when Sir Francis Drake's succeeded in 'singeing the king of Spain's beard', raiding the city, crucially depleting Spanish stores and ensuring that their Great Armada was delayed until the following year.

All in all, Ralegh was delighted by the prospect of the Cadiz action and he threw himself into preparations. No matter that Elizabeth appointed his rival, the Earl of Essex, as one of the commanders, and Charles, Lord Howard of Effingham (the Queen's first cousin once removed and the commander-in-chief during the Armada of 1588) as the other. This would be Ralegh's moment.

Scratch the glittering surface and a vivid picture of the frustrations of preparing for naval action emerges. First, getting hold of men to serve. This, on 3 May 1596, from Gravesend: 'I am not able to leave to row up and down every tide from Gravesend to London'. He sends a list of the men who 'refuse to serve her Majesty'. The next day he is bemoaning 'how little her Majesty's authority is respected, for as fast as we press men one day they run away another and say they will not serve'. The whole thing is getting out of hand. He can't write to the Earl of Essex because the messenger 'found me in a country village a mile from Gravesend hunting after runaway mariners and drugging [*sic*] in the mire from ale house to ale house, I could get no paper but that the pursuivant [messenger] had this piece'. One day he's in Northfleet, west of Gravesend, the next in Queenborough, a port on the Isle of Sheppey.

Second the weather: he's more 'grieved than ever I was in any thing of this world for this rough weather', as he writes 'from Blake Wale [Blackwall] ready to go down again this tide'. Essex and Howard are waiting at Plymouth with their ships. Ralegh is stuck in the Thames estuary, where the alehouses don't even have paper for him to write on. A week later, he's aboard ship but things are still not going well. He's had to let slip all their cables and anchors: if not, they would die. They've marked them with buoys, but someone needs to get out there to retrieve them from the northern part of the Goodwin Sands 'in five or six fathoms'. Someone agreed: the anchors and cables were retrieved and sent round to Plymouth by sea.

At last he gets to Plymouth on 26 May, with just enough time to write a quick letter in support of someone who aspires to be a prebend at Exeter Cathedral. The man would get the post later in the year. Ralegh the generous patron does his bit once again.

Then the journey south, destination Cadiz. The mud of the Thames is soon forgotten in the glory of sea battle. The English forces take Cadiz, facing little resistance as they go about their business of sacking, burning and hostage taking. It helps that the Spanish are disorganised and ill-equipped to face an attack. Their only significant action is to burn their own fleet, which is anchored in the bay.

Job done, Ralegh picks up his pen, writing 'to the westward of Cadiz, some 10 leagues, the 7 of July', a long letter to yet another cousin, Arthur Gorges. 'At the very opening of day, I weighed anchor and bare in crying Vive la Reigna d'Angleterre. I gat the start and led before all a good distance which, when it was perceived, the whole navy followed, as well those appointed as the rest.'

Ralegh is brimming with false modesty. The Earl of Essex was 'pleased to take my foolish advice before any else' and 'seemed much content with my bold reason'. The attack itself had Essex ('so great of heart that he could endure' waiting no longer and 'shouldered in through and came up as near me as wind and tide permitted') and Ralegh ('resolved to the keep the honour of the day, I let go all and hoist up topsail and foresail and got ahead again') jostling to take the lead. Ralegh was severely injured, receiving a 'grievous blow in my leg, larded with many splinters which I daily pull out. Yet I scrambled ashore'. There is no doubt who is the hero of the hour: Sir Walter Ralegh.

As ever, he is a powerful reporter from the frontline, recreating the chaos and horror of a sea battle, while also demonstrating his mercy and decency, in sharp contrast to the Spanish generals:

> Now began the *Philip* to faint as I approached, and with her the *St Matthew* and the *St Andrew* and *St Thomas* ran themselves aground, some [of the crew] saving themselves with boats, others leaping into the sea, the rest crying miserecordia. The noise and outcry was marvellous and the spectacle lamentable. The *St Philip* and *St Thomas* set themselves on fire, a most fearful and piteous sight to see so huge a flame, so many drowned, others burning in their shreds [shrouds, i.e. rigging], others half burnt and half drowned, with many wounded scrambling up through the mud. But before the other two gallies [galleons], the *Matthew* and *Andrew*, could rid [evacuate] the better sort, that they [the ships] might burn also, I recovered them [the crews] with boats and, sparing the lives of the greater part, saved the ships.

The sea battle won, Cadiz is taken, and 'All mercy was used'. This would be no Smerwick. Four thousand ladies, gentlewomen and merchants' wives were sent out from the city in all their glorious apparel, 'with their jewels about them, without any touched, with the greatest honour and respect that ever was used by any nation or in any war, to show that we all serve the greatest lady of the earth of most power and of greatest pity [compassion]'. Ralegh insists there were '16,000 eyewitnesses' to this great action. But above all else, as he wrote in a much shorter letter to Cecil, the King of Spain had never been 'so much dishonoured, neither hath he ever received so great loss'. Ralegh, unsurprisingly, holds back on the bad news: they didn't manage to achieve their military goal, the capture of the Spanish merchant fleet. Nor does he mention the knighthoods handed out to sixty-three gentlemen, presumably because it's not about him.

This letter was a crucial step in the race to get the news (*his* news) back to England. The letter's bearer, who 'hath seen all…can better report all then any letter or discourse', arrived at court on 31 July. Would Ralegh be ahead of the other generals? He was confident enough to praise his great rival, the Earl of Essex, who has 'conducted himself, I protest unto you by the living God, both valiantly and advisedly in the highest degree, without pride with cruelty [*sic*], and hath gotten great honour much love of all'.

In England, the wheels came off and the spoils of war evaporated. What to do with the soldiers and sailors now they were returned? The command went out that the army may 'for the most be returned unto their counties from hence, which, the sooner it shall be done, the less charge Her Majesty shall be at here with continuance of her sea charge'. The Privy Council agreed that the 2,200 soldiers from the Low Countries who had supported the English action should be sent home by sea after their ships and persons had been searched, presumably for some of the missing booty, and that the majority of the remaining soldiers should go at once to Ireland. The seamen should be sent home. It was all far from easy to manage, not to mention a reminder that the Elizabethan army and navy were inextricably linked. The navy, at least during the period when Ralegh was most at sea, had the most important strategic role in defending the Protestant English state but land and sea forces were deeply intertwined and needed to co-operate.

A year later, an even older, perhaps wiser (and most definitely war-wounded) Ralegh was back at sea. Elizabeth had sanctioned an expedition to the Azores; its goal to intercept and destroy the Spanish West Indian treasure fleet. The port of Ferrol would be taken and England would control the mid-Atlantic. The Earl of Essex was appointed admiral and general-in-chief, with Sir Thomas Howard, Earl of Suffolk as vice admiral. Ralegh was rear admiral.

It looked good on paper, but as usual, when it came to the preparations for war, everything came down to money, or the lack of it. The lordships have promised 'such sums of money as the vittels, wages and other charges should amount to...' Ralegh writes from Chelsea on 24 April 1597. By July, he's in Weymouth, writing to Cecil, and all is chaos: 'In this haste and confusion of businesses, among so many wants and so great haste.' Ralegh and his contemporaries were well aware of the Queen's changeability. An initiative would be agreed but the Queen would defer making a formal commitment. In the case of the Azores expedition, this meant having to make last-minute preparations despite the Queen having authorised it in April.

The months between the Cadiz and Azores expeditions provided an opportunity for a much-needed *rapprochement* between Ralegh and both Robert Cecil and the Earl of Essex. For all Ralegh's rhetoric, he and Essex had been as much rivals as collaborators in the Cadiz action, and in the aftermath they fought for every piece of gold and glory. The political rivalry between Cecil and Essex was just as heated, again because of Cadiz. The Queen had been frustrated and angered by the Earl's disobedience when in naval command. It was not just a matter of those knighthoods. In the heat of the action, Essex had demanded the English take and hold Cadiz, rather than merely destroy the Spanish treasure fleet. Only the other commanders' reminders of Elizabeth's clear instructions to get out and get back stopped him. Elizabeth expressed her fury and disappointment by appointing Robert Cecil, Lord Burghley's son, as her Principal Secretary, something she had promised Essex she would not do. It was yet another sign that, however strongly she might have been attracted to Robert Devereux, she was determined to appoint the best man for the political job, and Robert Cecil was that man. The continuing power and influence of Lord Burghley, Robert's father, is unmistakable and reveals, in the words of the historian Susan Brigden, that 'in Elizabethan politics, the pen was mightier than the sword'. Burghley ensured that his administratively competent younger son, stooped by a debilitating back problem to a mere five feet tall and the man the Queen called her 'little elf', would succeed over his more swashbuckling, not to mention taller, rivals.

It is therefore remarkable that Ralegh can write a letter which shows these three very different rivals as best of friends: 'I acquainted... [Essex] with your letter to me...He was also wonderful merry at the conceit of Richard the 2'. Ralegh was keen for the good times to last: 'I hope it shall never alter, and whereof I shall be most glad of, as the true way to all our good, quiet and advancement, and most of all for her sake whose affairs shall thereby find better progression'. (Whether Ralegh and Essex were bonding over the work of William Shakespeare is unclear. His *Richard II* was entered on the Register of the Stationers' Company in April 1597 but it was first performed in a private house in late 1595, when Robert Cecil was one of the audience.) Ralegh recognised that the Queen was frustrated by the conflict between her senior courtiers, and wished for concord 'for her sake' but he may have realised that in a straight competition with her 'little elf' Robert Cecil, son of the much loved Lord Burghley, and Robert Devereux, stepson of the much-loved Earl of Leicester, he himself might come a poor third.

The Azores expedition, when it at last took place, tested this fragile alliance. Not until 10 July did the full fleet leave England. Only eight days later, Ralegh was back in Plymouth giving his side of the story. The weather was against them: foul weather, thunder, wind and rain led to 'our disseverance' and a 'storm beaten fleet'. Ralegh had lost sight of 'my lord General' Essex and has no idea what happened to him. He is concerned that the Earl will return 'utterly heartbroken, although it be not in the power of man to fight against elements'. It is a neat shift to draw attention away from his own failure: he had not got close to the Azores.

The expedition was in meltdown. Ralegh has heard (much of Elizabethan warfare relied on rumours) that between thirty and forty of the expedition's boats have put in at Falmouth and he is trying to find out who is in them. He knows it's not Essex, but that's all. Heading to Falmouth, he finds a desperate situation; the majority of the soldiers are either ill or dying like flies and 'will shortly infect the rest'.

Essex limped back into Plymouth harbour on 19 July. Cracks immediately started appearing in the relationship between the two returned commanders. Was Sir Walter daring to ignore the Earl? Admiral Lord Howard didn't return until 31 July: 'This Wednesday morning my Lord General is expected here at Plymouth, being on Tuesday night put into Falmouth in great extremity and imminent peril of sinking in the sea'. Howard's vessel was leaking even before she left Plymouth. He'd been the scapegoat; the Queen – the same Queen reported to have cried when she heard that Essex had arrived home safely – didn't want her beloved Essex sailing in a 'crazed vessel'.

As a naval venture, the Azores expedition was proving an abject failure. But, remarkably, Essex and Ralegh started working together. The former rode 'all night post over the rugged mountains of Cornwall' to meet the latter at Plymouth, staying with Sir Walter on his ship. The two hold a council of war; their plan is to patch up the boats and try to rejoin Howard. They ride, haste, post-haste, to court to put Ralegh's proposal, for it is Ralegh's, to the Privy Council. It is accepted and the expedition rides again.

Disaster overtakes just as quickly as before. The first casualty of war is truth and this was nowhere more evident than in mid-Atlantic. The rumour circulates that Ralegh has persuaded a number of ships to follow him, rather than the rest of the fleet. The situation is complicated by the fact that, based on a false report (those rumours again), Essex has separated from the fleet to chase down the Spanish, while the Spanish treasure fleet is delayed by adverse winds in its efforts to get home. Ralegh, as ever, tries to give his side of the story: 'Haste post haste, haste for life. For Her Majesty's especial affairs, delivered at Tercera the 8th of September W Ralegh'. News of his attempted takeover, is of course, a 'monstrous untruth, raised out of malice'. His letter recounts a catalogue of shipping disasters: lost masts, lost sails, lost everything. And Sir Walter is not sleeping: 'And for my particular, I have never dared to rest since my wrecks and God doth judge that I never for these 10 days came so much as into bed or cabin'. The battered English fleet eventually got back to Plymouth, arriving from 26 October. Ironically, the Spanish had left Ferrol in the Azores on the ninth, the very day that Essex had departed.

As soon as Essex's ship reached harbour, he went straight to London, leaving Ralegh to mobilise the West Country against the expected invasion. Because this is what Sir Walter Ralegh, the sailor, did.

In the first half of the 1590s, all Ralegh wanted to do was get out and get at the Spanish by sea. By the end of the decade, if not before, he was tiring of the whole business, as he told his nephew John Gilbert, the young leader of a group of captains that seized numerous naval prizes, of dubious legality, in the final years of Queen Elizabeth's reign. The Queen was also weary; on 8 February 1599 she issued a proclamation that no one should seize ships and goods belonging to nations with which England was not at war. What is more, in the words of the historian Alexandra Gajda, Elizabeth was tired of 'ambitious naval and military incursions' (such as Cadiz or Azores) which 'would never achieve any tangible goal'. Ralegh's vision of defeating Spain at sea had come to nothing.

After Cadiz 1596: Ralegh and the Earl of Essex

Others thrived in the naval struggles of the 1580s and 1590s. A portrait of the Earl of Essex from 1596 shows a mighty figure, holding the baton of command, standing on a cliff as the city of Cadiz burns beyond. Essex wears a distinctive ginger square-cut beard, grown on the voyage: it would become his trademark. Other versions of the portrait show him either wearing the Order of the Garter of St George, a reminder of his privileged status, or clothes of black and white, a reminder of his loyalty to the Queen and her colours. In sharp contrast, a portrait ostensibly celebrating his triumphant action at Cadiz shows Sir Walter looking haggard, his hair thinning, his beard grey, crippled by his leg injury. Ralegh the sailor had paid a high price for his service to his Queen.

5

Lover

SOME ELEVEN YEARS before the Cadiz portrait the artist Nicholas Hilliard had captured Captain Ralegh, in an exquisite miniature, as an impossibly handsome, dark-haired man, with flowers in his hair. His beard does indeed appear to turn up naturally. There is nothing of the sailor or the soldier, let alone the statesman, in his face. This beautiful man is merely a decorated, almost effeminised, object dressed in the clothes of the moment.

Ralegh miniature, c.1585, by Nicholas Hilliard

What a moment it was: huge detachable cartwheel ruffs and jewel-encrusted codpieces were the order of the day. The codpiece, a hollow but padded protuberance at the groin ('cod' was a contemporary word for the testicles), was crucial to a man's image. It had come a long way from its functional origin as a flap of fabric between the two legs of the breeches, often the shirt-tails of a long linen shirt wrapped between the legs. Now, as padded, slashed, puffed, embroidered and bejewelled as other items of clothing of the period, the codpiece was 'a self-conscious and exaggerated symbol of virility', in the words of Anna Reynolds, a historian of dress. Sadly, no image of Captain Ralegh with codpiece survives.

Four years after Hilliard painted Ralegh with flowers in his hair, Sir Walter was still handsome (a contemporary described him as 'framed in so just a proportion and so seemly an order, as there was nothing in him that a man might well wish to have been added or altered') but in this portrait of 1588 (reproduced at the beginning of this book), he is not merely a disembodied pretty face. Admittedly, the artist shows neither Ralegh's codpiece nor his legs – a shapely, stockinged leg was another crucial indicator of manliness – but the painting announces that this is a serious man, a man to be taken seriously.

Both portraits exude Ralegh's personality; his confidence, his charisma. They proclaim, in different ways, his success at the court of Queen Elizabeth. Both also show him to be the Queen's man, and the 1588 portrait sends subtle, and not so subtle, messages of loyalty through its use of symbolism. *Amor et virtute* (love and virtue), Ralegh's motto (at least at that time), is inscribed in a corner of his portrait. It must therefore be true. His clothes are decorated in pearls, the Queen's favourite jewel, whose 'creamy colour and purity suited her preferred colour scheme of black and white', and 'symbolised virginity and the full moon'. The Queen herself was often similarly portrayed wearing large pear-shaped pearl earrings in one or both ears. Ralegh's homage to his Queen is not only shown in the pearl decoration on his clothing but also in the immense earring hanging from his left ear. For women, pearls complemented their prized pale skin. For Ralegh, they were a sign of his oneness with the Queen, his commitment to her inviolable chastity. The wealth on display is also a reminder that his intimacy with Elizabeth had brought him unimaginable wealth and power by 1588.

Was it all a self-serving fiction, this intimacy and loyalty? Was Ralegh as significant, and as close, to the Queen as these portraits suggest? Some historians are deeply sceptical, placing Ralegh firmly on the margins of real power. Looked at politically, they argue Sir Walter did not influence policy at any stage but was merely the deliverer – often a disgruntled and frustrated deliverer – of the Queen's political will. Looked at emotionally, both Ralegh and his Queen were merely performing the rituals of courtly love, with none of the true intimacy, perhaps even love, that Elizabeth expressed for men such as Robert Dudley, Earl of Leicester or Robert Devereux, Earl of Essex. But surely Elizabeth, that most canny of monarchs, would not have heaped so much wealth and status on Captain Ralegh, fresh from the Irish front line, unless there was something about the man that made him stand out from the other courtiers? Sir Walter and his Queen were lovers, but it is highly unlikely that their 'love' was ever physically expressed. It was an eroticised political relationship, not a political sexual relationship, and Elizabeth was on top.

The poetry exchanged between the two offers hints of the complex interplay between Walter and his Elizabeth. Ralegh's verses (for he was a man of many talents, who quickly became known as one of Elizabeth's 'crew of courtly makers, noblemen and gentlemen'), passionately celebrate the Queen's eternal power. She is the moon goddess Cynthia, and he is the sea, the 'water' (his nickname, from his Devonian pronunciation of his name). His every movement is governed by her power and the depth of his love mirrors the depth of the ocean. His is the voice of the fashionably lovesick character:

> Fortune hath taken thee away, my love,
> My life's soul and my soul's heaven above;
> Fortune hath taken thee away, my princess;
> My only light and my true fancy's mistress

And so it continues; on and on, and on. Intriguingly, Elizabeth's reassuring, but also deeply patronising, reply survives:

> Ah, silly Pug, wert thou so sore afraid?
> Mourn not, my Wat, nor be thou so dismayed.

The Queen ends her poem by commanding 'silly' (innocent but also foolish) Ralegh to get a grip:

> Revive again and live without all dread,
> The less afraid, the better thou shalt speed.

Sir Walter's position as Elizabeth's 'silly pug', the extent to which he would 'speed' under her command, depended not on these poetic exchanges, but on trust. It was essential to the mechanics of personal monarchy and particularly to the operation of the Privy Chamber.

The basic structure remained, regardless of which palace the Queen was resident in. Beyond the Privy Chamber, the Queen's (almost) private space, lay a series of rooms: a gallery, a great hall, a great chamber, but always a Presence Chamber, with the royal throne and its canopy. For Queen Elizabeth's subjects to reach anywhere near this throne, anywhere near the Royal Presence, sometimes took months of bribes, gifts and letters. Even then, the Queen might not emerge from her guarded and locked private chambers. But the wait would be worthwhile, since this was the only place that counted: all power rested in the will and person of the Queen. Access was everything.

The Privy Chamber was the Queen's chief refuge from the constant pressure of those who wanted that access. Only a handful of people saw the woman behind the royal performance and the portraits. Sir Walter Ralegh was one. As Captain of the Guard, he was in a uniquely privileged position.

Elizabeth did not merely trust Sir Walter; she knew how to exploit his particular and rare set of skills, in war and in peace, in England

and far from English shores. The Queen well understood that her 'silly pug' was far from silly; that, above and beyond the exchange of verses of love, his talent with words could be useful to her and the English state. In the autumn of 1591, when the news began to come that English ships had suffered a humiliating defeat at the hands of the enemy, Spain, he would be especially valuable to his Queen.

The very ship that Ralegh was to have sailed in (if only the Queen had permitted him to leave her side) had been taken by the Spanish. It was, astonishingly, the only English vessel lost during the many years of war. Elizabeth turned to Sir Walter: could he transform this actual defeat into a moral victory? Of course he could. Ralegh's tale, *The Last Fight of the Revenge*, tells the glorious story of a lone English captain's brave stand against a vast Spanish fleet. Yes, the ship was lost. Yes, the captain (Richard Grenville, late of Virginia) was killed. But all the glory was England's and her Queen's. Sir Richard Grenville's foolish, dangerous lone stand was transformed into an act of transcendent heroism. Ralegh's Queen is ordained by God to bring Spanish Catholicism to its knees and lead England to further Protestant greatness. Elizabeth, 'by the favour of God' will continue to:

> Resist, repel, and confound all whatsoever attempts against her sacred Person or kingdom In the mean time, let the Spaniard and traitor vaunt of their success: and we her true and obedient vassals guided by the shining light of her virtues, shall always love her, serve her, and obey her to the end of our lives.

Ralegh was very, very good at this kind of thing.

The only problem was that his words were empty. At precisely the time he was writing of love, service and obedience to his Queen, Ralegh was betraying her. He was risking every single political achievement and financial reward of the preceding decade – and there had been many. Perhaps even his freedom. Perhaps even his life. Whatever or whoever caused him to betray his Queen was powerful enough to make the risk worthwhile.

Bess Throckmorton and her family had known about the risks and rewards of Tudor life, riding the rollercoaster of religious and regime changes, for generations. Bess's father, Nicholas, was of the Queen's generation and in fact lived with Elizabeth when he was a very young man. Nicholas had turned his back on his family's Catholicism (of his eighteen siblings, only one other converted to the new religion) and had therefore been eligible to join the household of Henry VIII's sixth and last wife, the staunchly Protestant Katherine Parr. In Queen Katherine's house, Nicholas was joined by two young girls, Lady Jane Grey and the Princess Elizabeth, daughter of Henry VIII's ill-fated second wife, Anne Boleyn. The girls' futures would be entangled with Nicholas's for many years but he thrived in Parr's household. He moved on to serve the boy King Edward VI, Henry VIII's successor, as a Gentleman of the Privy Chamber and cemented his position at court through his marriage, in around 1549, to Anne Carew.

Anne, Bess's mother, came from another prominent courtier family with their fair share of experience of the dangers of royal service. Anne's mother was rumoured to be Henry VIII's mistress. More verifiably, she was the first cousin of Anne Boleyn and Catherine Howard, two of Henry's Queens. Anne's father, another Nicholas, was one of Henry VIII's closest friends from youth. He had even survived his King's first marital cataclysm; when Katherine of Aragon was discarded in favour of Anne Boleyn, Nicholas Carew remained loyal to Katherine. The King was, however, a dangerous friend. Years later, and with a suddenness that surprised no one in the final years of his despotism, Henry turned on his friend, now deemed a traitor. Carew was executed in 1539.

Survivors to their fingertips, Nicholas Throckmorton and Anne Carew thrived under Henry's son, Edward, who succeeded to the throne at only nine years old. The boy King's health was not good, however, and it became clear that he would not reach adulthood. The newly-married Throckmortons had to move very carefully. The King's choice of successor, or more importantly that of his chief adviser, the Earl of Northumberland, was Nicholas's erstwhile housemate, the young Lady Jane Grey, daughter of Frances, Duchess of Suffolk. Lady Jane's tenuous claim to the throne rested on the fact that she was the granddaughter of King Henry VIII's sister, Mary. But her real value lay in her Protestantism and in the prospect of her marriage to Northumberland's son, Guilford Dudley. King Edward himself encouraged this marriage, as part of his continuing attempts to set aside the claims of his older sisters, the Princesses Mary and Elizabeth. Northumberland feared the accession to the throne of the fiercely Catholic Princess Mary Tudor for good personal and political reasons, and Edward VI was ideologically opposed to any return to the religion of Rome. Between them, Edward and Northumberland overturned both Henry VIII's will and the Succession Act of 1544.

The pace of events quickened as the young King's health deteriorated. By June, Lady Jane Grey was suffering physically and mentally from the strain of the expectations laid on her. Edward VI died on 6 July 1553 but the public announcement of his death was delayed for two days. A further two days later, Lady Jane was brought by barge from Sion House, home of the Duke of Northumberland, to the Tower of London, pausing at Westminster and Durham House. At the Tower, she was proclaimed Queen. Only nine days later, and in the face of a hostile response to Queen Jane in London and elsewhere, Princess Mary Tudor was proclaimed Queen in London: 'a conciliar conspiracy had put Queen Jane on the throne; a popular rising deprived her of it' as the historian Susan Brigden puts it. It appeared that the issue of legitimacy (Mary was Henry VIII's daughter, while Jane was merely his great-niece) counted with the people, that Northumberland was widely distrusted if not hated and, probably most significantly, that the reformed religion Jane represented had not taken as firm a root in the country as its Protestant leaders thought or hoped.

Lady Jane Grey thus became yet another casualty of the power struggles of the mid-sixteenth century. One of the many tragic ironies of her situation was that her own father rallied support for Queen Mary and renounced the regal claims of his daughter. When it became clear that she would not be sister to a Queen, Jane's sister Catherine, who had been hastily married to Henry Herbert, was as hastily cast off by her new husband's family. The convenient, and possibly valid, excuse was that the marriage had not been consummated. Jane Grey's father and mother, the Duke and Duchess of Suffolk, were pardoned by the merciful new Queen Mary, but Jane's fate remained uncertain. Only a few months later, in the first winter of Mary's reign, her father was involved in a rebellion against the Queen's authority. His change of allegiance assured not only his execution but also that of his daughter; Lady Jane was beheaded on 12 February 1554.

Bess Throckmorton's parents, in particular her mother Anne, had backed the wrong Queen. Anne had been dangerously close to the Grey faction, even standing as proxy for Queen Jane as a godmother on the very day, 19 July 1553, that Queen Mary was proclaimed in London. The accession of Mary, and the subsequent execution of Lady Jane, was politically disastrous for both Anne and her husband Nicholas. Only a week after the execution of Lady Jane, Nicholas was imprisoned in the Tower for his part in the Duke of Suffolk's recent conspiracy. Anne, heavily pregnant with their first child, was preparing for her confinement. Two months later, in April, her husband's case came to trial at the Guildhall. The charge was treason.

For Anne Throckmorton, daughter of the executed 'traitor' Nicholas Carew, this was disturbingly familiar territory. Astonishingly, husband Nicholas was acquitted by the jury. Queen Mary was so distraught at the decision, one without precedent in a treason trial, that she allegedly took to her bed for three days. Once acquitted, Sir Nicholas moved to ensure that Anne – who in the meantime had given birth to a boy, christened William – would be provided for in case of further threats to his life.

Having survived the early months of Queen Mary's reign, Anne and Nicholas maintained a tactfully low profile until the accession of the Protestant Queen Elizabeth I allowed for their political resurgence. Their only daughter, Bess, was born in 1565, by which time the new Queen's rule was secure, or as secure as any monarch's of that time.

There would be one further twist in the tale linking the Throckmorton and Grey families. When Bess's father Nicholas died in 1571,

Anne remarried just six months later. Her new husband was Adrian Stokes, first the secretary, then husband, then widower of Frances Brandon, Duchess of Suffolk. That made him, significantly, the step-father of the one surviving Grey sister. Anne and Adrian's country estate was Beaumanor, the Duchess's former residence, and it was at Beaumanor that Bess lived for much of her childhood, in rooms that were still named for their Grey mistresses.

Such a tempestuous, deadly family history might have made a lesser woman than Anne Throckmorton aspire to a quiet life for her only daughter Bess. Instead, Anne was determined to place her daughter at court and, in 1584 (also a high point for Walter Ralegh), she achieved her goal. On 8 November Queen Elizabeth invested Bess, aged nineteen, as a Gentlewoman of the Privy Chamber.

Bess, like Sir Walter, now had access to the intimate space around the monarch. Elizabeth's women controlled admittance to her person and had intimate knowledge of the monarch's disposition, both invaluable political commodities in a personal monarchy. As a Gentlewoman of the Chamber, Bess could and did act as broker, of both influence and information, for the gentlemen who sought the Queen's favour. Even the Queen's most powerful male ministers knew that they had to speak, and listen, to the Queen's women. They aimed, before actually seeing the Queen, to learn 'her Majesty's disposition by some in the Privy Chamber with whom you must keep credit, for that will stand you much in stead'.

Just as women such as Bess Throckmorton shielded Elizabeth from the demands of her nation, her Captain of the Guard, Sir Walter Ralegh, protected the royal body from the very real threat of assassination. Both had to be loyal to the Queen, and the Queen alone. For six or seven years it is possible they were just that. But, in the summer of 1591, Bess became pregnant by Walter. In the autumn, the couple married in such secrecy that we still do not know the date. Ralegh's lines on his ideal woman celebrate both her mind and her body in delightfully explicit terms:

A violet breath and lips of jelly
Her hair not black nor over-bright
And of the softest down her belly
As for her inside he'd have it
Only of wantonness and wit.

But it was never just about sex. In an era in which the personal *was* the political, Bess's pregnancy and the couple's secret marriage were a challenge to the power, authority and future of the Queen herself. And it was never just about Bess and Walter, for, in that overheated summer of 1591, Ralegh achieved a telling *rapprochement* with his rival Essex. Perhaps Essex saw an opportunity to neutralise his competitor by bringing him into his circle, somewhere Ralegh (with more money than he knew what to do with, but also with a lurking and unfulfilled aspiration to be accepted into the aristocratic elite of the nation) may have been only too happy to be. It is certain is that the Earl of Essex did nothing to expose either the affair or the marriage, and there is evidence that he encouraged both. In return, Ralegh made his rival look good in *The Last Fight of the Revenge*, transforming Essex's inept and unwanted participation in the military action two years earlier in Portugal into a masterpiece of wartime strategy.

As her belly swelled, both Sir Walter and Bess pretended that nothing was happening. She maintained her position as a Gentlewoman of the Privy Chamber, while Sir Walter was busy with boats, finances and the brave new world. By November, and the Accession Day celebrations, all seemed to be going well. Elizabeth suspected nothing. Arthur Throckmorton, Bess's brother, reported in his diary that 'the queen spoke to me and made me to kiss her hand'. A couple of days later, Arthur recorded in his diary, in discreet French, that it was '*le jour que je saye le maryage de ma soeur*'; the day he found out about the marriage of his sister. Arthur promptly 'spoke' with Sir Walter in December but still there was no leak. It all stayed in the family.

Ralegh knew that it was possible to get away, if not with murder, then with the occasional sexual imbroglio. Unsurprisingly, frustration with the rule (and rules) of the Virgin Queen frequently led to eruptions of distinctly unchaste behaviour. The year 1591 was a particularly fruitful one for scandal, ranging from the banishment of Mr Dudley for kissing Mistress Cavendish, to Sir Francis Darcy being sent to the Tower 'about Mistress Lee who was brought abed in the court'.

Ralegh also knew that it was possible to father a child without the tedious necessity of marrying the child's mother. His will of 1597 left five hundred marks to his 'reputed daughter begotten on the body of Alice Goold now in Ireland'. This is around £333: the same will left £200 to Thomas Harriot, who also received 'all my books and the furniture in his own chamber and in my bedchamber at Durham House, together with all such black suits of apparel as I have in the same house'. It is possible that Alice Goold was the daughter of James Gold of Cork, Attorney General of Munster, who in the late 1580s was commissioned by Queen Elizabeth to survey the lands confiscated from the Earl of Desmond (and other rebels) for distribution amongst the English undertakers. But we don't know Alice and Walter's daughter's name, when she was born, or even if she was in fact Ralegh's child. What happens in Ireland, stays in Ireland.

Sir Walter Ralegh did not marry Alice Goold. He did marry Bess Throckmorton. An image of Bess from this time survives, although only as a black and white print of the lost original painting. She wears the conventional fashions of the 1590s: puffed sleeves ballooning, lace ruff immaculately starched, jewels ostentatiously displayed. There are a few details in the picture that might confuse the viewer. Bess wears the open ruff traditionally associated with an unmarried woman, but a large ring sits on the thumb of her left hand. Is this possibly a wedding ring? At that time, it was a matter of personal choice on which finger one wore the wedding ring. Is there even a hint of her pregnancy? Her stomach is certainly more rounded than in other women's portraits of the time. These details may or may not be significant; what is certain is that the woman portrayed, with her wide, flat cheekbones, long nose and slightly protruding bottom lip, may not be a conventional beauty but she nevertheless exudes a strange power.

The social and political reality was that Bess, the stepsister (admittedly via many steps) of Lady Jane Grey the nine-days' Queen, was of a higher rank than Ralegh, with familial ties to the monarchy, and a father, Nicholas Throckmorton, who was for many years Queen Elizabeth's trusted fixer in the tricky business regarding Mary Queen of Scots.

Most accounts of their relationship have Walter as virile and culpable and Bess as his sexual victim and political nemesis. One of the earliest biographies has him roguishly 'devirginating a Maid of Honour', which is deemed 'the worst Action of his whole Life'. Nevertheless, Ralegh does the honourable thing, by marrying 'the Object of his Love, the deflowered Lady'. The evidence suggests that Bess Throckmorton was far from a passive and innocent victim of Sir Walter's allegedly skilful seduction. This is not to diminish the man's attractions. His immense wealth and handsome face might have been enough for many women. He was charming, experienced, urbane and intelligent. His dark, Celtic good looks made him suspiciously similar in appearance and outlook to Bess's father. And he could write. But in the end, he was the fifth son of a Devon squire. Bess was a Throckmorton. Understand that, and Ralegh's ambitious plan starts to become clearer.

During the winter of 1591 he gave nothing away. His letters were studiously businesslike (if at times written so quickly as to be illegible, and hastily addressed to the wrong brother), concerned only with the organisation of his next great naval expedition against the Spanish in Central America. He was, gloriously, at last to be a full Admiral, in command of thirteen ships that would attack the Spanish silver fleet and, while there, sack Panama. Ralegh, being Ralegh, is preoccupied, quite rightly, with supplies for his men: fifty tons of cider in good casks; ten thousand dry Newfoundland fish to be sent to Plymouth. The serious planning for the Panama voyage began in early 1592; the ships were supposed to leave in February. Typically, there were delays. On 3 March Ralegh wrote again to his brother (getting the name right this time). He had wanted the sailors to be ready by 16 March but 'now, through many urgent occasions' he is 'constrained to defer' and asks John Gilbert to make sure the sailors are levied 'from places least infected' by plague, and to be ready on the twentieth.

Bess remained at court, still concealing, goodness knows how, her pregnancy. On 11 February, her ever-loyal brother Arthur paid twenty-eight shillings for a nurse 'for fourteen weeks from Monday next'. Bess came to his house in Mile End at the end of the month. She was cutting it fine, but if she could keep her non-attendance at court to under a fortnight, she would not need to obtain a licence to authorise her absence. Arthur wrote that his sister had come 'to lie here'. Both meanings are in play: Bess would both prepare for the birth of her child and continue to deceive the world, from Arthur's house.

Hiding in Mile End, Bess was physically not far from Sir Walter, who was often in Chatham Docks supervising preparations for the Panama expedition. To see each other was, however, simply too dangerous. Ralegh had invested an immense amount of money and time in setting up this voyage and its success relied on his charismatic leadership. An attack on Panama would serve his purposes well, enabling him to be as far away as possible if and when the news of his marriage and child broke on the Queen.

Despite his military, naval and political experience, Ralegh's temperament in this very different kind of crisis had not been truly tested. But it would be, by the ever-rising Robert Cecil. As the birth approached, Sir Walter explicitly denied any relationship with Bess in a series of lies to Cecil, who had been pushing Ralegh for some answers in the light of reports and rumours. Sir Walter claimed that there had been no marriage, that there would be no marriage and that he was attached to no one other than the Queen:

> I mean not to come away, as they say I will, for fear of a marriage and I know not what. If any such thing were I would have imparted it unto your self before any man living. And therefore I pray believe it not, and I beseech you to suppress what you can any such malicious report. For I protest before God, there is none on the face of the earth that I would be fastened unto.

What Sir Walter did not know, but probably should have guessed, was that Robert Cecil had belatedly found out about the secret marriage, most probably during the week at the end of February when Bess left the court. Therefore, when Ralegh wrote this letter on 10 March, Cecil knew that he was being lied to. Sir Walter thus destroyed any precarious bond of trust between these two profoundly dissimilar men. The letter, born of expediency, was political folly of the highest order: the request for Cecil to suppress the 'malicious reports' was naïve; and to swear 'before God' that he is telling the truth was downright blasphemous.

Bess went into labour on the morning of 29 March: that afternoon she 'was delivered of a boy between 2 and 3'. Sir Walter, still waiting for the wind at Chatham, heard of the birth of his son from Arthur Throckmorton's footman Dick, who rode down with the news that same afternoon. Sir Walter stayed away (what else could he do?) but he sent his half-brother, Adrian Gilbert to Bess, with fifty pounds of spending money. This generous sum, Gilbert later recalled, was spent 'at Mile End Green, and about London, when the Lady Ralegh was first delivered with child; and when most of Sir Walter's friends forsook him'.

Ralegh could not afford to let the news of the birth of his first son break his stride. Two days after the baby's birth, he was at Portland in the west of England, immersed in further expedition business, 'ready to take the first wind', picking up runaway mariners ('for we shall be undone if we miss them') and getting the all-important fish supplies on board.

On 10 April 1592 the boy child was christened, with the unusual name of Damerei. His godfathers were his uncle, Arthur Throckmorton and, surprisingly, given his history with the baby's father, the Earl of Essex. These were telling choices. Essex was supporting the marriage of his chief political rival to a woman from a solidly and aggressively Protestant family, just as he had allied himself in marriage to the widow of the Protestant soldier-hero Sir Philip Sidney, the daughter of the spymaster and foreign policy hawk Walsingham. The new political order envisioned, longed for, by Essex revolved around these marriages and their offspring. The marriage of Sir Walter Ralegh and Bess Throckmorton symbolised a vision for England: the honourable soldier and the Protestant gentlewoman would bring forth brave sons to fight for God's own nation. It was irrelevant that Essex had spent long periods of time apart from his own wife and had had numerous sexual relationships, including one with a maid of honour, Elizabeth Southwell, that resulted in the birth of an illegitimate son, Walter Devereux, at the end of 1591. This was not about sex; it was about establishing a political cabal.

Did Essex balk at the choice of the baby's name? The Raleghs' aspirations are nowhere more apparent than in the ambitious pretensions implicit in 'Damerei', so called because Ralegh had 'proved', with the aid of a genealogist, that he was descended from the Plantagenets. Yes: he had royal blood. In 1587, Ralegh, then in the ascendant at court, commissioned a history of Ireland from a well-known scholar, John Hooker. Hooker used his dedication to make public new evidence about Ralegh's royal ancestry. You had to go back to the Plantagenets to find it, and you had to accept that one Sir John de Ralegh had married the daughter of de Amerie or Damerei of Clare, a relation of Edward I, but if you accepted these facts it all made perfect historical sense.

Essex was not too alarmed by the royal name and nominated Ralegh to be a Knight of the Garter. This was the most exclusive social group in the realm: its numbers were limited to twenty-five and since the appointment was for life, new investitures depended on mortality. Only 'the best, most excellent, and renowned persons in all virtues and honour' could receive the honour, symbolised by 'a garter garnished with gold and precious stones, to wear daily on the left leg only; also a kirtle [tunic], gown, cloak, chaperon [head covering], collar and other solemn and magnificent apparel, both of stuff and fashion exquisite and heroical to wear at high feasts'. Ralegh would have looked very fine. Unfortunately, Essex was the only peer of the realm to nominate Sir Walter, who never did receive the Garter.

Ralegh had more pressing concerns at the end of April, as he waited for the tide to take the fleet out of Falmouth. He clearly wanted to be out of the way if and when trouble came. He began speaking about the expedition as a matter of life and death: 'if we live we hope to repay all again, if not we shall reckon in the kingdom of Heaven'. Bess, astonishingly, returned to court on 27 April, just four weeks after Damerei's birth. Her brother Arthur still paying the bills, the baby was sent with his nurse to Enfield, out of sight, but probably not out of mind. At the very moment when Bess audaciously re-established herself as a Gentlewoman of the Privy Chamber, the weather and sea conditions were at last propitious for Ralegh and he made his escape from Falmouth. The couple were back where they wanted to be.

Only a day after setting sail, however, Sir Martin Frobisher caught up with Sir Walter and demanded that he return to court, on the orders of the Queen. Ralegh, perhaps foolishly, ignored these orders, insisting that he needed to stay with the fleet until it was fully at sea. He was quick to understand that this was not just another example of Elizabeth's desire to have her dear pug near her. Rather, it was the first real threat to his special relationship with the Queen. The stalling over, on 16 May he was back in Plymouth and a few days later back in London.

Still the expected storm did not come from the Queen. Could Elizabeth really have been worried about Sir Walter's safety at sea? Relieved, Sir Walter and Bess, clearly both increasingly confident, took steps to regularise their relationship. For Ralegh, this meant asserting his financial and legal rights as a husband. He sent his man, Browne, to Arthur Throckmorton's house to draw up an *ex post facto* marriage settlement. For Bess, or rather Lady Ralegh, if only the world could know, this meant bringing her baby and his wet nurse back to the City of London from their exile in Enfield. She, Damerei and the nurse all went, on 21 May, to the house of her long-suffering brother in Mile End. Once again, Arthur paid the nurse.

The confidence implicit in these actions was ill-founded. A mere three days later, a representative of the Lord Chamberlain came to the house at Mile End. The writing was on the wall because the Lord Chamberlain was one of the three principal officers of the Royal

Household, with particular responsibility for the monarch's private and semi-private chambers, including the royal bedchamber. The messenger carried a warrant for the arrest and interrogation of Arthur and Anna Throckmorton. They were questioned to establish the extent of their involvement in the deception surrounding the two-month-old baby lodged in their house. This may have been when Bess realised just how much her brother and sister-in-law were risking; the point when she realised that it was time for her husband to stand up and be counted, the point when she had had enough of the lies. Whatever the case, there is a certain defiance in her next move. On 28 May 1592, baby Damerei was at last formally taken by his mother to his father's house. For a brief twenty-four hours, the Raleghs were a conventional family in their home, Durham House.

After the deceptive lull, the storm finally broke. First, the Queen's men came to question Sir Walter, who was placed under house arrest. For two days he was interrogated, allowed just one private visit from Arthur. The two men (if they had any sense) would have attempted to co-ordinate their stories. The Queen then moved against her Gentlewoman. Unlike Sir Walter, Bess was not allowed to stay in her own house but was taken by Sir Thomas Heneage, the Vice Chamberlain, to a 'courtyard' somewhere in London. Heneage was one of Elizabeth's most trusted spymasters, heir to the feared Walsingham; no doubt his team of secret agents had been collecting information for days, weeks or months. In happier times, Sir Walter and Sir Thomas had exchanged poems about the nature of love. Now Bess was in effect his prisoner and her husband was fighting for his political life.

Arthur quickly left London. Summoned for a second round of questioning, he replied that he was needed at his country estate at Paulerspury in Northamptonshire. He was nevertheless hauled back and made two formal statements on 10 and 12 June 1592. Suspiciously (and frustratingly for the historian), neither of these documents survives, but whatever Arthur said appeared to clear his name. He was allowed to return to the relative safety of the country and its pursuits; a few weeks later he was hunting with his best friend.

On one level hope flickered. Perhaps even at this stage the crisis could be managed, or at least suppressed, and the Queen, the most important player, might live and let live if only for the sake of min-imising the scandal. Indeed, Elizabeth appeared to be mellowing towards Sir Walter, confirming on 27 June 1592 the transfer to him of the estate of Sherborne. Granted Sherborne by his Queen, he was still not a free man.

Deprived of the lifeblood of personal contact with his monarch, Ralegh was struggling: 'the torment of my mind cannot be greater' he wrote in desperation. He was also angry. With typically bitter irony, he complained to Charles, Lord Howard, that Her Majesty thought it was, as he put it, 'profitable to punish' his 'great treasons', suggesting that on the one hand that it would *not* be profitable to punish him and that it would have been profitable to have been allowed to attack the Spanish treasure fleet, and on the other that his solitary 'unfortunate accident' was being grossly inflated into 'great treason'.

He continues, because he cannot stop himself:

> But I see there is a determination to disgrace me and ruin me, and therefore I beseech your lordship not to offend her Majesty any further by suing for me. I am now resolved of the matter. I only desire that I may be stayed not one hour from all the extremity that either law or precedent can avow, and if that be little would God it were withal concluded, that I might feed the lions as I go by to save labour.

Ralegh's attempts at irony fall very flat, as does his half-hearted joke about being thrown to the lions of the Tower of London (the monarch's personal zoo, as well as prison). His secret marriage, his secret baby, were, if not 'great treasons', then certainly a political and personal betrayal of his Queen. As for 'profit', Elizabeth would gain far more money from of Ralegh's downfall than she ever had from his success.

What is absent from his letters is any explicit acknowledgement of what he has done. This was not only true of Ralegh. There may have been a whispering campaign, but no one appeared willing to spell out exactly what had happened. There is a mysterious silence in the official records about why Ralegh, his wife, her brother and her sister-in-law were interrogated. It was even unclear whether it was indeed one 'unfortunate accident' or the 'several occasions' mentioned in one fascinated courtier's letter. The Earl of Essex's poetry vividly captures the atmosphere at court. He is no great writer but he knows at first hand that 'heavens, what hell! The bands of love are broken, Nor must a thought of such a thing be spoken'.

If the precise nature of the charges remains hidden, so do the Queen's motivations. The strangely stop-start progress of events suggests that the conventional interpretation, that the Queen, for whom 'vanity was the one constant force', was fired with sexual jealousy and banished Sir Walter from court 'when he seduced her maid' is inadequate. As the historian Susan Doran points out in her study of the Queen's courtships, there is no need to explain Elizabeth's behaviour in terms of deep-seated psychological damage and neurosis, let alone to suggest that she was motivated by vanity and jealousy; the Queen's anger at the secret weddings of her ladies and courtiers usually had a political cause. In general terms she wanted her privy chamber to be apolitical and consequently required her ladies to be free from loyalties to a husband and his kin. By marrying, her ladies risked their political neutrality; furthermore, when they married (often by necessity) secretly, they demonstrated to their mistress their untrustworthiness and divided loyalties. Marriages conducted without the Queen's 'privity' (her permission and knowledge) made her 'grievously offended'. Moreover, Queen Elizabeth's responses to the disloyalty of her female courtiers varied: Mary Shelton had her ears boxed, while Bridget Manners' husband was sent to prison.

Why was no one willing to talk about the issue in this case? More specifically, why was the Queen particularly aggrieved? In the short term, probably because Sir Walter could not keep quiet. Although it was clear that Her Majesty was not receiving his complaints well, Ralegh was unable to resist making one more attempt. His sense of urgency was compounded by the knowledge that the Queen was making final preparations for her summer progress, when anyone who was anyone would leave London.

Time was running out. A letter recounts how, catching sight of the royal barges assembling on the Thames at Blackfriars, Ralegh physically struggled with his keeper, his kinsman George Carew, saying 'that he would disguise himself and get into a pair of oars to ease his mind but with a sight of the queen, or else, he protested, his heart would break'. Tellingly, the correspondent (Ralegh's friend and cousin, so on paper a sympathiser) noted: 'all lameness was forgotten'. Even his friends saw through Ralegh's histrionics. He needed to calm down. He didn't.

He wrote to Robert Cecil, hoping that he would pass his words on to the Queen. Ralegh's letter is an extraordinary outpouring of intense emotion, ostensibly directed at a no doubt bemused, and possibly amused, Cecil but clearly directed to Elizabeth. Sir Walter certainly piles on the praise:

> I that was wont to behold her riding like Alexander, hunting like Diana, walking like Venus – the gentle wind blowing her fair hair about her pure cheeks like a nymph, sometimes sitting in that shade like a nymph [at this point, he crosses out 'nymph' and inserts 'goddess', having realised he has used 'nymph' already], sometimes singing like an angel, sometimes playing like Orpheus.

Sir Walter hints at the cause of the goddess Elizabeth's wrath but always euphemistically and always stressing the singularity of it all: 'once amiss…one frail misfortune…one drop of gall'. This is at best disingenuous, if it could be construed to mean the sexual act that created Damerei. Judged more harshly, it was a blatantly self-serving lie. Ralegh, as victim, presents himself as trapped in London (as he indeed was, under house arrest), with his beloved Queen going 'away so far off' while he remains incarcerated in 'a dark prison'. Significantly, when he revised the letter, he added the words 'all alone', thus not merely drawing attention to his prospective loneliness but also emphasising that Elizabeth had succeeded in separating him from his wife. By the end of a letter that becomes hysterical, Ralegh has completely lost sight of Cecil as audience and his words are addressed solely to his Queen. The letter completely failed in its purpose (the Queen left Greenwich on 25 July and was at the Nonsuch Palace by the 27th) and probably served only to exacerbate the situation. Ralegh was right to describe himself as 'a fish cast on dry land, gasping for breath, with lame legs and lamer lungs [first time spelt 'lunges', second time 'loonges']'.

Things became serious. House arrest, until now seen as punishment enough for both Sir Walter and Bess, was insufficient. The Tower was spoken of. The 'dark prison' of Ralegh's fantasy was to become, it was said, a harsh reality. Gossip went around London like wildfire. On Sunday night, Sir Edward Stafford wrote, with gleeful cattiness, to Anthony Bacon: 'If you have any thing to do with Sir Walter Ralegh, or any love to make to Mistress Throckmorton, at the Tower tomorrow you may speak with them, if the countermand come not tonight, as some think it will not be, and particularly he that hath charge to send them thither'. These revealing comments suggest first that the marriage between Ralegh and Bess was not common knowledge (Bess was still 'Mistress Throckmorton', although this could be irony) but clearly the existence of her baby was, made evident in the snide aside about her willingness to make love.

Second, they suggest a power struggle behind the scenes. The order to send Ralegh and his lady to the Tower had been drawn up but someone else was attempting to have that order countermanded. 'He that hath charge to send them thither' believed that the countermand would not be achieved. Who this is remains unclear but it is most likely Robert Cecil, who may well have been secretly delighted with the turn of events. No countermand came.

The Queen may have believed that the relationship was simply a matter of rampant hormones and could be ignored once a proper show of outrage had been manifest. But when she found out that there had been a marriage, that the baby was legitimate, that the boy's parents claimed he was descended from the Plantagenets, that the Earl of Essex was his godfather and that his mother had a family history of treachery and pretension to the Crown, she acted. Just over a year after Damerei had been conceived, four months into their son's life, Walter and Bess finally paid the price for their ambitions. Queen Elizabeth, at the Nonsuch Palace, signed the warrant for the arrest and imprisonment of her wayward gentlewoman and captain. On 7 August 1592, as the summer heat worked on the city's dirt, the pair were imprisoned in the Tower of London.

Ralegh the wordsmith turned to poetry, clearly not having learned from the failure of his earlier passionate letter to Robert Cecil. More than five hundred lines of (admittedly superb, if by turns self-pitying and aggressive) verse later, he must have felt he had captured the intensity of his feelings for his Queen. Having written out his poetic offering in his best italic hand, he sent it to Cecil in the hope that he would pass it on to Elizabeth. Cecil, unsurprisingly did not, although whether in an attempt to further marginalise his rival or tactfully, to protect Ralegh from the potentially problematic impact of his own words – Sir Walter is at his most bitter – remains unclear. In the mid-nineteenth century, a scholar working through papers held in Hatfield House, the Cecil family seat, stumbled upon these remarkable poems. For all their apocalyptic sense of urgency in 1592, the manuscript had lain unseen for some 250 years.

Bess attempted to get the support of her noblewomen friends and risked a gentle criticism of Robert Cecil. Perhaps he has been 'deceived in his judgement' and 'it may be he findeth his error'. She is 'daily put in hope of' delivery from the Tower of London (a hope that would be dashed again and again), but she is also aware that she may do 'harm' to Sir Walter 'to speak of my delivery'. Her studied cheerfulness and practicality almost conceal the perilous situation that she finds herself in but there are clear indications that she is both ill and frightened. The 'plague is greatly seized' and coming closer and closer to the Tower. Bess's opening lines refer to the end, to her sick estate and to her illness, which continues 'even so still'. There are moments of studied optimism, but she acknowledges that her future, even if she is released, is uncertain. 'Who knoweth what will become of me when I am out?' she asks. And yet, despite her obvious fears and sickness, Bess celebrates her marriage, never showing anything other than complete loyalty and devotion. She writes to her friend that 'I assure you truly, I never desired, nor never would desire my liberty without the good liking nor advising of Sir W R' and she goes on defiantly, 'we are true within ourselves, I can assure you'. Proud to the last, she signs the letter ER, a public proclamation of her married status and, disconcertingly, the Queen's cipher.

Safely out of reach, in her palace at Nonsuch, of the encroaching plague in London, the other ER received news of the capture of the richest prize ever taken by English ships, the Spanish treasure galleon *Madre de Dios*. English ships? They were also Ralegh's ships. Elizabeth had denied her errant courtier the opportunity to sail with his fleet to Panama but on paper he remained the expedition's leader and it had succeeded beyond anyone's dreams. The *Madre de Dios* contained half a million pounds' worth of treasure and all the spices and gold, ebony and ivory, that could be dreamed of by an ambitious adventurer. But the distribution of the booty was being grossly mishandled and by the time the looters had finished their business, the cargo was worth less than 150,000 pounds. Robert Cecil was horrified by the chaos: 'Fouler ways, desperate ways, no more obstinate people did I ever meet with'. Sir John Hawkins, on the spot in Dartmouth and desperate for support, knew who was needed: 'Sir Walter Ralegh is the especial man'.

Soldier Ralegh and sailor Ralegh saw his opportunity. As soon as the *Madre de Dios* came into Dartmouth, he began offering the Queen and her council a financial deal in return for his release from the Tower of London. On 11 September 1592 he wrote to Lord Burghley, promising hard cash: 'Four score thousand pound is more than ever any man presented Her Majesty as yet. If God have sent it for my ransom I hope Her Majesty of her abundant goodness will accept it'. Ralegh's offer of hard cash is framed by some very familiar rhetoric. Writing from his 'unsavoury dungeon', he has a 'faithful mind and a true desire to serve her' (which neatly glosses over the actions of his unfaithful body), and once again his letter ends with an implied plea direct to the Queen herself.

Whether it was promise of eighty thousand pounds or the declarations of a 'faithful mind' and 'true desire', the strategy appeared to work. A few days later, in mid-September, the Queen signed the order for Ralegh's conditional release. The following day he was out. In hours he was riding westwards, dashing off a letter of thanks to Lord Burghley from London, and yet another from Hartley Row, on the road west between Basingstoke and Bagshot. Burghley's son, Robert Cecil, capturing the essence of the man, noted that Ralegh's 'heart is broken, as he is extremely pensive, unless he is busied, in which he can toil terribly'.

It could have been worse. Ralegh was forbidden to appear in court and could not exercise his duties as Captain of the Guard, but he had been permitted to keep the Sherborne estate and his offices in the West Country. Ralegh was back in business, asking, from Hartley Row, for a commission to make enquiry into which goldsmiths and jewellers have gone down to Devon, intending to intercept them on their way back as, he promises, 'many things will be discovered'.

His wife had no such possibility of escape. Some who had supported and encouraged Lady Ralegh a few months earlier, not least the Earl of Essex, were quick to fade into the background in her time of trouble. All she had was a husband who would not even acknowledge her (there is continued and complete silence about Bess in Sir Walter's letters for fully the next three years). Did he believe she had ruined his political career?

Unable to offer eighty thousand pounds to the Queen and unwilling to deny her relationship with Ralegh, Bess remained alone in the Tower. As September continued, the heat in London did not abate. It was the end of one of the hottest summers in living memory and London was a city of drought; the Thames itself dried up. Conditions in the Tower deteriorated as the weeks went by but worse was to come in October, as the plague took a stranglehold on the city. Those who had returned to attend to business or the start of the new law term quickly packed up and left; even the legal sessions moved to Hertford, well north of London. The theatres closed; playwrights either fell silent or found other ways to earn their keep: this was the summer William Shakespeare turned to poetry. The Queen eventually returned from her summer progress but kept clear of the City of London and Westminster, preferring to stop at Hampton Court on 10 October. The heat and the plague acted on the weak; on those who could not leave. It was most probably in October that baby Damerei died, at only six months old. There is silence in the official records about this small tragedy and about the fate of the infant's mother. Was it a coincidence that Bess and her baby were left in prison in a plague-ridden London? ER, the Queen, may well have hoped that ER, her treacherous gentle-woman, would follow the baby Damerei, carrier of such an ambitious name, into the anonymity of a public plague pit.

At last, in deepest midwinter, Bess was allowed to leave the Tower. She went straight to the Sherborne estate. Her fallen husband, unlikely to be given any form of military, naval or political command any time soon, and estranged from both his Elizabeths, remained at Durham House. He had escaped being 'deciphered' as a traitor but it appeared that his fall from grace would be as rapid and complete as his rise to power.

6

Explorer

JUST OVER TWO YEARS later, Sir Walter Ralegh – the man who could not sleep on board a boat, who was by his own admission a poor 'footman' (walker) and a person of such an intellectual bent that he travelled with a chest full of books – found himself in a canoe up the Orinoco river in South America, thousands of miles from home.

The promise of £80,000 for Elizabeth had been enough to ensure his release from the Tower. Delivering the money, which duly found its way into the Crown's coffers, ensured that Ralegh stayed out of prison. It was not enough, however, to ensure his political rehabilitation. Ralegh was now therefore on a quest for the 'great and golden city of Manoa, which the Spaniards call El Dorado', which, if found, would make that eighty thousand pounds appear small change. The journey to what he called the 'large, rich, and beautiful empire of Guiana' (now part of Venezuela) was dressed in the clothes of gaining an empire for his Queen. But it was also a naked grab for money and power, both essential if Sir Walter were to regain anything close to the glory of the 1580s.

Ralegh also had a new personal motivation: a second son, Wat. His attachment to Wat, conceived at Sherborne in the early months of 1593 just weeks after Bess's release from the Tower of London, and christened there in November, is unquestionable. When, in the late summer of 1594, plague struck again, the new father was desperate: 'I had a post this morning from Sherborne. The plague is in the town very hot. My Bess is one way sent, her son another way, and I am in great trouble therewith'. Presumably, the plan was to separate mother and baby to minimise the chances of both succumbing. They both survived, this time.

This brush with plague not only shows a father's concern but also Ralegh the married man. This is the first letter in which Sir Walter acknowledges his marriage of three years before. Plague appears to have finally put an end to Ralegh's public amnesia about his wife. Once he has mentioned Bess, he does not stop; she features in his very next letter to Robert Cecil. For a man as complex, as capable of deception both of himself and of others, as Ralegh, it is very hard to assess the nature of his feelings for his wife. In part he is driven by a desire, a need, to confirm his son's legitimacy and secure his inheritance. Sir Walter may have lost vast tracts of political ground but he remained extremely wealthy and was determined his wealth should pass to Wat. Provision for his wife was simply not a priority. When he reviewed his finances in 1594 (and then later when he wrote his will in 1597) Ralegh allowed Bess a mere two hundred pounds a year after his death, which certainly would not have kept her in the manner to which she was accustomed. Everything else was to go to Wat.

While not particularly surprising, this is certainly not generous. Ralegh appears to take steps actively to exclude Bess from his financial dealings. He wrote in one letter that 'all the interest [the equity] is in my son', since the lease on the Sherborne estate has been assigned to young Wat 'without power of revocation'. If or when Ralegh dies, Bess receives no property and no influence over the property, just her two hundred pounds a year. Even so, Sir Walter expresses anxiety about this and desires his correspondent to keep quiet about the details: 'And besides by that means my wife will know that she can have no interest in my living, and so exclaim'. This statement is ambiguous: does Ralegh mean 'interest' in the sense of equity, in which case he is anxious that Bess will realise that she has absolutely no stake in his property and land (his 'living') and will thus complain of her unfair treatment? Or does it mean that Ralegh is worried that Bess would see the two hundred pounds as something valuable and that she would therefore have no interest in him living and more interest in a regular income after his death? Either way, his worry is that Bess will 'exclaim'. This evocative word carries its modern sense of crying out vehemently but had two other possible meanings in Ralegh's time, both characteristic of Lady Ralegh's behaviour. One was to 'accuse loudly', the other to 'expose an injustice'. As one of Christopher Marlowe's characters says at a particularly bloody moment, 'I curse thee, and exclaim thee, miscreant'.

Biographers – let alone film-makers – have not always done justice to Lady Ralegh's undoubted feistiness, nor have they acknowledged the tensions between her and her husband. Bess has been described as 'a devoted honourable wife' with 'blue eyes and blonde hair' (think Abby Cornish in *The Golden Age*), the marriage as 'without doubt, a happy one' and Ralegh as 'being obviously genuinely relaxed in his wife's company'. The documents, in contrast, suggest Ralegh was rarely 'relaxed' about Bess and often feared her reaction. Was Bess 'relaxed' in the company of Ralegh, the husband who would not even acknowledge her existence for the first three years of their marriage and who actively sought to constrain her financially in the event of his death? For a woman who appeared to value honesty and straight-talking so highly, what did she make of Ralegh's lies and evasions?

It has been suggested that deception on the scale Ralegh used reveals a man either devastatingly clear-sighted or completely self-hypnotised. Or perhaps both. He was a heady combination of these qualities, a man characterised by duality: intellectually brilliant but unable to control his passionate emotions, capable of extraordinary exertion (even Robert Cecil acknowledged that he could 'toil terribly') but also of periods of extreme passivity and depression. Bess Throckmorton had allied herself to one of the most visionary, mercurial men of her generation. It might be difficult to be relaxed in the company of a man who lived so intensely but it may well have been exciting.

When he was up, he was up, which explains why he was in a canoe on the Orinoco in the spring of 1595. Having seen off accusations of atheism and the threat of plague, by the end of 1594 the 'very gallant' Sir Walter was increasingly in London, a freewheeling adventurer again. In early December the Queen at last granted Ralegh permission to 'offend' the King of Spain and by Christmas he had organised the boats and men necessary for a voyage in search of the gold of El Dorado.

Bess attempted to stop him. She pleaded with Robert Cecil to use his power to 'stay' her husband. As Ralegh made his preparations to sail, his lady insisted that a bond should be drawn up between her and William Sanderson, the man who had been responsible for raising much of the money for the voyage. Bess demanded some protection against the possibility of a lawsuit from Sanderson to recover his investment from her if Ralegh did not return. If she herself was not going to gain from Ralegh's death at sea, she did not want to be saddled with his debts. Bess believed there were other, safer, ways in which Sir Walter could achieve his political rehabilitation.

He chose to make the voyage. It is tempting to conclude that Ralegh risked the crossing of the Atlantic not merely because he was driven by a vision of El Dorado but because at sea he could escape both the political elite with which he had to work and the political fictions that he himself had helped to create and by which he had to live. At sea, the strange blend of qualities that characterised the man come fully into play: he could be practical, pragmatic and task-oriented but also visionary and imaginative; he could be full of curiosity and wonder but equally full of scepticism. He could be in sole command.

Ralegh seems more comfortable pitting himself against the ocean than struggling with human enemies on dry land. The Commission into his atheism the previous summer had been a reminder of the very real dangers he faced from those enemies, just as the arrival of plague in Sherborne the same summer had been a reminder that death could come at any time, in any place.

As with all the expeditions, voyages and battles in which Ralegh was involved, the quest for El Dorado – whether understood as the 'golden one', the King who ruled an empire of gold or the empire itself and its great and golden city of Manoa – was one element of a far bigger picture. Any attempt on 'the empire of Guiana' entailed a direct challenge to Spain, always a good thing in Ralegh's mind. He understood, and for years had explained at length to anyone who would listen, the significance of what he called 'Indian' gold to England and Europe. Substitute the oil of our own time for the gold of his and the geopolitics become clear. Gold 'disturbeth all the nations of Europe, it purchaseth intelligence, creepeth into Councels, and setteth bound loyalty at liberty, in the greatest Monarchies of Europe'. Put simply: 'Those princes which abound in treasure have great advantages over the rest'.

Now, England could have its own Indian gold, from a land so rich in it that its King, El Dorado, the Golden One, bathed in it. It was a place of 'great plenty of gold, pearl, and precious stones'. The report of El Dorado might seem strange but Spain had the wealth of the Incas, therefore, Ralegh urges us, if we consider 'the many millions which are daily brought out of Peru into Spain, we may easily believe the same'. Ralegh even had a picture: 'How the nobility of Guiana would cover themselves in gold when feasting', inspired by his meeting with Toparimaca, cacique of Arowacai. Glittering marcasite, used as body paint, can look very like gold. It was an easy mistake to make but surely not a deliberate misrepresentation on Ralegh's part.

Who would not seize the chance to find the Emperor of Guiana and his court, as described in a Spanish history of the Indies, helpfully translated by Ralegh for his English audience?

> All the vessels of his house, table and kitchen were of gold and silver, and the meanest of silver and copper for strength and hardness of the metal. He had in his wardrobe hollow statues of gold which seemed giants, and the figures in proportion and bigness of all the beasts, birds, trees, and herbs that the earth bringeth forth: and of all the fishes that the sea of waters of his kingdom breedeth.

The Spanish had already been busy, with two great families competing for the title to the territory. Expedition after expedition of *doradistas* had headed into the interior but all was still there for the taking by England, if only it could be found. If it were not found, then the English would be quite happy to take some workable gold mines. That suited Ralegh; mining was part of his heritage, whether as a West Country boy and man, or as Lord Warden of the Stannaries, with direct responsibility for Cornwall, England's most important mining region.

Mining had not been part of the nascent vision of the English empire in North America, for the obvious reason that there were no precious metals or mines in 'Virginia'. Ralegh's colonial ambitions had instead been centred on what Thomas Harriot called 'vegetable gold': planting not mining, settlement not plunder. (This was one of the reasons Ralegh became the nineteenth and early twentieth centuries' poster boy for what was seen as a more decent form of imperialism. He was the true precursor of the British Empire because he attempted settlement in Virginia while others, such as Francis Drake and John Hawkins, were merely concerned with trade and plunder.) This privileging of 'vegetable gold' allowed England to demonise Spain for its mining activities. It was not hard to do. Opencast mining was, and is, horrific in terms of human labour and the destruction of the environment. The lives of mineworkers, then and now, are cheap. But ten years on from Virginia Ralegh wanted real gold, whether that of El Dorado's well-hidden empire or the more realistic chances of workable mines beyond the Orinoco delta. Plantation, 'vegetable gold' of any kind, came a very poor third behind trade and plunder.

Virginia and Ireland had all too clearly shown Ralegh the challenges inherent in empire-building. Would 'the large rich and beautiful empire of Guiana' be third time lucky? Ralegh wanted Elizabeth to think so, asking her to 'undertake the enterprise' of annexing what he (and the Spanish) believed, or hoped, to be the last undiscovered Inca kingdom. Whether the empire of Guiana and its King would willingly agree to this was left hazy. The ideal was the willing acceptance of the legitimacy of English supremacy by the indigenous people. Conquest was, however, not off the agenda. Precisely because the voyage took place in the very earliest stages of the English imperial mission, anything was possible; the colonial rulebook had not yet been written.

It was, unfortunately, not the best moment for such a voyage. In the mid-1590s, England was reeling from famine and plague. The Crown's military resources, such as they were, were spread across the Netherlands, France and Ireland and serious threats were reported (by Ralegh) from Spain. Having already paid for assaults, led by Drake and Hawkins, on the Spanish in Puerto Rico the cautious Queen was unlikely to support, financially or in any other way, the Guiana dream.

An empire in, or close to, the Indies; impoverishing Spain; the quest for El Dorado; a back route to the Incas. Gold. All these were enough to send Ralegh across the Atlantic, with or without the support of his Queen. But there may well have been a very raw, very personal ambition at work in the early months of 1595. This restless, driven man hungered for a land he could call his own: Raleghana.

To all these ends, Captain Jacob Whiddon was despatched to reconnoitre the region in 1594. He returned with more than a report; he brought the first South Americans to reach England since a Brazilian 'king' in 1531. Later in the year, to Ralegh's horror, Robert Dudley, the illegitimate son of the Earl of Leicester, surveyed Trinidad and the lower Orinoco delta. Another rival expedition departed in January 1595. The good news was that Dudley's report confirmed Ralegh's belief in the potential for gold-working. The bad news was that his competitors were getting there ahead of him. Ralegh was rightly anxious that they would 'attempt the chiefest places of my enterprise'. He 'shall be undone', while they, lacking his skills and experience, 'will be beaten and do no good'. They would not, they must not, take the opportunity that Sir Walter was determined was his; to seize the empire that only he had the ability to seize.

Did he have it in him? He was not young (in his early forties) and for many years his life had been centred on the court and his developing estate at Sherborne. Even one of his admirers, the early twentieth-century imperialist historian V.T. Harlow, is doubtful of Ralegh's ability as a sailor and explorer. He was not a 'first-rate seaman', 'found wanting' in stormy weather on various occasions. It was not that he was a 'coward…he was simply not a sailor', says Harlow, as is revealed by Ralegh's deeply suspicious practice of taking a trunk full of books to sea: 'an outward and visible sign of his character'. Harlow's words, steeped in a very English anti-intellectualism, are variations on a theme that emerged in Ralegh's time, as he well knew. People, acknowledged the man himself, think he is 'too easeful and sensual to undertake a journey of so great travel [travail?]'. Undertake it he would. And undertake it he did.

Late 1594: Ralegh – as ever – is waiting on the weather. 'I stay but for the wind to bring about the ship.' He is looking for the arrival of his ships from the Thames, anxious because 'the passage down the Channel' is 'often more hazardous than the crossing of the Atlantic'. Five days later: 'this wind breaks my heart'. It should be carrying him away; instead it is keeping his 'ships in the river of Temes'. He was still waiting on 1 January. The month came and went:

> [His] body is wasted with toil, the purse with charge and all things worn. Only the mind is indifferent to good fortune or adversity. There is no news from hence worth the writing. If I were more fortunate I should be the more worth the commanding. As I am, you may dispose of me. And thus for the present I leave you to all good fortune, and my self *quo me fortuna retrudet*.

Ralegh had used some of these lines before, in the weeks leading up to the birth of Damerei. He never knowingly wasted a good phrase.

At last they sailed, reaching Trinidad on 22 March, where Ralegh coasted around the island 'in my barge close aboard the shore and landed in every cove, the better to know the island':

> This island of Trinidad hath the form of a sheephook, and is but narrow; the north part is very mountainous; the soil is very excellent, and will bear sugar, ginger, or any other commodity that the Indies yield. It hath store of deer, wild porks, fruit, fish, and fowl; it

hath also for bread sufficient maize, cassavi, and of those roots and fruits which are common everywhere in the West Indies. It hath divers beasts which the Indies have not; the Spaniards confessed that they found grains of gold in some of the rivers; but they having a purpose to enter Guiana, the magazine of all rich metals, cared not to spend time in the search thereof any further.

The message is that Trinidad may be wonderful but Guiana is even better. However, to seize 'the magazine of all rich metals' Ralegh had to control Trinidad, as Spain well knew. His cover story for circum-navigating the island was that his fleet was heading north to relieve the Virginian colonists but had been blown off course, and sheer curiosity led him to ask questions. In a sign of Spain's weakness, rather than her strength, the Spanish Governor, Berrio, who had founded the town of San José de Oruña just before Ralegh's arrival, let him.

Ralegh understood Spain's vulnerabilities. The Spanish were not like the Portuguese, who could travel from Lisbon to north-eastern Brazil in about thirty days and return in forty to fifty. The Portuguese royal house could manage its colony at a distance, with no need to establish a separate colonial law code, printing press or university in the new world. The Spanish had a far harder task. The Caribbean ports were two months from Seville, and it took even longer to reach New Spain and Peru. The journey home was often five to six months. The distances made Spain vulnerable to European competitors, something not lost on Ralegh. They also made Spain see her American territories as remote, a world apart. A world over which viceroys ruled almost autonomously, using a separate legal code. A place where, far from Madrid, the great families of Spain competed for dominance.

In the Orinoco region, 'Vides governor of Cumana, and Berreo were become mortal enemies', Ralegh happily noted. Both men had attempted to ally with a significant indigenous leader, Morequito, with whom Governor Berrio had lived for seven months. In a typical counter-move, Vides's men headed into the Orinoco delta and 'carried off about three hundred stolen souls whom they sold like negroes'. Unsurprisingly, when Berrio returned to the region, Morequito was hostile. No wonder that the governor was alarmed by the arrival of the English (blown off course? Berrio was not so sure) and secretly sent for reinforcements. A local leader, a *cacique*, went straight to Ralegh with the information and he decided to act immediately, otherwise he might have 'savoured much of an ass':

> Taking a time of most advantage, I set upon the Corps du garde in the evening, and having put them to the sword, sent Captain Caulfield onwards with sixty soldiers, and myself followed with forty more, and so took their new city, which they called St. Joseph, by break of day. They abode not any fight after a few shot, and all being dismissed, but only Berreo and his companion (the Portuguese captain Alvaro Jorge), I brought them with me aboard, and at the instance of the Indians I set their new city of St. Joseph on fire.

Spanish historians have described the attack as a 'crime' and compared Ralegh's butchery of the inhabitants to his actions in Ireland. Sir Walter, at the time, legitimised the slaughter, praising the bravery of the 'Indians' who:

> Come aboard to trade with me upon pain of hanging and quartering (having executed two of them for the same which I afterwards found) yet every night there came some with most lamentable complaints of his cruelty [...] that he made the ancient Casique which were lords of the country to be their slaves, that he kept them in chains, and dropped their naked bodies with burning bacon, and such other torments, which I found afterwards to be true: for in the city after I entered the same, there were five of the lords or little kings (which they call casiqui in the West Indies) in one chain almost dead of famine, and wasted with torments.

In other words, it was Ralegh's moral duty to attack, 'at the instance of the Indians', the Indians who have been so appallingly treated by the conquistador Spaniards. It is, of course, his social duty to spare Berrio and Jorge, men of his own rank. Indeed, he subsequently has a gentlemanly discussion with the governor, gathering:

> From him as much of Guiana as he knew. This Berreo is a gentleman well descended, and had long served the Spanish King in Milan, Naples, the Low Countries, and elsewhere, very valiant and liberal, and a gentleman of great assuredness, and of a great heart. I used him according to his estate and worth in all things I could, according to the small means I had.

Ralegh listened, learned and finally told Berrio of his intention to become an English *doradista*:

> Berreo was stricken into a great melancholy and sadness, and used all the arguments he could to dissuade me; and also assured the gentlemen of my company that it would be labour lost, and that they should suffer many miseries if they proceeded. And first he delivered that I could not enter any of the rivers with any bark or pinnace, or hardly with any ship's boat, it was so low, sandy, and full of flats, and that his companies were daily grounded in their canoes, which drew but twelve inches water. He further said that none of the country would come to speak with us, but would all fly; and if we followed them to their dwellings, they would burn their own towns. And besides that, the way was long, the winter at hand, and that the rivers beginning once to swell, it was impossible to stem the current; and that we could not in those small boats by any means carry victuals for half the time, and that (which indeed most discouraged my company) the kings and lords of all the borders of Guiana had decreed that none of them should trade with any Christians for gold, because the same would be their own overthrow, and that for

the love of gold the Christians meant to conquer and dispossess them of all together.

Berrio did his best to put Ralegh off but he remained undaunted, even though 'many and the most of these I found to be true'. He was resolved to 'make trial of whatsoever happened'. It was not going to be easy, but that just made the whole expedition more heroic, more exciting. The empire of El Dorado might be 'environed with impassable mountains on every side as it is impossible to go over them with any company and more impossible to victual any company' but still they would go. Somewhere, there were fierce Amazons, and a people living on 'that branch which is called Caora' whose 'heads appear not above their shoulders...their eyes in their shoulders, and their mouths in the middle of their breasts, and that a long train of hair groweth backwards between their shoulders'. And still they would go.

The adventure began. It makes a gripping yarn. The first challenge is to cross the Orinoco delta and find a way inland. Ralegh reconnoitres and finds numerous entrances all 'at least as big as the Thames at Woolwich' but none suitable, due to their shallow reach. They decide to make the sea crossing (a distance 'as between Dover and Calais'; Europe is never far from Ralegh's mind) in their smaller wherries and – reading between the lines – trust to luck. There were so many streams and branches to the river, 'all so fair and large, and so like one to another', that it was impossible to do anything else.

By chance – Ralegh as ever unwilling to see God's hand at work – they find a way in. The river they are navigating has no name in the minds of the English, so it is promptly christened 'the river of the Red Cross'. Ralegh may see his successes and failures as matters of chance, not providence, but he remained a man of his time.

Once into the Orinoco delta, the going got harder. Ralegh and his men were:

All driven to lie in the rain and weather, in the open air, in the burning sun, and upon the hard boards, and to dress our meat, and to carry all manner of furniture in them, wherewith they were so pestered and unsavoury, that what with victuals being most fish, with the wet clothes of so many men thrust together and the heat of the sun, I will undertake there was never any prison in England that could be found more unsavoury and loathsome, especially to my self, who had for many years before been dieted and cared for in a sort far differing.

Durham House, silk stockings and fine dinners are a long way away. After yet another gruelling episode, 'nothing on earth could have been more welcome to us next unto gold, than the great store of very excellent bread which we found in these canoes, for now our men cried, let us go on, we care not how far'. Gold remains the goal but survival is becoming the priority: bread, and living with the maddening 'overgrown mosquitos (a fly that biteth very grieviously)'.

Ralegh almost glories in the fact that on the expedition he was 'dieted and cared for in a sort far differing'. It must surely be false modesty that makes him insist that he is unable to endure long marches in the tropics because, in the end, that is what he and his men do. Each day brings a new challenge and a new vista. Ralegh makes clear that the thrill of the expedition runs through everyone, not just him:

When we were come to the tops of the first hills of the plains adjoining to the river, we beheld that wonderful breach of waters which ran down Caroli [Ralegh's version of Caroni]; and might from that mountain see the river how it ran in three parts, above twenty miles off, and there appeared some ten or twelve overfalls in sight, every one as high over the other as a church tower, which fell with that fury, that the rebound of water made it seem as if it had been all covered over with a great shower of rain; and in some places we took it at the first for a smoke that had risen over some great town. For mine own part I was well persuaded from thence to have returned, being a very ill footman; but the rest were all so desirous to go near the said strange thunder of waters, as they drew me on by little and little, till we came into the next valley, where we might better discern the same.

Ralegh's men inspire him to continue but the way does not get easier:

> The third day that we entered the river our galley came on ground, and stuck so fast, as we thought that even there our discovery had ended, and that we must have left sixty of our men to have inhabited like rooks upon trees with those nations: but the next morning, after we had cast out all her ballast, with tugging and hauling to and fro, we got her afloat, and went on.

A 'goodly river' follows, but then a 'violent current' meaning 'every gentlemen and others taking their turns to row'. The company runs low on food ('our bread even at the last, and no drink at all') and the heat increases, 'breeding great faintness'. Ralegh lies to his men that it was only one more day's 'work more to attain the land where we should be relieved of all we wanted, and if we returned that we were sure to starve by the way, and that the world would also laugh us to scorn'. It might have been a mixed message but it worked. They were saved by the fruits, flowers, fowl, fish and trees of the country and would not starve. Even at this moment, Ralegh has time for wonder:

> We saw birds of all colours, some carnation, some crimson, orange tawny, purple, green, watched [blue or blueish], and of all other sorts both simple and mixed, as it was unto us a great good passing of the time to behold them.

If anything, however, things get even more challenging. It was:

> Dark as pitch, and the river began so to narrow itself, and the trees to hang over from side to side, as we were driven with arming swords to cut a passage through those branches that covered the water.

Their stomachs 'began to gnaw apace'. At last 'about midnight we saw a light, and rowing towards it we saw the dogs of the village'. It is one of many moments when, with the entire expedition on the brink of disaster, everything comes right. The Indians bring them 'good store of bread, fish, hens and Indian drink'. The men sleep well and in the morning, the landscape is one of beauty, a plain of 'twenty miles in length, the grass short and green'.

The final moments of the expedition are no less demanding, no less exciting, no less human:

> When we were arrived at the sea side then grew our greatest doubt, and the bitterest of all our journey forepassed, for I protest before God, that we were in a most desperate estate: […] there arose a mighty storm, and the river's mouth was at least a league broad […] I confess I was very doubtful which way to take, either to go over in the pestered galley, there being but six foot water over the sands, for two leagues together, and that also in the channel, and she drew five: or to adventure in so great a billow, and in so doubtful weather, to cross the seas in my barge. […] about midnight we put our selves to God's keeping, and thrust out into the sea, leaving the galley at anchor, who durst not adventure but by day light. And so being all very sober, and melancholy, one faintly cheering another to show courage, it pleased God that the next day about nine of the clock, we descried the island of Trinidad, and steering for the nearest part of it, we kept the shore till we came to Curiapan, where we found our ships at anchor, than which, there was never to us a more joyful sight.

As he journeyed, Ralegh saw his own country, and his own people, mirrored in Guiana. Some islands in the river were 'as big as the Isle of Wight, and bigger'; the deer 'came down feeding by the water's side, as if they had been used to a keeper's call'; there were 'diverse copses scattered here and there by the river's side, and all as full of deer, as any forest or park in England'; a mountain 'appeared like a white church tower of exceeding height'; the waterfalls like church towers, the spray like smoke from a town. And the women? The women were beautiful, as beautiful as the women in England:

> In all my life I have seldom seen a better favoured woman: she was of good stature, with black eyes, fat of body, of an excellent countenance, her hair almost as long as herself, tied up again in pretty knots, and it seemed she stood not in that awe of her husband, as the rest, for she spoke and discoursed, and drank among the gentlemen and captains, and was very pleasant, knowing her own comeliness, and taking great pride therein. I have seen a Lady in England so like her, as but for the difference of colour I would have sworn might have been the same.

For all his thoughts of home, Virginia and Ireland had taught Ralegh that he and his men were reliant on the indigenous population, so he made the crucial contacts, recruited interpreters, collected intelligence, made use of the 'two Indians' who had been brought to England the previous year and who were 'familiar with the English language' (as the Spanish noted, enviously) and – in contrast to the Spanish – insisted that his men did not involve themselves with the local women:

> [When] the poor men and women had seen us and that we gave them meat, and to every one some thing or other, which was rare and strange to them, they began to conceive the deceit and purpose of the Spaniards, who indeed (as they confessed) took from them both their wives and daughters daily, and used them for the satisfying of their own lusts, especially such as they took in this manner by strength. But I protest before the majesty of the living God, that I neither know nor believe, that any of our company one or other, by violence or otherwise, ever knew any of their women, and yet we saw many hundreds, and had many in our power, and of those very young, and excellently favoured which came among us without deceit, stark naked.

For Ralegh, there is a sense that this is not simply strategic, although it was certainly that. He is fascinated by the politics and society of the lower Orinoco and listens eagerly when the old chief Topiawari provides detail after detail of his people's lives. His account of the expedition has been judged a profoundly valuable ethnological text, 'a fundamental source for the historical anthropology of the Americas', precisely because Ralegh is so engaged with this land far from home. His interest in the landscapes and peoples that he encountered (however brutal and incomplete that encounter might be) allows us, four hundred years on, a glimpse of a vanished world. It is a world that he, his men and his ideology helped to destroy but it is also a world that Ralegh explored with wonder, providing a rare glimpse of the peoples of the Orinoco delta during a period of almost first contact.

Others simply see a man asserting his cultural and political supremacy. For many, there is nothing to admire in Ralegh's treatment of the indigenous people. Their 'very acceptance of Ralegh's dissembled gifts betokens their uncomprehending entry into the circulations of England's nascent imperial economy – an economy to be fueled, in the future, by their own gold', argues Louis Montrose. 'Uncomprehending' does not quite do justice to the communities in the Orinoco delta or their history; they had had a century of dealing with, and resisting, Spanish and Portuguese intrusions on to their territories. Indeed, his allies were not quite as loyal as Ralegh hoped or believed. When Ralegh made his parting attack on the Spanish, in Cumaná, he suffered heavy losses because (according to Spanish sources) the Englishmen's native guide, Juan Caraca, 'knew what he had to do' and 'led them by a devilish road overlooked by two forts'.

The Lieutenant Governor of Cumaná, Lucas Fajardo, entertained Ralegh, Berrio and Jorge at around the same time, as the four gentlemen deliberated the terms of release of Berrio and Jorge. Such is war. Such is the military elite.

As Michael Oberg writes, the native peoples made use of Ralegh, 'whom they saw as a potentially valuable ally in their struggles against

European and Native American foes'. Indigenous politics were far more complex than local tribes seeking to replace the Spanish with new English overlords. There were power struggles between the tribes and regular attempts to play the Europeans off against each other:

> That Ralegh traded with them, established the reciprocal basis for an alliance, exchanged emissaries, and pledged through his interpreters to protect them from their enemies offered evidence that here was a foreigner whose friendship was worth cultivating.

A friendship worth cultivating? Others have been more scathing about the disjunction between the apparent consideration and courtesy (friendship) demonstrated towards indigenous cultures on the one hand and the quest for gold and the need for conquest on the other. This disjunction is built into the period's colonialist discourse, to paraphrase Stephen Greenblatt, one of the great scholars of early-modern culture and a man who cut his academic teeth on Sir Walter Ralegh's life and works. Ralegh is perpetrating 'a most massive deception of the Indians', 'simultaneously covetous and generous, cynical and patriotic'.

At the time, one of the propagandist poets Ralegh drew to his cause insisted that the goal was 'conquest without blood'. Guiana was a place where Sir Walter Ralegh could be 'King of the Indians', a place where the captain of the *Destiny* could fulfil his own destiny. In 1595, in Guiana, the fifth son of a Devonian gentleman could be a king. It would not be treason, for he remained, ever and always, a loyal servant to his own Amazonian Queen, the *cacique* of the guard of the great Ezrabeta Cassipuna Aquerewana, as he took care to translate 'Elizabeth the great princess or greatest commander'.

Ralegh's fascination with the Amazons may either be strategic, in that to write of their power was to flatter Elizabeth, or might be born of his long years of service to a queen. Either way, it is powerful. Amazonian tribes are found all over the world, he lectures his reader, channelling his not-so-hidden social anthropologist but:

They which are not far from Guiana do accompany with men but once in a year, and for the time of one month, which I gather by their relation to be in April. At that time all the kings of the borders assemble, and the queens of the Amazons, and after the queens have chosen, the rest cast lots for their Valentines. This one month, they feast, dance, and drink of their wines in abundance, and the moon being done, they all depart to their own provinces. If they conceive, and be delivered of a son, they return him to the father, if of a daughter they nourish it, and retain it, and as many as have daughters send unto the begetters a present, all being desirous to increase their own sex and kind, but that they cut off the right dug of the breast I do not find to be true.

Returning to the hard sell and his royal audience, Ralegh imagines the Amazons hearing the 'name of a virgin, which is not only able to defend her own territories and her neighbours, but also to invade and conquer so great empires and so far removed'. How could Ezrabeta Casspina Aquerewana resist?

She could resist because, in the end, plain Sir Walter Ralegh, no king of the Indians he, returned from the 'large, rich and beautiful empire of Guiana' with nothing. Whether Ralegh failed because there was, in fact, no gold to be found has long perplexed historians and commentators. The foremost modern Spanish historian of the region and the time, Pablo Ojer, argues that 'the Caroni mine' was revealed as a measure of the indigenous peoples' trust in Ralegh. The anthropologist Neil Whitehead spells it out: 'We now know that it did exist, that it was known to the Spanish in 1595, and that it was still known and considered for exploitation at the end of the eighteenth century'. But it is hard to work out exactly where it was. Perhaps Mount 'Iconuri', a day's march inland from the river? Maybe on the river Caroni? It doesn't help that sixty-two of the seventy references to gold made by Ralegh when writing about his expedition are general. Joyce Lorimer, a Ralegh scholar who trusts her subject as far as she can throw him, points out that 'actual gold mines' are hardly mentioned and even the more sympathetic Whitehead argues that Ralegh 'badly serves himself' by inflating the indications of gold working to conform more closely to the El Dorado legend of a 'Golden King'. Ralegh's words bring the gold close, but the reality was that, although he was 'safely landed' on English shores by the end of September 1595, he landed empty-handed.

A few days later, Sir Walter was back in London. People were excited that he had brought a 'supposed prince' from Guiana. On 9 October, he dined with John Dee at Durham House. Dee, mathematician, astronomer, astrologer, supporter of colonialism, was Ralegh's kind of man: sceptical, enquiring, expert. People noticed a change in Sir Walter. He 'is here and goes daily to hear sermons, because he hath seen the wonders of the Lord in the deep: 'tis much commended and spoken of'. It was all quite fascinating, but what of the much-anticipated gold?

Ralegh does his best: every stone promised 'either gold or silver by its complexion' but the rocks are too hard to mine: 'like flint, and in all as hard or harder'. He has a barrel full of the 'rocks like unto gold ore'. Writing to Charles, Lord Howard and to Robert Cecil, he claims that there is hardly a piece of 'rich' rock that doesn't contain 'some metal, either, gold, silver, copper, steel of all which we have brought some quantity to make trial'. Unfortunately, he admits that he had had:

> Neither Pioneers, bars, sledges, nor wedges of iron to break the ground without which there is no working in mines, but we saw all the hills with stones of golden colour, and some of the colour of silver and we tried them to be no marquisite, and therefore I hope, they will prove of the right stamp, and if any of many which we saw by chance without search prove rich, I will undertake to load 1,000 ships with the ore of any one of a dozen, which we passed over as we went to view the country.

It is a huge claim (a thousand ships? Really?) but the lack of appropriate men and equipment is a shocking admission. Ralegh had hired a 'refiner and trier of metals' in London but he 'came not to me at all, which hath fallen out I know now to what loss, for we had neither man nor means to try which mine was good, or which was bad'. This embarrassing omission in their company was revealed in a manuscript account of the voyage, written by 15 October. It marked Ralegh's first attempt to paper over the cracks, the most obvious crack being that he had not brought even one ship laden with gold back to England, let alone a thousand.

Nevertheless, he was the talk of London. Lord Burghley wanted to see the manuscript account and so did others. (Just one copy, that addressed to George Carew, survives in the Lambeth Palace Library, but there were obviously more in circulation.) One courtier writes to another that he has been promised a copy of Ralegh's 'discourse to the queen of his journey', suggesting that the work's most important reader might be Elizabeth. Ralegh certainly hoped so.

His courtly readers remain unconvinced. A month later, Ralegh is becoming desperate at the lack of a follow-up expedition. He piles on the rhetoric, writing from 'this desolate place' (he is at Sherborne), with 'no hope' and, for good measure, channelling recent Shakespearean play titles: 'We that have much ado to get bread to eat have the less to care for, unless much lost labour and love awake us'. He challenges Robert Cecil, his correspondent, directly:

What becomes of Guiana I much desire to hear, whether it pass for a history or a fable. I hear Master Dudley and others are sending thither. If it be so, farewell all good from thence, for although myself like a coxcomb did rather prefer the future in respect of others, and rather sought to win the kings to Her Majesty's service then to sack them, I know what others will do when those kings shall come simply [innocently] into their hands. [...]

For conclusion I will only say this much, take good heed lest you be not too slow; expedition in a little is better than much too late. But your ministers of despatch are not plentiful, neither is it every man's occupation.—From Sherborne, the 10th of November.

A couple of days later, he's repeating the same message: 'You may perceive by this relation that it is no dream which I have reported of Guiana'. He knows:

> the like was never offered to any Christian Prince. I know it will be presently followed both by the Spanish and French, and if it be foreslowed by us I conclude that we are curst of God. In the meantime I humbly beseech you to move her Majesty that none be suffered to foil the enterprise, and that those kings of the borders which are by my labour, peril, and charge won to her Majesty's love and obedience be not by other pilferers lost again. I hope I shall be thought worthy to direct those actions that I have at mine own charge laboured in, and to govern that country which I have discovered and hope to conquer for the Queen without her cost. I am sending away a bark to the country to comfort and assure the people that they despair not nor yield to any composition with other nations.

There's more, of course, because this is Ralegh. There are maps (produced by Harriot) that he can send; there are promises of 'both diamond and pearl' (he can send two stones to Cecil and is sending one 'which I think is amethyst, and hath a strange blush of carnation'); there is a further assurance that everything he writes is backed up by 'Spanish letters' (a package of extracts from Spanish manuscripts, seized in 1593 by George Popham and handed to the Privy Council in early November). There is a characteristically ironic comment about the success of Ralegh's old enemies: 'if the Spaniards had been so blockish and slothful we had not feared now their power, who by their gold from thence vex and endanger all the estates of Europe'.

He's writing quickly: from 'Sherborne, this Wednesday morning, an hour after the receipt of your letter, the 13 November'. This note, crammed into the left-hand margin, is a sign of his haste: if it was Wednesday, it was 12 November. Two weeks later, he is still writing quickly ('haste post haste W Ralegh'); his letter making its way from

Shaftesbury at 'one of the clock; Received this letter at v of the clock in the afternoon, the 26 day of November, '95, Sarum. Received at Andover at eight of the clock afternoon, and at Basingstoke at xi of clock at night. Hurtford Bridge, the 27th day of November at i of the night. Staines, 8 a clock in the morning'. This was good going, but not as good as another correspondent wished when he wrote: 'Haste, for thy life, post, haste; for thy life, post, haste, haste; for thy life, haste, haste, haste, haste, for thy life, post, haste' and presumably not as good as Ralegh desired. He is begging for clarity from the Crown:

> I beseech you let us know whether we shall be travellers or tinkers, conquerors or crounes [novices?], for if the winter pass without making provision, there can be no victualling in the summer, and if it be now foreslowed, farewell Guiana for ever! Then must I determine to beg or run away; honour and gold, and all good, for ever hopeless. I do not hear how you like the white stone; I have sent for more of each; as soon as they come you shall have them.

Ralegh attempts to keep the letter short. He turns to a brief summary of the defences of Devon and Cornwall (and indeed Dorset), but Guiana is always on his mind. He is trying to make the point that even though the news was all of the Spanish preparations for another attack, this should not prevent a renewed attempt on the empire of Guiana because, crucially, 'your lordship [Charles Howard] doth find that it is the surest way to divert all attempts from home'. Ralegh's global perspective, seeing Dorset on the same map as Guiana, is characteristic of the man. But by the second week of December, even Ralegh was starting to accept that those with the power to support him – Cecil, Howard, the Queen – were not going to. On 13 December, he is a 'banished man from court' and thinking about going to the Netherlands. There would be no follow-up expedition.

Queen Elizabeth had no reason to support a second voyage at a time when her kingdom was threatened. In Ireland, even as the Spanish continued their preparations for a new Armada (it would be destroyed in a storm in October 1596, but in 1595 Elizabeth could not know that), the Earl of Tyrone was in open rebellion. And on 23 July, while Ralegh was in Guiana, the Spanish landed in Cornwall, making a series of what have been described as commando raids on ports in the far west, including Penzance and Mousehole. The Spanish ships came from Brittany (the same Brittany, with its superb harbours, that Ralegh had been keen to raid earlier in the decade), where their fleet had a footing and was supporting the Catholic side in the continuing French civil wars. It was yet another manifestation of the stop-start nature of the ongoing war between England and Spain, far more characteristic of the conflict than the Great Armada of 1588 and revealing of the fact that Spain still viewed English maritime exploits as a threat to its power.

As 1595 closed, Ralegh was among those advocating an attack on the Spanish mainland. Attack looked like being England's best form of defence but would also be rather helpful to Ralegh's dreams of empire in Guiana, since it would ensure the Spanish were unable to send reinforcements to the Orinoco region. Meanwhile, Ralegh attempted to find more evidence of the 'empire of Guiana', sending Lawrence Keymis – a friend since university, a member of Sir Walter's household since the early 1590s and his trusted lieutenant for the Guiana voyage of 1595 – in a tiny expedition across the Atlantic in January 1596. It was the best he could do.

His next step became one of his trademark moves. Having reluctantly recognised that the Queen was unwilling to take over the search for El Dorado and his empire – Ralegh should have known by now that Elizabeth used her subjects to fight her wars whenever she could – Sir Walter shifted his focus to private individuals. It was a shift that led to the publication of what, for many readers, is Ralegh's most iconic work:

> The Discovery of the large, rich, and beautiful EMPIRE Of GUIANA; with a Relation of the great and golden CITY of MANOA, which the Spaniards call EL DORADO, and the PROVINCES of EMERIA, AROMAIA, AMAPAIA, and other

Countries, with their rivers, adjoining. Performed in the year 1595 by Sir WALTER RALEIGH, KNIGHT, CAPTAIN of her Majesty's GUARD, Lord Warden of the STANNARIES, and her Highness' LIEUTENANT-GENERAL of the COUNTY of CORNWALL.

It was a publishing sensation; three editions were rushed out in 1596 alone.

Ralegh subtly changes his manuscript for public consumption, another mark of the man: he always thought about his audience. His main aim appears to be to make the English look good. For the print version, he removes the moment when, to ensure his loyalty, they took their Indian guide's wife hostage and he keeps quiet about the demands made by the same guide in recompense for his ill-treatment: 'a shirt, a hatchet and a knife'. While sanitising his own and his men's behaviour (bread, not wine, is offered to the Indians in the print version), Ralegh also removes some of the Spaniards' more problematic statements that he had reported previously. He didn't wish to publicise the idea, promulgated by the Spanish, that the 'English nation sought for Indians, and to take their children to sell in England for bardasos' (young boys who were prostituted to older men). Nor does he care to mention that one particular indigenous leader thoroughly supported the Spanish.

While some changes make Ralegh himself look better – there is no more talk of the refiner who didn't turn up – others were designed not to give too much away; there is no mention of a barrel of rocks taken from a 'round mountain'. Some of the most interesting moments end up on the cutting-room floor: an account of the beast Jawari, a joking allusion to the tendency of men to get distracted by women, a passage concerning the ways in which Guiana is a wonderful destination for drunkards, womanisers and smokers, the attack by two jaguars while Ralegh's men were feasting on roasted armadillo (the armadillo stays in, the jaguars are cut) and Ralegh's love of pineapples and hammocks:

in mine opinion there is nothing more necessary for soldiers, for they are light to carry, and easy to lodge in, and will keep them from the cold and wet ground, the lying whereon breedeth so many fluxes and agues in every camp, and they are bought there for the value of a 2 penny knife, or less.

Joyce Lorimer, who has edited the two versions, believes that in the interim between manuscript and print, Ralegh's friends, household or political colleagues 'took the humiliated author in hand', disciplined his prose and eliminated soaring hyperbole. But whoever encouraged, or told, Ralegh to edit the manuscript version did not always get their own way. Sir Walter was asked to change 'know' to 'think'. He kept 'know':

For I know all the earth doth not yield the like confluence of streams and branches, the one crossing the other so many times, and all so fair and large, and so like one to another, as no man can tell which to take: and if we went by the sun or compass, hoping thereby to go directly one way or other, yet that way we were also carried in a circle amongst multitudes of islands, and every island so bordered with high trees as no man could see any further than the breadth of the river, or length of the breach. But this it chanced, that entering into a river (which because it had no name, we called the River of the Red Cross, ourselves being the first Christians that ever came therein), the 22. of May, as we were rowing up the same, we espied a small canoa with three Indians, which by the swiftness of my barge, rowing with eight oars, I overtook ere they could cross the river. The rest of the people on the banks, shadowed under the thick wood, gazed on with a doubtful conceit what might befall those three which we had taken. But when they perceived that we offered them no violence, neither entered their canoa with any of ours, nor took out of the canoa any of theirs, they then began to show themselves on the bank's side, and offered to traffic with us for such things as they had. And as we drew near, they all stayed; and we came with our barge to the mouth of a little creek which came from their town into the great river.

There is hyperbole here but the reader also hears, loud and clear, that Ralegh had been there, had navigated the 'great river', had seen the 'high trees' and the 'multitude of islands'; had eaten armadillo, manatee and the eggs of the tortuga. Perhaps there were not millions of oysters growing on the branches of mangroves; perhaps the Spaniards had not martyred and tortured hundreds of the Indians, but hammock-loving Ralegh's voice loses something between manuscript and print. Though not much.

Sir Walter promised his readers a discovery, in the older sense of uncovering or revealing something. He delivers it, describing Guiana as a beautiful virgin just longing to be taken by the right man:

> To conclude, Guiana is a country that hath yet her maidenhead, never sacked, turned, nor wrought; the face of the earth hath not been torn, nor the virtue and salt of the soil spent by manurance. The graves have not been opened for gold, the mines not broken with sledges, nor their images pulled down out of their temples. It hath never been entered by any army of strength, and never conquered or possessed by any Christian prince.

These have become (in)famous lines, offering a 'prospect of virgin penetration, gratefully invited', in the words of one critic. Or as Ralegh puts it: 'There is a way found to answer every man's longing'. It is no surprise that feminist and post-colonial analyses condemn outright Ralegh's 'literary acts of colonial appropriation'; the way in which his masterful rhetoric is harnessed to the service of the rapist imperialist. The *Discovery* is an example of (to quote Michel Certeau) 'writing which conquers'.

There's absolutely no doubt that Ralegh could produce 'writing which conquers'. Conquering the actual territory of Guiana was another matter. Ralegh had been right to feel a desperate urgency, since the Spanish re-established themselves swiftly. By the time Keymis's small expedition arrived in the region, he was too late. Berrio, as soon as he was released from Cumaná, rushed back to the Orinoco and established a small garrison close to the delta. His son sent a further cohort of soldiers from New Granada, which allowed the rebuilding of the settlement on Trinidad. The 'principal Indians of that coast' were instructed by Spain that 'in future they must not admit nor receive in their country any foreigners except Spaniards who should come in the name of your Majesty'.

Ralegh had instructed his surrogate Keymis 'to comfort and assure the people, that they despair not, nor yield to any composition with other nations' but, due to the Spanish reclamation of the Caroni river (predicted by Ralegh), Keymis swiftly moved to a previously-agreed alternative. He worked on finding other routes in to the delta, making landfall on 14 March 1596 at the mouth of the river Arrowari, far to the south of the Caroni. Further north, the Indians were waiting for Ralegh 'during the whole moon of the month of March'. Keymis attempted to reach Topiawari's port but found to his 'grief' that the Spaniards were lying in ambush 'to defend the passage to those mines, from whence your ore and white stones were taken the last year'. Keymis headed back to search for the other friendly leader, Putijma, 'in the mountains', the plan being that 'if the Indians should think themselves too weak, with our help to displant the Spaniards: to set some of these to work, for hatchets and knives to return us gold grains, and white stones from such places, as they should be directed unto'. Putijma could not be found, so the native guide:

> offered to bring us either to the mine of white stones near
> Winicapora, or else to a gold mine, which Putijma had showed
> him, being but one day's journey overland, from the place where
> we now stayed at an anchor. I saw far off the mountain adjoining
> to the gold mine, and having measured their paths near the same
> place this last year, could not judge it to be fifteen miles from us.
> I do well remember how coming that way with Putijma the year
> before, he pointed to this same mountain, making signs to have
> me go with him thither. I understood his signs, and marked the
> place, but mistook his meaning, imagining that he would have

showed me the overfall of the River Curwara from the mountains. My Indian showed me in what sort without digging they gather the gold in the sand of a small river, named Macawini, that springeth and falleth from the rocks where this mine is.

So near and yet so far. In 1595, there might just have been an opportunity to steal Guiana for the English. Just a year later, Spain was closing the door. Keymis came back empty-handed, even though, for anthropologist Neil Whitehead, Keymis's account is 'direct confirmation of the location of many of the gold deposits mentioned by Ralegh and his contemporaries'. Whitehead identifies one of historians' problems with Ralegh, a man who so often "sexed up his dossier": the misrepresentations (if we are being harsh, the lies) don't actually 'undermine or make invalid the representations of native social practice, or indeed the presence of gold. It's just that it's hard to tell where truth ends and fiction begins'. Indeed.

This is also true of Ralegh's proud claim that none of his men died on the expedition into the interior:

> Moreover the country is so healthful, as of an hundred persons and more, which lay without shift most sluttishly, and were every day almost melted with heat in rowing and marching, and suddenly wet again with great showers, and did eat of all sorts of corrupt fruits, and made meals of fresh fish without seasoning, of tortugas, of lagartos or crocodiles, and of all sorts good and bad, without either order or measure, and besides lodged in the open air every night, we lost not any one, nor had one ill-disposed to my knowledge; nor found any calentura [fever] or other of those pestilent diseases which dwell in all hot regions, and so near the equinoctial line.

This may well be true but Ralegh keeps quiet about the botched raid on Cumaná, focusing on the threat of diseases rather than Indian arrows and Spanish muskets.

In late June 1596, it was the straight-talking Lady Ralegh who spelt out the truth of the collapse of Ralegh's dream of Guiana. There has been nothing done of 'much worth: for that the Spaniards are already possessed in Guiana'. Or, as she makes clear, deploying her idiosyncratic spelling: 'I mean along the shorre, so as they durst not land: and also Topeaware the king, that was heer Magisti's subgect, is ded, and his sun returned'. Thomas Harriot did his best to give a more positive gloss to the voyage. Writing on 11 July, he admitted that 'although Captain Keymis be not come home rich, yet he hath done the special thing which he was enjoined to do, as the discovery of the coast betwixt the river of the Amazon and Orinoco, where are many goodly harbours for the greatest ships her Majesty hath and any number'.

Ralegh, and his supporters, made several more efforts to sell Guiana. Keymis produced a *Relation* of the second voyage to Guiana or as he now calls it – tellingly, wistfully, as with each passing month the dream of King Walter further receded – Raleana. Keymis adds a new religious gloss to the initiative, something singularly lacking from Ralegh's *Discovery*, with Biblical authorities aplenty and a prayer that 'God grant that we possess this promised land'. The core message remains the same: the Guiana empire would be 'profitable', it was 'necessary' to counter the Spanish and it would be easy, oh so easy, to achieve. The Spanish are hated by the Indians, the sea journey is straightforward and the country easily defended. In the *Relation*, gold is less important than farming and trade: 'Brazil wood, honey, cotton, balsam and drugs' are all available for the taking. A third text, recounting the voyage of Captain Leonard Berry on the *Watte*, appeared. It is even less rhetorically sophisticated than Keymis's *Relation*, being primarily concerned with navigation. It showed that little further was achieved, except to continue a tentative dialogue with the local people, who still came to the Englishmen, still used 'us kindly, and brought us victuals and other things'. Ralegh's epic journey in search of gold for his Queen has been supplanted by a more mundane, but more realistic, analysis of the economics of colonialism and the mathematics of navigation, relevant to the predominantly non-courtly adventurers who invested in these early initiatives.

The *Discovery* was, and remains, glorious travel writing. Ralegh's fascination with and admiration for the people he encountered, and for their lives, shines through.

> These Tivitivas are a very goodly people and very valiant, and have the most manly speech and most deliberate that ever I heard of what nation soever. In the summer they have houses on the ground, as in other places; in the winter they dwell upon the trees, where they build very artificial towns and villages.

This is one of the reasons that, literally and metaphorically, his name lived on for so long in the region. During the late 1590s and beyond, Ralegh's readers enjoyed his words but were unwilling to support future expeditions: they 'only to entertain idle time, sit listening for Guiana news, and instantly forget it, as if it were nought else, but a pleasing dream of golden fancy'. El Dorado, let alone Raleana, remained a 'pleasing dream of golden fancy'. Ralegh's personal, rich and beautiful empire was not to be.

The Warao People, descendants of the Tivitivas, still inhabit the Orinoco delta.

7

Writer

SOLDIER AND SAILOR, courtier and lover, explorer and colonist. This should have been enough for one man but Ralegh's
need to write ran like a seam through all these lives. Lives that
were, at least in part, made possible by his talent with words. He lived
in an era characterised by phenomenal innovation in the English language, an exceptional fecundity of literary talent and a magnificent
explosion of new forms. Although English writers arrived late to the
Renaissance literary ball, once in, there was no stopping them. Spenser
plundered Ariosto to create his own British epic, Sidney transformed
Petrarch into a very English (and very funny) sonnet sequence, Donne
channelled Ovid's filthy wit and Jonson mined the Roman drama of
Terence and Plautus. The techniques of satire are timeless. As for
Shakespeare, he responded to anything and everything he read and
saw, working his alchemy and creating a distinctly English literary
language that has endured for centuries, enriching our lives even now.
It is sometimes hard to remember that, in his lifetime, Shakespeare
was seen as good but not that good. He was only a playwright, turning
out shows that might run for a few nights.

Among this brilliant crowd, Ralegh's talent for rhetoric stands out.
He was the master of persuasion, a man who could make you believe
that defeat was victory, that black was white. He seduced people
with his words in his own time and for centuries after his death by
appealing to the idea that he, and only he, is being honest, telling it

as it is. Readers then and now believed him. It was one of the reasons he was hated.

Take this bravura moment from the *Discovery of Guiana* when Ralegh writes 'for the rest, which myself have seen, I will promise these things that follow, which I know to be true' and follows up by offering the reader a seductive, compelling vision:

> The common soldier shall here fight for gold, and pay himself, instead of pence, with plates of half-a-foot broad, whereas he breaketh his bones in other wars for provant [poor provisions] and penury. Those commanders and chieftains that shoot at honour and abundance shall find there more rich and beautiful cities, more temples adorned with golden images, more sepulchres filled with treasure, than either Cortes found in Mexico or Pizarro in Peru. And the shining glory of this conquest will eclipse all those so far-extended beams of the Spanish nation. There is no country which yieldeth more pleasure to the inhabitants, either for those common delights of hunting, hawking, fishing, fowling, and the rest, than Guiana doth; it hath so many plains, clear rivers, and abundance of pheasants, partridges, quails, rails, cranes, herons, and all other fowl; deer of all sorts, porks, hares, lions, tigers, leopards, and diverse other sorts of beasts, either for chase or food.

If critics such as Mary Fuller are right to see the literary recuperation of failure as 'noble, strategic, even a form of success' – an English sub-genre of its own – then Ralegh is one of its greatest exponents. His Queen knew it, of course. He had come to Elizabeth's attention through his letters from battlefields and oceans; during the 1580s and 1590s, he continued to write regularly about the arts of war, navigation and politics. No wonder that the Queen commissioned Sir Walter to write about the *Last Fight of the Revenge*, in which he turns abject naval defeat into a glorious moral victory.

Even more importantly, he knew how to make others look magnificent: as poet, propagandist and speechmaker, Ralegh was responsible, as much as any man of his time, for the construction of the image of the Virgin Queen, whether as Belphoebe, Diana or Astraea. His ability with words was one of the most powerful drivers of his success, the oil in the courtly machine, a clue to what Queen Elizabeth found compelling in the man: he could both charm and persuade with authority and panache.

The court was not Ralegh's only literary arena. He embraced the brave new world of print, reaching beyond the boundaries, and readerships, of manuscript circulation. Once again, Ralegh stands in sharp contrast to his competitor the Earl of Essex, who feared the literary world beyond the court. The Earl wrote anxiously that he was being written about, even performed, throughout London: 'The prating tavern haunter speaks of me what he lists; the frantic libeller writes of me what he lists; already they print me and make me speak to the world, and shortly they will play me in what forms they list upon the stage'. Essex is far from happy at the thought: 'The least of these is a thousand times worse than death'. This was not just a nobleman's pride. It was the equivalent of being on the front page of the today's tabloid newspapers or the subject of an unauthorised biopic.

What Essex feared, Ralegh appeared to relish. It was another mark of the man. If this were the new media then Ralegh would make it work for him. His move from manuscript circulation to print publication for *The Discovery of Guiana* was a spectacular success, at least in terms of sales. Readers throughout Europe delighted in the Englishman's vision of El Dorado's gold, with the *Discovery* translated into numerous languages and reproduced in lavish illustrated editions. Because Ralegh understood that words mattered and that print would matter, he harnessed others' talents to his cause, Thomas Harriot among them. Harriot's only published work is an account of his experiences in Virginia in the mid-1580s but at the end of that decade, Ralegh became the literary patron of the poet Edmund Spenser, who he brought to London from Ireland. In return, Spenser dedicated his epic poem *The Faerie Queene* to 'the Right noble, and Valorous, Sir Walter Raleigh knight'.

Ralegh became a poet because that's what young men did to get noticed, whether at Oriel College, Oxford or the Middle Temple. He became a satirical poet because it was the kind of writing that these young men exchanged among themselves, targetting unfortunates such as the Henry Byng lampooned here:

> What is the cause that maketh Binge so great?
> Is it because his prating maketh sport,
> Or for his father keeps a bawdy court?
> The gold that he by whores and knaves doth spend,
> Will bring his greatness to a pocky end.

Occasionally, a poem from this world was printed, which is how we know that 'Walter Rawely of the middle Temple' wrote a verse in praise of *The Steel Glass* by Gascoigne in 1576. The poem was prescient of Ralegh's future sense of grievance:

> For whoso reaps renown above the rest,
> With heaps of hate shall surely be oppressed.

Ten years on, Ralegh continued to be a poet not only by virtue of his place at court but also because it turned out he was very, very good at this crucial part of political life. Now, instead of aspiring young lawyers, it was established courtiers who dashed off a few stanzas, which would be circulated in manuscript, responded to (often critically) by others, then set to music by yet someone else. Sex and satire remained the literary currency, although there was little mention of whores, knaves and the pox. Nevertheless personalised exchanges were the order of the day. A man of 'renown' himself ten years after his poem in praise of Gasgoigne, Ralegh found himself 'above the rest' and oppressed with 'heaps of hate' from his rivals; hate often delivered in prose or verse.

In 1589 Sir Walter was named among a 'crew of courtly makers, noblemen and gentlemen of her Majesty's own servants, who have written excellently well, as it would appear if their doings could be found out and made public with the rest'. Someone did make the poetry public, printing both the poem from Ralegh addressed to his Queen ('Fortune hath taken thee away, my love') and, even more excitingly, her response ('Ah, silly Pug, wert thou so sore afraid?').

Ralegh's trademark cynicism is strikingly absent from this poem to his Queen. Perhaps he was wise enough to allow her to be the cynic in their relationship. His cynicism is present almost everywhere else. The courtier Thomas Heneage, he who would be Bess's keeper in the crisis of 1592, writes in praise of love. In response, Ralegh bids 'Farewell' to 'false love, thou oracle of lies...fever of the mind'. Christopher Marlowe begs his mistress (or master) to 'Come live with me and be my love, and we will all the pleasures prove' on 'beds of roses', no less. Ralegh responds by acknowledging the attractions of love, or maybe simply escape from the world, but reveals those attractions as empty fictions, supplied by the deceitful 'shepherd's tongue'. It is perhaps his most well-known poem, the nymph's reply to the shepherd:

> But could youth last and love still breed,
> Had joys no date nor age no need
> Then those delights my mind might move
> To live with thee, and be thy love.

The poem is a reminder of the power of time and death to ensure the failure of any attempt at happiness. It is an incitement to scepticism. If it is not by Ralegh, it should be. He was adept at exposing the fictions, or more harshly the lies, on which his society was based. His eloquent, brutal, satirical poem 'The Lie' is the most obvious example and the contemporary responses to the poem, with their relentless riffs on Ralegh's alleged atheism and his humble origins, show – in part – why he was hated.

When the power struggle between Essex and Ralegh resumed in full-throated form in 1597 after the uneasy *rapprochements* of baby Damerei's christening in 1592 and the swashbuckling Cadiz action of 1596, it was a power struggle conducted, in part at least, in poetry, some of better quality than others: Ralegh's 'Lie' prompted the Earl to condemn 'so rawe a lye', and that 'rude Rawly'. The two men had traded poetic insults since 1590, when Ralegh composed a commendatory poem for the first part of his protégé Edmund Spenser's *The Faerie Queene*. Essex took offence at the lines 'the praise of meaner wits this work like profit brings, / As doth the Cuckoo's song delight when Philomena sings', horrified to be described as having a meaner wit than his rival. Echoing Ralegh's imagery in his answering poem, 'Muses no more but Mazes be your names', Essex retorted 'But foul befall that cursed cuckoo's throat, / That so hath crossed sweet Philomela's note'. It is no coincidence that Sir Walter is characterised as a bird, whether a cuckoo or a parrot, someone who can 'never cease to prate'. Essex also plays with Ralegh's nickname, 'Water', a backhanded homage to his Devonian pronunciation of his own name: 'filthy water makes unwholesome broth'. 'It is too much to think, / So pure a mouth should puddle water drink'. How can Elizabeth stoop so low, gasps the Earl? Crucially, it is not simply Ralegh's low filthiness (Sir Walter is dismissed with 'I know what he has been and what he is') but his ability with words that Essex is so keen to attack; his 'wretched skill' with language.

The disdain goes deeper and is inextricably linked to Ralegh's talent for poetry. The Earl of Essex, whose own verses draw on the common stock of poetic devices in his time (Elizabeth is a phoenix, capable of self-renewal, for example), on the common stock of forms (repetition and paradox) and the common stock of dramatic poses (the broken-hearted lover, the hermit retired from court) is quite sure that he, himself, is not really a poet, let alone a poet of love:

> I sing not I, of wanton love-sick lays
> Of trickling toys to feed fantastic ears.

Real men aren't poets. They certainly don't write 'lovesick lays'. You can almost see Essex thinking of that miniature by Hilliard, the one in which Walter wears flowers in his hair.

Ralegh's contemporary, George Puttenham, surveying the poets of the era, called Sir Walter 'lofty, insolent, passionate'. He is not being complimentary. The man himself is 'lofty': high, but also haughty, insolent and proud, while his poetry is elevated in style or sentiment. The Oxford English Dictionary is determined to give the adjective 'insolent' a positive spin, even while acknowledging that the word is invariably pejorative, used to describe a person who is 'proud, disdainful, haughty, arrogant, overbearing; offensively contemptuous of the rights or feelings of others', not to mention 'extravagant, immoderate, going beyond the bounds of propriety', and used about 'the powerful, rich, or successful, their actions'. None of these conventional meanings applies to Ralegh, the OED announces, since Puttenham meant 'swelling, exulting: in good sense. [Rare]'. The use is indeed rare; so rare that it applies only to Puttenham's analysis of Ralegh. Insolent, in all its meanings, seems a superbly apposite description of Sir Walter Ralegh.

'Passionate', like Puttenham's other terms, can refer both to the poet and the effect of his poetry. It suggests anger and excess, a person easily swayed by emotions, perhaps even effeminate: 'Thou art passionate, hast thou been brought up with girls?' wrote one playwright. Again, the word captures Ralegh's almost embarrassing excesses of emotion, a quality that generations of imperial historians have been keen to brush out of the picture of their national hero.

It was not Puttenham, nor even Essex, but Edmund Spenser, whose *The Faerie Queene* seems at first glance to be a sustained celebration of his patron Sir Walter, who would offer the most sustained critique of 'passionate' Ralegh. Spenser imagines Ralegh as Timias, a young squire, who – after some heroics – is wounded in the thigh by an opponent who symbolises the lust of the flesh. Timias's lust is directed towards Belphoebe, the 'fair virgin' committed to 'spotless fame of chastity'. Almost possessed, Timias struggles to suppress his futile desire: 'Long while he strove in his courageous brest, / With reason due the passion to subdue' but in doing so, 'his heart wax sore, and health decayed'. For one literary scholar, the result is

Timias's 'anguished experience of his insufficiency' (his symbolic castration).

If not castrated, he is certainly feminised and eroticised. Timias is 'wasted' by his 'service' to (or the lack of opportunity to service, if thinking simply and crudely about the sexual act) the chaste Belphoebe. The quite terrible poetry he produces when corrupted by lust is yet another indicator of his emasculation and impotent desire. Spenser risks making Timias's verse sound like a poor imitation of Ralegh's, with relentless erotic puns about dying: 'Die rather, die, then ever so fair love forsake'. (To die was a euphemism for orgasm, '*le petit mort*', in Ralegh's time).

Worse is to come in Book IV of *The Faerie Queene*, written after Ralegh and Spenser had truly fallen out, although you could be forgiven for thinking all was not well even in 1591. Belphoebe calls Timias a man of 'foul dishonour'; this may well be the author's assessment of Ralegh. Lust achieves its victory over Timias/Ralegh and his only hope is to learn his lesson: 'Abstain from pleasure, and restrain your will / Subdue desire, and bridle loose delight', writes Spenser.

The later books of *The Faerie Queene* show nothing of Ralegh the man of action, naval and military leader, explorer, coloniser, fluent propagandist, West Country landowner, parliamentary fixer, eloquent propagandist and Spenser's former patron. Spenser's image of Ralegh, a man in thrall to loose delights, endures. Critics write of Sir Walter's relationship with Queen Elizabeth that 'he alone dared to proclaim a specifically sexual attraction, based on compelling physical desire', or that 'his erotic appeal to her as a woman, through the constantly deferred promise of sexual gratification' ensured that the Queen was attracted to him. Not only does this overplay the sexual element (which may not have existed at all) between Queen and courtier but it also misrepresents Ralegh as a writer and a man. There may be nothing casual about this. The Elizabethans knew a thing or two about fake news; misrepresentation can be a powerful political tool. There is a theory, explored seriously by Michael Rudick, a modern editor of Ralegh's poetry, that 'The Lie', his bitterest poem, was in fact anti-Ralegh propaganda, his opponents seeking to incriminate him as 'the author of someone else's nihilistic, irreverent, anti-establishment satire'.

Ralegh was a man of passion, however that word is understood. For this very reason, his voice is like no other in his time. He may stand out from the crowd in his rhetorical, persuasive writings (*The Last Fight, Guiana*, 'The Lie'), but when it comes to his longest, greatest work of poetry, he stands apart.

The work was born in that summer of 1592, when Ralegh's political career was in freefall. In a remarkable cluster of poems, written in his beautiful italic hand, he eloquently reveals himself to be in a state of radical isolation. This was, of course, his physical reality at the time but in the poems Ralegh reconfigures isolation as psychic imprisonment and disintegration.

He opens with a riddle (still unsolved), continues with an exquisite sonnet ('My body in the walls captived […] / Despair bolts up my doors, and I alone / Speak to dead walls'), then launches into a long, disjointed, prisoner's lament of 522 lines that ends in dejection ('her love hath end, my woe must ever last'). The manuscript closes with a few verses bemoaning Ralegh's 'unrepaired loss', a poetic false start, an uneasy end. The final, unfinished, poem is titled 'The end of the boockes, of the Oceans love to Scinthia, and the beginninge of the 22 boock, entreatinge of Sorrow', leading to the manuscript often being called 'Ocean's Love to Cynthia'. One of the many mysteries surrounding the poems is where, if anywhere, are the other twenty 'books' of Ocean's love?

Less mysterious is Ralegh's portrayal of himself as Ocean. He had represented himself as water in his earlier poetry (for example, 'Our Passions are most like to Floods and streams') and he had been attacked as 'Water' by Essex, among others. Now, Ocean is Ralegh and Cynthia is the Queen. It is sleight of poetic hand, however, because the Queen is now imagined as water and Ralegh is no longer the ocean but merely a river bank, overwhelmed by floods. He is no longer Shepherd of the Ocean (as his protégé Edmund Spenser named him) and master of himself. He is being destroyed by the ocean and within the metaphoric framework of the poem that ocean is both himself and the Queen.

Ralegh's genius is to write about, to write out, dysfunctionality in that tormented summer of 1592. Any attempt to move towards calm and resignation in the content, towards control and closure in the form, malfunctions. Even a moment of poetic exchange in the '21st and last book' – the kind of exchange on which Ralegh had cut his poetic teeth – becomes warped. Christopher Marlowe had recently retold the story of the doomed lovers Hero and Leander, which in its classical form ends with the sea-god Neptune orchestrating the death of Leander by drowning. Marlowe's take on Hero and Leander is witty, erotic and teasing; he leaves his lovers in bed as the poem breaks off. Ralegh, in 1592, offers a clumsily eloquent retelling of his own, which not only begins abruptly, but ends in incoherence and paradox: 'She sleeps thy death'.

> She is gone, she is lost, she is found, she is ever fair.

There is no sea-god, lascivious or otherwise, at work here; merely a female nemesis. The moral, such as it is, is fatalistic rather than regenerative: 'Do then by dying what life cannot do'. In Ralegh's hands, the Hero and Leander episode demonstrates the erotic disintegrating into stasis and death. It seems the most natural of movements for the man.

Ralegh claims that it is not his body that suffers but his mind, tormented by memories of what has been. He insists that he has done so much for Elizabeth: he has been 'to seek new worlds, for gold, for praise, for glory' and, yet again stressing his isolation, his only reward is to stand 'alone, forsaken, friendless on the shore':

> So my forsaken heart, my withered mind –
> Widow of all the joys it once possessed,
> My hopes clean out of sight with forced wind,

To kingdoms strange, to lands far-off addressed,
Alone, forsaken, friendless, on the shore
With many wounds, with death's cold pangs embraced,
Writes in the dust, as one that could no more,
Whom love, and time, and fortune, had defaced;
Of things so great, so long, so manifold,
With means so weak, the soul even then departing,
The weal, the woe, the passages of old,
And worlds of thoughts described by one last sighing.
As if, when after Phœbus is descended,
And leaves a light much like the past day's dawning,
And, every toil and labour wholly ended,
Each living creature draweth to his resting,
We should begin by such a parting light
To write the story of all ages past,
And end the same before the approaching night.
Such is again the labour of my mind.

What is so telling about this superb passage is that Ralegh does not merely imagine himself as shipwrecked and wounded, which is powerful and painful enough, but also as a man forced to attempt an impossible task. Every other living creature can look forward to sleep at the setting of the sun. Only he must begin 'to write the story of all ages past' before the 'approaching night'. All Ralegh's despair at the futility of his efforts is present here. But, imprisoned for his secret marriage to Bess Throckmorton, Ralegh was not only melancholy. He was also angry and he poured his anger into his poetry.

These remarkable poems recount a journey, albeit a beautiful and haunting journey, to the dark side of love, whether understood as inertia, disillusion, or death. In the context of the crisis of 1592, this poetic journey has a dangerously satiric, political edge. Ralegh was not the only courtier to feel anger against the Queen, fuelled by dissatisfaction with a feminine, and feminised, court. Male courtiers valued military honour and achievement and were concerned that the court was now no place for their heroics. Ralegh spells it out: under a female Queen, 'the hardest steel' has been 'eaten with softest rust'. His lament for lost heroism comes dangerously close to a wider critique of a world gone soft.

The passages of panegyric of his Queen – his goddess – jostle with powerful critiques of Elizabeth the woman. It is as if Ralegh is raging against his dependency on a mere female. She is no goddess now. That is an 'outworn conceit'. A list of the beauties and perfections that seemed to last forever is countered by the reality:

> These were those marvelous perfections,
> the parents of my sorrow and my envy
> Most deathful and most violent infections
> These be the Tyrants that in fetters tie
> their wounded vassals, yet nor kill nor cure,
> but glory in their lasting misery.

'These' are 'seeming beauties'. They are fictions, fantasies, images and conceits that produce 'powerful empery' [dominance]. Fantasy here is delusion that must be countered by rational knowledge of the physical reality: Cynthia is a woman and 'so doth she please her virtues to deface'. Elizabeth is also and only a 'woman', full of the viciousness of 'her kind', a tyrant exacting a cruel and unjust punishment: 'Judgement hath been given…the limbs divided, sundered, and a-bleeding'. It is brutal stuff; Ralegh offers a self-portrait as a hung, drawn and quartered traitor.

Cynical and sceptical to his fingertips, frustrated and embittered, he could not keep his views to himself. But did he really think, in that summer of 1592, with his political career in tatters, that it was wise to depict his own death as a traitor or that his Queen would want to read his vicious critique of her mask of youth? To write that:

> Belphoebe's course is now observed no more
> that fair resemblance weareth out of date

> our Ocean seas are but tempestuous waves
> and all things base that blessed wear of late

is one thing. To copy it in his best italic hand and to attempt to send it, via Robert Cecil, as a presentation to the Queen is quite another. Behind closed doors, similarly challenging, indeed even more insulting, verses were circulating amongst the Essex circle, but the Earl and his friends made sure those particular lines never fell into enemy hands, let alone were printed. Cecil probably did Ralegh a favour by quietly burying the manuscript in the archives of Hatfield House.

This quiet stifling of his longest poetic work is just one reason we do not know Ralegh the writer as well as we should. If he had lived in any other age than Shakespeare's, perhaps we would know his work better or, if his other talents and achievements were not so distracting, maybe we would pay his literary endeavours more attention. Then again, historical or political non-fiction, one of the genres in which Ralegh flourished, is barely read, barely taught and hard to track down. Gone are the pursuits of earlier generations, forced as children to wade through the dense histories of Macaulay, Gibbon and their like. Ralegh's poetry is easy to find and his work can be, and is, anthologised. But individual poems can seem like throwaway toys to modern readers; poems born of a political moment, part of an elaborate game at court, ephemera.

Scholars complicate matters by agonising whether Ralegh is in fact the author of a particular verse, forgetting that authorised versions, including Shakespeare's plays and John Donne's poems, are thin on the ground from his era and the quest can be a distraction. There are no extant Shakespeare plays written in his own hand. They forget too that, for Ralegh, we have that most remarkable of entities, an autograph manuscript of a substantial body of poetry. And yet, and yet. 'Ocean's Love to Cynthia' is riddling, fractured, unfinished and downright strange. It is almost impossible to anthologise, such is the stream of (diseased, dis-eased) consciousness that runs across the page.

Perhaps even Ralegh realised he had gone too far; realised the dangers of pouring out his anger in ink. After 1592, as far as we can tell, his poetry is almost entirely recycled from earlier material. His literary focus would be prose; he would be a statesman, not an erotically-focused dabbler in passionate poetry. Most of the time.

8

Rival

I T WAS A WISE STRATEGY. Slowly but surely, as the decade
wore on and despite the lack of Guiana gold, despite the absence
of any apology to his Queen and, as ever, without the support
of a noble family, Ralegh clawed his way back to something like his
former glory. Since his teens, Walter's energy, vision and intelligence
had been intertwined with arrogance, violence and deception. It was a
potent mix, allowing him to survive sea battles and sex scandals, atheism enquiries and guerrilla warfare, coups, plague and the Orinoco.
Probably only Ralegh himself was unsurprised by the fact that, by the
late 1590s, this man of many parts – and great ambition – was not
merely standing but appeared to be rising again.

By 1598, Sir Walter Ralegh was Warden of the Stannaries, Vice-
Admiral in two counties, the possessor of the increasingly magnificent Sherborne Castle estate in Dorset and the already magnificent
Durham House on the Thames in London, an active member of
parliament, Lord Lieutenant of Cornwall, controller of the lucrative wine monopolies and, probably most significantly, restored to
his position as Captain of the Queen's Guard. With the death in
August 1598 of Lord Burghley, Queen Elizabeth I's most important
counsellor, Ralegh even hoped for the prize of a place on the Privy
Council. Six years after that allegedly singular 'frail misfortune' of
1592, Sir Walter's loyalty to his Queen appeared, at last, to be paying
dividends.

Unfortunately for Ralegh, his rivals' positions were equally buoyant. Robert Devereux, Earl of Essex, may have come a poor second to Ralegh in the courtier poetry wars but he had gained his Privy Council seat in February 1593. Essex and his associates were quietly confident that, once William Cecil, Lord Burghley was dead, the Earl would take his rightful place as England's leading statesman. Ralegh's most important task in the summer of 1598 was to make sure that didn't happen.

The Earl made things easier with his loose talk; his frustrations ran deep. He told a French envoy that England's government was hampered by 'two things': 'delay and inconstancy, which proceeded chiefly from the sex of the queen'. Not only that, but the peacemakers (the English courtiers who were working towards ending the years of war with Spain) were anything but blessed in the Earl's eyes: 'injurious are they to the country which bred them', injurious 'to her Majesty who hath ruled them' and, the sucker punch, 'injurious and most unthankful to God himself'.

Essex was barely able to maintain an appropriate deference towards his Queen. As June turned to July, he was so angered by one of her decisions he turned his back on her. Shocked at his lack of regard for her royal, quasi-divine, status, Elizabeth struck Essex across the head. He reached for his sword (possibly a reflex action?) and was immediately restrained. Far from seeing the incident as a breach of royal protocol on his part, Essex saw it as a great 'affront and indignity' to himself. The gossips said that he made a bad situation worse by telling the Queen that she was 'as crooked in her disposition as in her carcass'. (Ralegh took note of that carcass line. He was canny that way.)

Essex had crossed a line that even the often-outspoken Ralegh dared not and he was banished from court. His exile did not last long, however, because the Queen needed him in Ireland, where her claims to imperial control were once again being challenged; Hugh O'Neill, the Earl of Tyrone, was rebelling against English rule. On 27 March 1599 Essex left for Ireland, his mandate the crushing of Tyrone. He went as the head of the largest Tudor expeditionary force ever sent to Ireland, although it was only just under half the size of the army taken to France by Elizabeth I's father, Henry, in 1544.

Elizabeth's choice of Essex was a blow to Ralegh, although she obviously valued his perspective on Ireland, appointing him to a commission to advise on the best way to conduct the war. Ralegh's priorities and values were clear: the need to feed and pay his soldiers, the need to have a consistent military policy and to stick with it, the natural aversion of the ordinary man to the horror of war, the sense that people far from the battlefield had no idea of the reality and needed to be told and that English control of Ireland remained essential to the nation's security. Elizabeth wanted Ralegh's advice but she would not give him command of an army.

Ralegh watched, helplessly. Why had he not been sent? But his jealousy turned to relief: thank goodness he had not been put in command of inadequate resources to fight an impossible war against a relentless enemy. Essex came to a similar conclusion, abandoning the planned attack on Tyrone in the north, instead taking his troops south and engaging in a protracted – and in the end futile – campaign in Leinster and Munster.

At court his enemies, Ralegh among them, had a field day. By mid-September, the Earl, keen to return home, had made a truce based on a deal made with Tyrone in a private conversation. Unfortunately, this was completely contrary to Elizabeth's orders: no conciliation. Essex compounded his error when he returned to England by forcing his way into the Queen's bedchamber, desperate to justify himself in person. Sir Walter Ralegh, Captain of the Guard, protector of the body of the Queen, had his rival where he wanted him. The Queen, far from amused, placed Essex under house arrest and he was stripped of his offices at a tribunal on 5 June 1600.

And yet, as Essex's star waned, Ralegh's did not rise. Or at least it did not rise with the speed he might have hoped. He was acutely disappointed when, in April 1600, he was not appointed Vice Chamberlain, let alone Privy Councillor. He left court, licking his wounds: 'Sir Walter

Ralegh is gone into the country, unsatisfied', wrote one commentator. The Queen appointed him Governor of Jersey but it was not enough. How bitter was that disappointment? How deep did it run?

There was so much at stake in these closing years of the century, for the Queen was an old woman; an impressive, regal, old woman, but an old woman nevertheless. In 1598 a German visitor wrote that the face of the sixty-five-year-old Elizabeth was:

> oblong, fair, but wrinkled, her eyes small, yet black and pleasant; her nose a little hooked, her lips narrow and her teeth black; her hair was of an auburn colour, but false; upon her head she had a small crown. Her bosom was uncovered, as all the English ladies have it till they marry. Her hands were slender, her fingers rather long, and her stature neither tall nor low; her air was stately, and her manner of speaking mild and obliging.

In an audience with Elizabeth a year earlier, the French ambassador noted that she was 'for ever twisting and untwisting' the sleeves of her dress and would 'often rise from her chair, and appear to be very impatient with what I was saying'. She wore a 'great reddish-coloured wig, with a great number of spangles of gold and silver' and kept the 'front of her dress open' so that 'one could see the whole of her bosom, and passing low, and often she would open the front of this robe with her hands as if she was too hot'. These signifiers of youth fooled no one, since her face 'is and appears to be very aged. It is long and thin, and her teeth are very yellow and unequal, compared with what they were formerly, so they say, and on the left side less than on the right. Many of them are missing so that one cannot understand her easily when she speaks quickly.' The ambassador continues, with the confidence of the patriarchal voyeur, that the Queen's bosom was 'somewhat wrinkled as well as one can see for the collar that she wears round her neck, but lower down her flesh is exceeding white and delicate, so far as one could see'. It would be a few years before elite women's necklines plunged so much that the nipples were exposed but Elizabeth lived, dressed and ruled in an era of extreme *décolleté*; not the kindest of fashions for an older woman.

Little wonder that a 1596 order from the Privy Council commanded public officers 'to aid the queen's Sergeant Painter in seeking out unseemly portraits which were to her great offence and therefore to be defaced'. No more images of Elizabeth were to be produced unless approved by the Sergeant Painter, which meant that all portraits showed the Queen to be young. Courtiers caught on quickly, one writing, tactfully if absurdly, that Elizabeth is 'very youthful still in appearance, seeming no more than twenty years of age'.

It was all a response to the scrutiny of the Queen's ageing body. It also made good political sense, reinforcing a narrative of female power that had enabled Elizabeth's long rule. These images made the claim that the Queen was ageless and that this agelessness was a product of her active virtue, her virginity and chastity. Ralegh was one of this claim's chief architects, albeit using pen and ink rather than paint and canvas. He had created Elizabeth as Belphoebe, the 'fair virgin' committed to 'spotless fame of chastity'; the image he had so brutally dissected in his poetry of 1592. The scholar Helen Hackett spells it out: whether in numerous miniatures or large canvases such as the Rainbow portrait, images of the ageless Queen implied 'that her sexual intactness had brought with it resistance to bodily decay'. There were convenient biblical overtones: 'triumph over sexuality was interpreted as triumph over the Fall, in turn enabling triumph over the penalty of the Fall, mortality. Elizabeth's motto, *Semper Eadem*, "Always one and the same," came to signify not only constancy, integrity and singularity, but also a miraculous physical purity and immutability'.

The 'mask of youth', as it became known, may have been politically expedient but for many male courtiers it not only symbolised the grotesque falsity of court life but also exacerbated their (entirely conventional) misogyny. It was hard to serve a woman, for men lived in a society built on the fundamental premise that women were faulty versions of men. Some male courtiers found the combination of power, femaleness and age so disturbing that they nicknamed the

Queen 'Juno', the goddess whose female irrationality tormented the hero Aeneas. Yet, however disturbed they might be by this old woman's power, to serve her, they nevertheless had to engage, day in, day out, in an eroticised politics. All Elizabeth's courtiers loved her and she loved them. However frustrated, when describing their Queen most courtiers, not least those who wished to succeed, took care to avoid mention of the wrinkles and blackened (or yellowed, depending on your source) teeth.

The mask of youth, constructed in words and images, did little to conceal the body within. Every political move, by every political player, was inspired by the prospect of the old, childless Queen's death and the glaring reality that she did not have a successor. Not that one could talk about it. There were to be no reminders of Elizabeth's mortality and the Queen and her ministers were determined that her age, and the prospect of her death, were taboo, at least in public.

Behind closed doors it was a different story. Like all his contemporaries, Ralegh was keeping a keen eye out for each and every rival's manoeuvre regarding the succession, while trying to position himself for the inevitable regime change. Sadly, dangerously perhaps, nothing was working for him. As he wrote to a new friend, Henry Brooke, Lord Cobham, in April 1600 from Sherborne: 'I can write your lordship nothing from hence but that we live'. If he were to continue to be sidelined at court, then 'I must begin to keep sheep by time'. Cobham was doing better, entertaining the Queen at his house in Blackfriars in June and embedding himself even more firmly into the political elite by his marriage to the daughter of Charles Howard, Earl of Nottingham. The Howards were one of the most powerful families in the country, so entrenched that the Protestant Crown usually overlooked their Catholic sympathies. Lord Cobham and Ralegh became closer with each month: 'I will remain yours before all the world', wrote Walter to Henry.

Historians tend to be harsh on Ralegh's new friend ('but one degree from a fool', writes Anthony Weldon) but he was on the rise. Ralegh remained in the country through the autumn of 1600, relentlessly busy and not looking forward to a further 'miserable journey into Cornwall'. He recognised that, 250 miles west of London, he was dangerously removed from the real business of government. No matter that, as Lord Lieutenant and Warden of the Stannaries, he was politically, economically and militarily in control of a county of crucial strategic importance for coastal defence, whose tin mines offered huge financial rewards. No matter that Ralegh was the perfect man for the job. With no powerful local magnate and the Crown unable to maintain order (tin miners, sailors, pirates and smugglers were all renowned for their troublesome ways), there was a power vacuum in Cornwall. A vacuum that someone such as Sir Walter Ralegh had – if at times grudgingly – been willing to fill. Or maybe not so grudgingly? Some have seen Ralegh, the Governor of Jersey, and his new ally Cobham, Warden of the Cinque Ports, as part of a small but powerful cabal quietly striving to gain control of the key military, naval and fiscal resources of the kingdom. If so, it was a long game. In the short term, although Ralegh proved adept at dealing with miners, sailors, pirates and smugglers, and knew how to make good money from them, those deals were not the same as a seat on the Privy Council.

Winters proved more glamorous. For three years in succession, the Queen used Sir Walter for ambassadorial duties, managing the diplomatic spectacles, elaborate ceremonies and royal feasts when the great men of Europe came to stay. Ralegh took care of Virginio Orsini, Duke of Bracciano, nephew of the Grand Duke of Tuscany, at the first night of Shakespeare's *Twelfth Night* at court. A few days later, Ralegh, with Lord Cobham, escorted Orsini to Hampton Court, then Orsini and 'Guatteralli', as the Italians styled him, rode from Gravesend to Chatham to view the fleet.

With an even higher profile than Orsini, the Duc de Biron, acting as emissary from the French King Henry IV, arrived in September 1601 with a large retinue. The English political goal, that France might declare war on Spain, was not achieved, but in diplomatic terms the embassy was a success. During the French visit, Ralegh was tireless: 'Haste post haste for life, W Ralegh' he writes (accompanying the instruction with a sketch of the gallows, just in case the messenger hadn't grasped the urgency), furious that the Duke had been terribly neglected, with 'not one nobleman nor gentleman' accompanying or guiding him. So Ralegh takes over; to Westminster 'to see the monuments', then to the Bear Garden 'this Monday…which they took great pleasure to see'. There's a hitch; 'their horses will not be provided till Wednesday morning', but fortunately Sir Walter is on to it: 'I sent to and fro and have labored like a moyle [mule] to fashion all things'. The result was that the French party reached the Hampshire country house, The Vyne, on Thursday, where the Queen met them. (There were grumblings on both sides. Biron felt neglected, at least at first, but Elizabeth reckoned his entertainment at her subject's house in Hampshire cost her more than if she had hosted the French at her own court.)

It was still not enough for Ralegh, frustrated by his lack of progress and recognition while the Queen lived, fearful of what would happen when the Queen died. He must have known that others were making their own moves and alliances, not least Robert Cecil, Burghley's son and successor.

Ralegh was close to Cecil during what was turning out to be a political endgame, but it was a complicated, perilous closeness. A remarkable letter, written from Ireland in October 1598, shows Ralegh's ruthlessness and his ability to work dangerously close to the wire but, above all, shows him covering Cecil's back, presumably in the hope that his loyalty would pay political dividends. Or, more cynically, that Cecil would one day owe him, big time. Ralegh was in Ireland because the temporary ceasefire between the Irish lords and the English, brokered the previous year, had expired in June 1598; therefore his, and the Queen's, lands and titles were again under direct threat. Many English settlers were fleeing the island, among them Edmund Spenser, whose castle at Kilcolman was destroyed by O'Neill's forces in October.

Sir Walter writes home from the Irish front line, where there is news of the killing of a rebel leader. Ralegh swiftly moves into jus- tificatory mode, since 'the lives of anointed princes are daily sought and we have always in Ireland give [*sic*] head money for the killing of rebels, who are evermore proclaimed at a price'. The rebel killing was the assassination of the Earl of Tyrone, on the instructions of Robert Cecil, now the Queen's chief minister, who had written to the Secretary of State for Ireland, Sir Geoffrey Fenton. His justification (of sorts) for the killing of a prince (of sorts) was that at the beginning of August a serious rebellion had yet again rocked Munster, and O'Neill had triumphed over English forces at the Battle of the Yellow Ford. Fenton urged Cecil to communicate with the utmost secrecy but the assassination went ahead. In his letter, Ralegh shows himself well aware that things are done in wartime from which leaders wish to distance themselves while still reaping the rewards. Robert Cecil is 'not to be touched in the matter' and Ralegh is also careful to cover himself. In one of his telling postscripts (the man's postscripts are a genre in and of themselves), he writes that 'he hath nothing under my hand but a passport'. There is no paper trail to link Cecil or Ralegh with the cold-blooded 'killing of a rebel'.

A letter written some fourteen months later reveals another aspect of Ralegh's relationship with Cecil. Dated 2 February 1600, it appears at first sight to show a close friendship, cemented by the presence of Will Cecil, Robert's much-loved son, at Sherborne. Motherless Will, coming up to his ninth birthday, was born a year before the ill-fated Damerei Ralegh and was two and a half years older than Ralegh's surviving son, Wat. Ralegh flatters Cecil with a vision of young Will's future glory (he 'shall be able to keep as many men at his heels as he, and more too') and, the next month, writes in paternal fellowship of the boy's progress:

> Because I know you can receive no pleasinger news from hence than to hear of your beloved creature, I thought good to let you know of his good health […] better in health and strength than ever I knew him. His stomach that was heretofore weak is altogether amended and doth now eat well and digest perfectly […] He is also better kept to his book than any where else.

Quite apart from the fact that Ralegh appears unaware that presenting himself as the ideal father figure (and the boy did indeed admire Sir Walter) might alienate rather than flatter Will's actual father, a post-script in another letter from this time reveals the fault lines in this most slippery of political relationships, one that that had never been robust but had always ticked over. Ralegh admits that he is uncertain of Cobham's loyalty and friendship ('I never received one word from my Lord Cobham, neither of his suit nor of his coming or other matter this 3 weeks') but he's just as concerned about Cecil as an ally: 'You have many letters of mine: I pray return some answer. Candlemas Day'. Ralegh is uncomfortable with being ignored; no wonder, in this volatile political situation.

Uncertain of Cecil, Ralegh nevertheless had a clear political target: the Earl of Essex was in trouble again. Another doomed Irish campaign and Sir Walter does not hold back. Essex is a 'tyrant' whose 'malice is fixed'. Cecil should not show mercy, because the tyranny and malice of the Earl:

> Will not evaporate by any your mild courses, for he will ascribe the alteration to her Majesty's pusillanimity and not to your good nature, knowing that you work but upon her humour, and not out of any love towards him. The less you make him, the less he shall be able to harm you and yours, and if her Majesty's favour fail him, he will again decline to a common person.

That was the aim: to ensure that Essex would return to the ranks, the same ranks from which Ralegh had risen. There's more: young Will Cecil would only rise if Essex were kept down. If not, he will 'be able to break the branches and pull up the tree, root and all. Lose not your advantage. If you do, I read your destiny.—Yours to the end, W.R'.

It was indeed only a matter of time before Essex attempted to pull up the tree, root and all. After his disastrous 1599 Irish expedition and his even more disastrous invasion of the Queen's Privy Chamber, the Earl was 'an earl without place or income; a patron without patronage;

a commander without an army', as Susan Brigden writes. The Privy Council had for a time been concerned about the 'concourse of people and great resort of Lords and others to Essex House', the Earl's London residence on the Strand (complete with forty-two bedrooms, a picture gallery, a chapel and a banqueting suite). There were whispers, getting louder all the time, that Essex and his followers were intent on restoring him to what they believed to be his rightful place at the centre of government. Ralegh was not the only frustrated courtier in town. The Earl was summoned to explain the meetings but, 'in bed & all a sweat after tennis', he refused and, when summoned again, again refused.

By February 1601, the Earl, increasingly and to some extent rightly paranoid (there were indeed spies in his household and his handwriting had indeed been forged) was convinced that the Privy Council was attempting to lure him from his home to one end: his death. Essex revealed the threat to his life after a private command performance of *Richard II*, given by Shakespeare's theatre company, the Lord Chamberlain's Men, although whether it was Shakespeare's take on the deposition of King Richard we do not know. Essex had received word from 'friends in the City' that 'some hard measure' was intended against him. More specifically that Sir Walter Ralegh 'had a band of men ready to murder him and that an ambush had been prepared if he went to the Privy Council'. These friends were ready to defend him 'against the malice of his private enemies'.

Private enemy number one was obviously Sir Walter Ralegh, Captain of the Guard, now in command of double the usual number of men. Essex and his supporters knew Ralegh was ready for them and therefore a direct attack on the court (and the Queen) was too dangerous, so they chose a softer target. They would 'move the city', to make the 'Citizens to take arms in his behalf'.

It is quite possible that the whole thing was a set-up and Ralegh's murderous band of men merely a story put about to precipitate foolish action. If so, it worked. The notoriously impulsive Essex acted the very next day when, with about a hundred followers, he marched on the City. He led his band from Essex House through Ludgate and into the

City chanting 'Murder, murder, God save the Queen'. The words of loyalty fooled no one. The citizens of London would not follow the traitor, who returned to Essex House by river. A short siege later, the Earl was taken by soldiers of the Crown. He would not see his Queen again.

Early on the same day, two men had met in a boat on the Thames. One was Ferdinando Gorges, loyal to Essex. The other was Sir Walter Ralegh. The men were cousins; Ralegh urged Gorges to flee while he could, since the Council knew about Essex's foolish plan and were making ready to repel him. Even the young lawyers of the Inns of Court had been asked to take up arms. Gorges in turn urged Ralegh to take refuge in the court, since he remained optimistic about the Earl's chances.

Ralegh, at least this time, knew better. Essex never got close to achieving his *coup d'état*, not least because he seriously over-estimated the degree of support he would get from the citizens of London. Above all, he jumped too soon. Or was, perhaps, pushed to jump too soon.

The end came quickly. Essex began by denying his treachery but, over six days, the Crown gained a signed confession. He was executed on 25 February 1601. From the scaffold, he spoke of his sinfulness ('this my last sin, this bloody, this crying, this infectious sin') and prayed for the Queen, her nobles and her ministers of church and state, although he had to be prompted to pray for his enemies. Laying his head on the block, he echoed Christ: 'Lord into thy hands I commend my spirit'. It was a pitch-perfect death; no wonder a mob attacked the executioner as he left the scaffold. With tensions rising, the ports were closed and the trained bands (local amateur militias charged by the Crown to defend the realm) around London were readied for action. Preachers were instructed to deliver sermons denouncing the Earl, the subject who wished to become another Henry IV, who desired only to have 'set the Crown of England upon his own head'.

The Essex Rebellion divided, and still divides, opinion. Was it a spectacular failure, a revolt quickly contained with great ease by the government's forces, a footnote to the series of more serious rebellions that punctured the Tudor monarchs' quiet? Or was it a desperately needed and genuine attempt at a peaceful transition of power? In which case, the launch of a *coup d'état* a week ahead of schedule was precisely what Essex was 'trying not to do', according to his modern biographer, Paul Hammer. Was the attempted coup merely an opportunity for the Queen to punish Essex for his earlier profound discourtesies? This was certainly the view of Arbella Stuart, who, as great-great-granddaughter of King Henry VII and Elizabeth of York, niece of Mary Queen of Scots and granddaughter of the for-midable, and ambitious, Bess of Hardwick, understood this world as well as anyone. Arbella Stuart believed that Essex had been doomed from the very moment he had burst in on his Queen without warning, puncturing the façade of the eternal goddess, even as he kissed 'that breast in his offensively wet riding clothes'. Ralegh's take was similar but cruder: it was not Essex's 'insurrection' that had ensured his death, but rather that he had 'told Queen Elizabeth that her conditions were as crooked as her carcass'.

It is possible that Ralegh acted as *agent provocateur* but equally possible that the Earl didn't need much provoking. It is also possible, but unlikely, that Ralegh smirked (and smoked) as Essex was executed, watching from a window of the armoury at the Tower of London. As Nicholls and Williams suggest in their biography, it was Ralegh's duty, as Captain of the Guard, to attend the execution and it might have been tact that led him to stand off-stage during the Earl's final moments. It is a matter of record that Essex rounded on Ralegh at his trial, insisting that Sir Walter swear on the Bible and that even then the man could not be trusted: 'What booteth it to swear the fox?' Essex was not the first, and would not be the last, man to call Ralegh a liar but he was one of the most powerful. Ralegh's mendacity, and his 'bloody pride' (according to one ballad of the time), were the two qualities that would hang like millstones around his neck.

For all the venom directed against him – it is astonishing and telling how much of the popular literature that survives is preoccupied with attacking Ralegh – one of Sir Walter's most significant rivals had been eliminated. As his brother-in-law, the rather less mercurial Arthur

Throckmorton, noted, 'it seems the state was sick. I hope this letting blood will do it good.' The state was indeed sick, but in the short term 'this letting blood' might serve Ralegh's turn very well. The questions remained. With 'the earl who would be king' removed, who would now be King? Or Queen? Whoever succeeded Elizabeth, could Ralegh prosper? Could he do more than prosper?

9

The last days of Elizabeth

T HE SAFE MONEY and significantly, the money of Robert Cecil, was on James Stuart, King of Scotland to succeed Elizabeth. James was Protestant, experienced and conveniently, male. More problematically, he was the son of Mary Queen of Scots, whom Elizabeth had had executed. But that was nearly fifteen years ago, in another time. Now it was understood that the Queen herself favoured James VI of Scotland, who in his turn had made it clear that his mother's treason did not affect his title to the English throne.

James's claim was, nevertheless, far from incontrovertible. As for Elizabeth, she refused, despite pressure from the Scottish King, to formally recognise him as her heir. Her reasons were political and they were sound. The Queen distrusted both James and her own subjects. So did Ralegh. In 1593, he had warned that England needed to be ready for a military response from Scotland if James did not become King of England. At the time, Ralegh was, ostensibly, writing in support of a clampdown on any discussion of the succession, in the aftermath of a foolhardy attempt by Peter Wentworth to have the matter debated in parliament. As one MP and lawyer put it, 'if we should enter into dealing with titles of the Crown we had need (I think) hold a parliament a whole year long'. Ralegh concurred but could not resist weighing in with his own advice to the Queen, mocking those who sought to influence her and warning her of the potential threat from James if he were overlooked.

The Queen's commitment to not naming a successor may have made shrewd political sense but it did nothing to silence the political whispering in the post-Essex era. In 1601, one observer identified twelve competitors who 'gape for' the death of the Queen: 'Thus you see', he declared, 'this crown is not like to fall to the ground for want of heads that claim to wear it, but upon whose head it will fall is by many doubted'. The ambition and the anxiety of these years are hard to underestimate, not least because, just over the Channel, France had suffered its own war of succession, creating fears of something similar in England.

Nor did it help that all the claims to the Crown were problematic. Edward and Thomas Seymour had a strong case by right of their lineage: they were the sons of Katherine Grey who, being the granddaughter of Henry VIII's younger sister Mary and sister of the nine-days' Queen, Lady Jane Grey, had been the most likely successor to Elizabeth in the first years of the Queen's reign. Elizabeth ensured that the boys' lineage meant nothing; she had Edward and Thomas proclaimed bastards, excluding them from the succession. The reason: their mother had made the grave error, as a 'virgin of the blood royal', of marrying Edward Seymour, the Earl of Hertford, without the Queen's permission, and becoming pregnant. This was not a moral issue but one of national security, reflected in the act of 1536 that had made it treason for a person of royal blood to marry without the monarch's approval. Katherine ended up in the Tower of London, where her son Edward was born in 1561. That her child was a boy made a bad situation worse, since a Protestant male heir could so easily become a rallying point for those of Elizabeth's subjects who might not tolerate the (necessarily monstrous) regimen of a woman. In 1562, Seymour and Katherine's marriage was declared void and their children illegitimate. The story of Katherine's next six years makes painful reading. This younger sister of the nine-day Queen was, her biographer argues, probably anorexic and certainly deeply melancholy. She died, still a captive, on 27 January 1568.

Sir Walter Ralegh knew all about the unhappy Grey sister, Bess's stepsister, the previous occupant of her childhood bedchamber. Sir Walter also knew all about the consequences of secret marriages and less secret male heirs. He had a clear grasp of exactly how likely it would be for Elizabeth to overturn the Seymour brothers' illegitimacy. It was not going to happen.

Ralegh was, it seems, looking elsewhere. His monarch-in-waiting was not James but – and one has to add 'it seems', because Ralegh would not put such a thought in writing in such dangerous times – Arbella Stuart. He was not alone: Lord Burghley was rumoured to support the claim of this great-great-granddaughter of Henry VII. The Queen, for her part, did not and ensured her cousin was kept isolated in faraway Derbyshire.

Others were quite sure that the new King would come from Scotland. The words and actions of two men were to seal Ralegh's fate. One was the elderly, intellectual, crypto-Catholic Lord Henry Howard, the Earl of Northampton, a political outcast for much of his career despite being a member of one of the great ancient noble families of England. He re-emerged after 1600 and became someone to whom James was willing to listen. Howard, with Robert Cecil, instigated a secret correspondence with the Scottish court, in which he savaged the claims of other English courtiers. The two men created a picture, partially true as all powerful fictions are, that James had many enemies in England and that only they could defend him.

Enemy number one was Sir Walter Ralegh, closely followed by Henry Brooke, Lord Cobham. They were easy targets, not least because of their perceived animosity to the Earl of Essex, who James much admired.

Ralegh appears to have no idea how much he was hated or how brutally his political hopes were being undermined. Perhaps he had become inured to the vitriol. After all, he had survived thus far. He continued to foster the friendship between Will Cecil and his son, continued to send Cecil gifts of gloves and cheerfully passed on his wife's 'best wishes notwithstanding all quarrels', noting happily that it only took two days and two nights for Cecil's letter to reach him. He writes, oblivious: 'I pray believe that when all hearts are open and all desires tried that I am your poorest and your faithfullest friend to do you service'. Meanwhile, Sir Walter was being ripped to shreds in secret letters for his 'accursed duality'.

The fact that Howard and Cecil saw Ralegh as a threat was quite an achievement. Not a Privy Councillor, not from a great family, someone who was used by his Queen to take foreign princes to the theatre. Why was he so feared? Was he a contender in the struggle to control the succession? Howard thought he might be and intended to stop Ralegh before he ascend 'into those high regions'.

Ralegh may have been unaware of the secret correspondence but he was not entirely open with Cecil, despite his assurances. When he received a letter from Cecil, he immediately forwarded it to his friend Cobham, keeping him informed as to what their rival was saying, while responding equally promptly to Cecil. This kind of moment shows why Ralegh was perceived as a threat, since it exudes the sheer energy of the man. He writes 'Sherburn the 13th of August at night when I received yours' on his letter to Cecil, then copies Cecil's letter and writes to Cobham. The thrust of his letter to Cobham is to suggest that he was right to get away when he did: 'if you were not loose [travelling? or a free man?] you should be tied above [at Court?] for a while. If you needs will unto Cornwall, then make haste or I think you will be sent for. I can say no more.' Hints and warnings abound and there's even a postscript from Bess: 'And if I could disgest this last word of Sur Waltars letta I wold expres my love likewies, but unly this I agree and am on in all with Sur Waltar and most in his love to you. I pray hasten your returne for the elecket sake, that we may see the bathe to gether. Your trew poour frind, E Ralegh.' Lady Ralegh was clearly important to the Ralegh/ Cobham alliance, or her husband thought she was, because her voice becomes increasingly audible in their correspondence, whether writing about elections or the danger of her oysters and partridges becoming stale.

Ralegh with his son Wat in 1602 (artist unknown)

Ralegh had plenty of energy but he (and Cobham) were not perhaps as powerful as Henry Howard feared or Ralegh and Cobham desired. For all their stratagems, on 14 July 1601 Ralegh found that he had once again not been made a Privy Councillor, despite Essex's removal: 'You hear of our new counsellors. I am left out till the parliament, they tell me, but I take no thought of it'. The senior knight of Cornwall doth protest too much. Ralegh could entertain foreign dignitaries, offer advice about Ireland and Cornwall and he knew a lot about boats. But there were limits, always limits.

Once again, he found himself on the sidelines. Once again, he pulled himself up, dusted himself down and re-entered the fray. Ralegh's renewed confidence in 1601 is visible in a portrait of him with his son. It is an image of quiet ambition. Both are dressed in splendid costumes: Ralegh's jacket is embroidered with seed pearls and his son's blue suit is silver-braided. Man and boy – young Wat mimics his father's confident stance – stand in the balletic pose favoured by the Elizabethans: 'one foot in front of the other and each slightly turned out to emphasise the shapely male leg, the ideal form of which was lean, muscular and exaggeratedly elongated with a curving calf and strong swelling thigh disappearing into the trunk hose' (according to the historian Anna Reynolds).

Ralegh knew that he was useful to his Queen, if only as a man of action. He wanted to be a warrior for Elizabeth: 'I my self went it in half a day less, and if there [be is crossed out] were any danger it would be no otherwise handled'. The danger is, as ever in Ralegh's mind, Spain: 'If they hover about the mouth of the Channel, I am here nearer my charge than at London'.

The parliament of the winter of 1601 was remarkable because Elizabeth did at last allude to a time when she would not be Queen. Her acknowledgement of her mortality, even her exhaustion, was embedded in a speech characterised by words of humility and service. She began:

> To be a king, and wear a crown, is a thing more glorious to them that see it, than it is pleasant for them that bear it: for myself, I never was much inticed with the glorious name of a King, or the royal authority of a Queen, as delighted that God hath made me His instrument to maintain His Truth and Glory, and to defend this kingdom from dishonor, damage, tyranny, and oppression. But should I ascribe any of these things to myself, or my sexly weakness, I were not worthy to live, and of all most unworthy of the mercies I have received at God's hands, but to God only and wholly all is given and ascribed.

Elizabeth claimed that if it were merely her 'own disposition I should be willing to resign the place I hold to any other, and glad to be freed of the glory with the labors, for it is not my desire to live nor to reign longer than my life and reign shall be for your good'. It was an astonishing admission, immediately softened by her claim that, although

Parliament would have had 'many mightier and wiser Princes sitting in the Seat, yet you never had nor shall have any that will love you better'.

With the Queen now speaking of her end, was Ralegh's star at last in the ascendant? Attacks on him certainly increased. Howard wanted the present Queen's (as well as the potential King's) eyes opened as to what was going in Durham House and had some very practical suggestions. They could expose Ralegh's secret communications with the Duke of Lennox in Scotland. They could encourage Ralegh to negotiate with Spain. Or they could deny him money and see what he did. Howard was going for Sir Walter's jugular; coming from a great family himself he knew very well that Ralegh had no similar dynastic safety net. Starved of cash, Ralegh, the fifth son of a mere gentleman from Devon, with expensive tastes, would reveal his true colours, his 'great sauciness'. Breeding would out.

A fourth strategy was to launch an all-out attack on Durham House, 'to prove what sport he could make in that fellowship'. It is just possible that a burglary in April 1602, in which only two 'linen pillowbears... fitted with silk and gold worth 10 pounds [and] a linen cushing cloth adorned with silk and gold, worth five pounds' were taken, was cover for an attempt to get evidence against Ralegh.

Intriguingly, there are hints, and sometimes more than hints, that the real power at Durham House lies with Lady Ralegh. She is a 'most dangerous woman', 'full of her father's inventions', writes Howard. Here, he invokes the ghost of Sir Nicholas Throckmorton, the Queen's representative in Elizabeth's dealings with, and execution of, Mary Queen of Scots, the Scottish King's mother. Howard notes that the 'league is very strong' between Lady Ralegh and Lady Shrewsbury, better known as Bess of Hardwick, and, significantly, grandmother of Arbella Stuart. The word is that Bess is very close to regaining her old place in the Privy Chamber. The Queen, writes Howard, 'must be told what canons are concluded in the chapter of Durham, where Rawley's wife is precedent: and withal how weakly Cobham is induced to commend the courses that are secretly inspired by the consent of that fellow-ship'.

The horrific inversions of Durham House are laid bare. Lady Ralegh commands her husband and the monstrous couple control the spine-less Cobham. There was more: Ralegh's 'wife, as furious as Proserpina with failing of that restitution in court which flattery had moved her to expect, bends her whole wits and industry to the disturbance of all motions, by counsel and encouragement, that may disturb the possibility of others' hopes, since her own cannot be secured'. Bess is Proserpina, the daughter of Zeus and Demeter, abducted by Hades to be his Queen, dangerously 'precedent' in the lower world, her move-ments between hell and the upper world a symbol of the naturally fecund cycle of the seasons. Ralegh is no better: 'the greatest Lucifer'. Howard reveals Bess and Sir Walter as monarchs of hell, although even 'Hell did never show up such a couple'.

Howard was wrong. The Raleghs were getting nowhere, again. Sir Walter was still courting Robert Cecil, vaguely aware that he is being more and more pushed to the side. His letters to Cecil make queasy reading, lurching between passages of business (between men of the world) and expressions of love and flattery (obviously, and optimisti-cally, addressed to the Queen). Ralegh was grieved to:

> Find with what difficulty and torment to my self I obtain the small-est favour. Her Majesty knows that I am ready to spend all I have, and my life, for her in a day, and that I have but the keeping of that I have for all I have I will sell for her in an hour and spend it in her service. Let the Queen then break their hearts that are none of hers: there is little gain in losing her own. These things should not torment me if I were as other[s] are, but it is true, *ubi dolor, ibi amor, exue amorem, exueris dolorem* [where there is pain, there is love; cast off the love, you cast off the pain].

These passionate lines, whose Latin phrases are taken from Ficino, the Renaissance poet of neo-Platonic love, are embedded in a letter whose main theme is parliamentary proceedings and some business about taverns. All the lovesick (and egotistical) lamenting in the world

An exquisite miniature from a time of extraordinary success, with wealth, land and power all bestowed on him by his Queen.

The manner of their fishing.

John White, sent by Ralegh to sketch the landscapes and indigenous people of the New World, returned with a powerful record of the people of Roanoke or 'Virginia'.

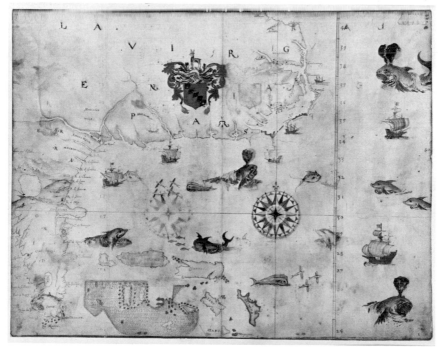

The moon, the pearls, the colours, the motto: all show Ralegh's loyalty to his Queen in 1588.

A sketch of the ageing Queen Elizabeth I in 1592.

Some ten years later, the 'mask of youth' is in place for the now ageless Queen.

A portrait of quiet ambition: Ralegh with his son, Wat, in 1602.

James I soon after his accession to the English throne. Already hostile to Sir Walter while still King of Scotland, James would grow to hate the man he called 'Rawly'.

Henry, James's son, who as a teenage Prince of Wales established a rival and very different court to his father, full of 'gold, the learned and the militant'.

Ralegh's 'dear Bess', defiant even as her husband 'withered' in the Tower.

wasn't going to do any good. The time for this kind of language from Ralegh had long gone, even if Cecil intended to pass the message on to the Queen. Which he didn't.

Ralegh understood how court life worked. It was a world dependent on personal access. What mattered was being close, physically, to the person in charge. Ralegh had been there: he knew he was nowhere near it now. It was particularly galling that others were using the same language of love with more success, suggesting it was not the language that had gone out of fashion but the man. Lord George Carew was fulsome in praise of the Queen's beauty, which adorned the world for which he, George, would of course sacrifice himself at her feet. Cecil, who supported Carew, was rather pleased with the effort, and reported that the Queen 'liked your letter very well'.

Meanwhile, Cecil was playing Ralegh and not just regarding the secret correspondence with Scotland. He even invested £2,000 in one of Sir Walter's naval ventures. Ralegh is all gratitude: 'If we cannot have what we would, me think it is a great bond to find a friend that will strain himself in his friend's cause in whatsoever as this world fareth'. Cecil, more canny, asks Sir Walter to 'conceal our adventure'. Cecil had, of course, 'no other meaning than becometh an honest man in any of my actions'. Ralegh fell for it.

By the spring of 1602, Ralegh was in Jersey, politically increasingly impotent and thoroughly despondent. Even his enemies were less concerned about him. One wrote to James in Scotland, labelling Ralegh 'insolent [and] extremely heated' but having, nevertheless, 'excellent good parts of nature'. Sir Walter likes to think of himself, and be regarded, as someone able 'to sway all men's fancies' but the truth is that, when the time comes, he won't do James 'much good nor harm'. Ralegh's status as B-list courtier could not have been made clearer. The man himself knew that he was cut off, politically and physically. The wind is in the wrong direction; he is in 'desolation'. He sends the same letter to Cobham and to Cecil, one a dangerous friend, the other a dangerous enemy: 'I arrived here the 3rd so I have walked here this 17 days in the wilderness'.

August 1602; a glimmer of hope at court: the Lord Chamberlain has died. Is this Cobham's chance? His father had held the office. September; Ralegh is 'in pain and cannot write much'. Cobham is not Lord Chamberlain.

It was not the despair that Sir Walter could not stand, it was the hope. And every time, those hopes had been dashed. Then, something in the winter of 1602–3 prompted Ralegh to act to protect himself. This is new territory. He was driven not by a desire for power but by fear for his own life.

Perhaps he heard that the Queen's physical and mental health was deteriorating rapidly. It may have been a genuine crisis of funds: Ralegh had complained of poverty so often that it is hard to assess whether his claim that his estate was 'weak and far in debt' was true or not. Or his actions might have a far more sinister significance: Ralegh was on the brink of risking everything.

He took two crucial steps. One was to sell his Irish estates for a paltry £1,000 to Richard Boyle, later the Earl of Cork, on 7 December 1602. The other was to place his estate at Sherborne in trust. The first straightforwardly increased Ralegh's liquid assets but the second suggests a deeper anxiety. Lying behind this legal move was the spectre of treason charges. Ralegh knew precisely what happened, physically, to those convicted of treason but he also knew there were those who gained from others' falls: he had done so himself. The process was grounded on the principle of 'escheat', whereby if no successor was qualified to inherit under the original grant, the property and land (the 'fief') of a tenant reverted to the lord when the tenant died. As, according to the doctrine of corruption of blood, an attainted person could have no legal heir, his property suffered automatic escheat: his heirs, however innocent, could not inherit. Instead the estate 'lapsed' into the control of the Crown. The fear of escheat provoked Ralegh to place Sherborne in trust for his ten-year-old son. If convicted of treason, Ralegh could not forfeit to the Crown what he did not possess. If he lived, he could receive income from the estate. If he died the property would stay in the Ralegh name.

The tantalising question remains: did Ralegh fear a treason charge because he was plotting treachery, or did he fear his enemies' ability to frame him for the crime?

He set up the Sherborne trust just in time. The Queen had been 'by fits troubled with melancholy some three or four months'. By the close of February 1603, her end was drawing close. For two weeks she was 'extremely oppressed': she would neither eat nor see a doctor, nor go to bed to rest. Finally, her will gave way and she was persuaded to lie down. She knew that death was near. The most important men of the land, led in prayer by the Archbishop of Canterbury, stood to watch her die. Then night fell, and the important men departed, leaving the Queen in her Privy Chamber alone 'all but her women that attended her'. The Queen died at 2:30 in the morning.

The path to the scaffold

T HE POWER VACUUM lasted for only a few hours. 'At about
10 o' clock King James was proclaimed in Cheapside by all
the Council with great joy and triumph.' This had been a
long time coming and the Privy Council – *sans* Ralegh, of course –
was ready for its crucial task of ensuring the peaceful installation of
a successor to the childless Queen. The slick transfer of power after
so many years of suppressed, whispered anxiety about the succession
was a triumph for Robert Cecil and a relief for those who had feared
'commotions'. The crowds were strangely quiet but this was interpreted,
conveniently, as a mark of respect for the dead Queen. At least there
was no violence; five hundred soldiers were levied in London for the
coronation to 'withstand any tumults and disorders'. 'In an hour, two
mighty nations were made one', wrote Thomas Dekker; the union of
Scotland and England had been achieved. He also noted, less com-
placently, that 'some English great ones that before seemed tame, on
the sudden turned wild'.

Ralegh was one. He joined the hordes of courtiers riding north,
hoping to be among the first to be noticed and favoured by King James.
But, in an ominous move, he was stopped in his tracks by Robert Cecil
and forced to return to London. Cobham was also frozen out: Lord
Henry Howard, Earl of Northampton, was already at the King's side
in Scotland and, according to one letter-writer, working 'to possess
the king's ear and countermine the Lord Cobham'. Howard, in person,

repeated the message of his letters, possessing the King's ear with an image of Elizabeth's court as 'a world…of fractions', of vicious cabals working tirelessly against each other. Days into the new regime, things did not look good for Ralegh. He moved swiftly to seal the deed that conveyed the Sherborne estate to trustees.

His actions suggest that, in March, Ralegh still hoped (foolishly, optimistically) that the new King might look favourably on him or, failing that, that the new King's wife might look favourably on Lady Ralegh. Her opportunity came in mid-April. King James, having travelled as far south as Yorkshire, gave orders that 'some of the ladies of all degrees who were about the [old] Queen…or some others whom you shall think meetest and most willing and able to abide travel' should travel north to meet his Queen, Anne of Denmark. Lady Ralegh had most certainly been 'about' the old Queen and had shown she was 'willing and able to abide travel'. James's letter was, however, addressed to Robert Cecil, who was in no mood to do the Raleghs any favours. Bess was not on the guest list.

Lady Anne Clifford was, and she gives a graphic account of her participation in the struggle to be the first to meet the new Queen. First there is a problem about horses, which delays Anne and her mother, but once they are mounted there is no stopping them as they attempt to catch up with the main party. 'My Mother & I went on our journey to overtake her, & killed three Horses that day with extremities of heat.' They arrive late at night at a great house 'where we found the doors shut & none in the House, but one Servant who only had the Keys of the Hall, so that we were forced to lie in the Hall all night till towards morning, at which time came a Man and let us into the Higher Rooms where we slept 3 or 4 hours'. In the morning they were off again, still hoping to be amongst the first to greet England's new Queen Anne in her progress south. However quickly they travelled and however many horses were sacrificed to their political ambitions, the 'diverse ladies of honour' nevertheless had to halt their journey just south of the Scottish border. News filtered through that Queen Anne had suffered a miscarriage. She was not well enough to travel out of Scotland.

Some of the aspiring ladies used their initiative. The Countess of Kildare, wife of Lord Cobham (but, to complicate matters, no friend to Lady Ralegh or her husband), 'quit her companions at Berwick and went to Edinburgh', where Anne was due to make her first appearance after the miscarriage. The Countess's initiative seemed to pay dividends, because even before the Queen crossed the border at Berwick on 6 June, Kildare had been appointed governess to the young Princess Elizabeth, King James and Queen Anne's only daughter. Anne then travelled slowly south towards her new court in Westminster.

Bess, obviously not one of Cecil's chosen few, did her best under the circumstances. She rode north, belatedly. Did she know that Robert Cecil was recording her every move? The very man she begged to accompany her to meet the new Queen was Cecil's spy. He later wrote to his real master: 'I was entreated by his wife to ride another idle journey to my charge to meet the Queen, where she received but idle graces'. Queen Anne was clearly either unwilling or unable to offer Bess any support. 'Idle graces' were not what was needed as spring turned to summer in 1603.

Ralegh was not having much more success. Prevented from gaining physical access to James, Sir Walter attempted to write to his King. On 25 April 1603, an informer reported back to the increasingly powerful Robert Cecil that Ralegh's opinions 'hath taken no great root here' although his letters had indeed been presented to the King.

It is possible that Ralegh succeeded in meeting James. The diarist John Aubrey, writing decades later, tells of an encounter between the two men at Burghley House near Stamford. There is no other evidence for the meeting but as Aubrey tells it, both James and Ralegh are utterly recognisable as characters. Suffice to say the story does not involve a meeting of minds. James commented that he could, if necessary, carry the country by force. Ralegh, conveniently 'walking close by', suggested the matter should be put to the test. The King, understandably nonplussed by the proposition (he might have been expecting a flattering courtier to reassure him that there was no need for bloodshed, such was the universal affection for the new King), asked Ralegh to explain himself, which he promptly did: 'Because that then you would have known your friends from your foes'. Aubrey says the comment was 'never forgotten or forgiven'. James's mind had already been poisoned against Sir Walter, thanks to Howard and Cecil, something the King allegedly admitted to Ralegh's face: 'O my soul, mon, I have heard rawly of thee'. These words offer both an indication of James's accent and a reminder of how Ralegh's name was pronounced by a Scot.

If Ralegh didn't realise at this stage he had been stitched up by his enemies, he never would. He then made a bad situation worse by advocating war with Spain. The shifting political sands in the spring of 1603 are nowhere more visible than in England's conflict with Spain, begun in 1585. James, as potential successor to Elizabeth, had been a staunch opponent of peace; his opposition rooted in his anxiety about the claims of the Archduchess Isabella, the Spanish Infanta, to the English throne. This created an opportunity, before Elizabeth's death, for men such as Howard to damn Ralegh and Cobham as supporters of a deal 'in the matter of this peace'. Once installed as King of England, James was far more conciliatory towards Spain: there would be no Queen Isabella. The irony of course is that Ralegh, a long-standing military hawk, was just as wary as James was of Philip III of Spain's plans to place his daughter on the English throne and even more wary of those English courtiers who seemed to welcome the idea. Ralegh, like Essex before him, did not trust the peacemakers. Always a political outsider, despite his wealth, achievements and service to the Crown, Ralegh was now well and truly on the margins. Was it at this point that he began to consider a more dangerous way back to power? For the moment, he turned – once more – to writing.

Despite James being newly pro-Spain, Ralegh put together his arguments for active intervention on behalf of the Netherlands against Spain in *A Discourse touching a war with Spain*. His reasons were pragmatic rather than ideological. The Netherlands was unable to defend itself, so would be forced to turn to another country for protection. It was best that country be England. In another typical move, Ralegh ends the tract with a defence of the honest adviser, the man who tells truth to power, a necessary part of any monarch's court. Those who remain silent when they can 'declare' and 'publish' their advice are no better than those who flee the kingdom, he writes. He might have been better off fleeing.

For a brief moment, Ralegh remained an ostensibly powerful, and highly visible, figure. His position as Captain of the Guard meant that at Queen Elizabeth's funeral he walked at the head of his 150 'men of the guard, with the points of their halberts downwards'.

But it all unravelled very swiftly. First, Ralegh was stripped of the Captaincy of the Guard. In May, he lost his control of monopolies. Worse was to come. On 31st May, Ralegh was given notice to leave Durham House, another indication that others had succeeded where he had failed in the crucial months after James was proclaimed King. The Bishop of Durham had preached sermons to James at Berwick on 6 April and at Newcastle on 10 April, with the happy result of the return of the palace to his possession. Ralegh was given notice to leave by 24 June and warned not to remove any panelling, glass or

Ralegh at the head of the Queen's Guard during her funeral procession

metalwork. The 'stables and garden' were taken over by the ascendant Robert Cecil, who planned to clear them to make space for his 'New Exchange'. All that Ralegh could retort was that even the poorest man would have been given three months' notice and the whole process was 'contrary to honour, to custom, and to civility'. He had held the house for nearly twenty years and had spent nearly £2,000 of his own money on it. He had 'made provisions for 40 persons in the spring' and has a 'family (that is, a household) of no less number and the like for almost 20 horse'. He thinks it 'very strange'.

No one was listening.

15 July 1603: George Brooke confesses. The Cinque Ports are closed and proclamations issued for the arrest of the conspirators. Men are being tortured. Thomas Gayton, writing from Gray's Inn to his wife, notes that he's bought the cloth she wanted and that Anthony Copley has been racked. Wild stories are the stuff of this summer: news of the King's death briefly circulates, and is swiftly quashed. Ralegh is placed under house arrest; his keeper Thomas Bodley, his temporary home Bodley's house in Fulham, west of London. The Crown has only hearsay evidence about a plot to overthrow James but it is enough to justify an interrogation of Cobham, who cracks. Cobham admits that he had intended to inspire rebellion and bring about a Spanish invasion. The result? The death of the King and the placing of Arbella Stuart on the throne. His co-conspirator? Sir Walter Ralegh.

Ralegh's nerve is being severely tested and he does not handle it well. Asked about his involvement with Cobham, he makes the mistake of claiming different things, one after the other: he first denies any knowledge, then hints at his suspicions (clearly attempting to extricate himself by pointing at others) and then, most damningly, gets in touch with Cobham to reassure him that he had not revealed anything incriminating.

It was never going to turn out well. On 19 July Ralegh was moved to the Tower of London. A day later, Cobham was informed of Ralegh's double-dealing towards him: 'O wretch, O traitor' he cried, with 'many exclamations and oaths' against Ralegh. More details emerged. The two men were planning to go to Flanders before travelling to Spain, where they would get 'five or six hundred thousand crowns' (600,000 crowns equates to an astonishing £150,000 in the present day, and this an era when most people never even had one crown in their hand). Then they would meet in Jersey, where Ralegh was governor. The plan, which always had a back-of-an-envelope quality, was that 'they would take advantage of the discontentments of the people and thereupon resolve what was to be done'.

Cobham's confession made clear that there were two, very loosely connected, plots. The goal of what was now deemed the secondary, or so-called 'Bye Plot', was to force a degree of religious toleration. It brought together such unlikely bedfellows as radical, sectarian Protestants and Catholic priests, both groups seeking a measure of freedom to practise their religion. The more ambitious, and deadly, aim of the 'Main Plot' was to stir up rebellion, invite a foreign invasion, kill the King and his two sons and put a puppet (and conveniently female) monarch, the young Lady Arbella Stuart, on the throne. The huge sums of money necessary to achieve these goals were, it was claimed, being raised by Ralegh and Cobham by means of the Spanish envoy, the Count of Arenberg. Ralegh *and* Cobham? No, said Cobham. He would never have done anything without Ralegh's 'instigation'. The man 'would never let him alone'.

It was damning (and plausible) stuff. There were only two problems. One, the state had no material evidence. Ralegh had learned a little over the years about the dangers of putting things in writing. And, two, almost immediately, Cobham retracted almost every word of his confession. Over the following four months, Cobham, remarkably, refused to repeat his accusations, which meant that the Crown, seeking prosecution, would have to rely on 'certified statements' if it came to trial.

Perhaps it would not come to that. Ralegh, in his own mind the victim, besieged by 'persecutors and accusers' and 'overthrown' by them, was in complete despair. He 'stood still upon his innocency, but with a mind the most dejected I ever saw', wrote the Lieutenant of the Tower, reporting to his superiors. It got worse. Two days later, the Lieutenant is losing all patience: 'I never saw so strange a dejected mind as is in Sir Walter Ralegh. I am exceedingly cumbered with him, 5 or 6 times in a day he sendeth for me in such passions as I see his fortitude is [not] competent to support his grief.'

While Ralegh's abandoned any pretence at 'fortitude', his family remained both traumatised and under threat. Henry Howard, for one, was determined to bring both the Raleghs down, warning Lady Ralegh against any attempt to exonerate her treacherous husband. Torn between painting Bess as a devious conspirator (has she an 'unspotted conscience', he wonders) and as a foolish woman standing by her man, Howard points out that before she 'conclude him to be a martyr', Lady Ralegh must prove Sir Walter's innocence. If she proved his innocence, however, then she charged 'the state it self with injustice'.

Arthur Throckmorton, Bess' brother, forwarded a letter from her to Robert Cecil on 23 July. His covering letter, written from his estate in Northamptonshire, reeks of understandable fear for himself and his sister. Unlike Bess, he is wary of showing support for Sir Walter: all he wishes to do is offer simple brotherly support to a 'sorrowful sister' in her time of need, to share their correspondence because he hopes it will show that they are innocent bystanders. All he asks is that he should be given 'leave to come up unto her' to give her 'the lawful brotherly comforts I may'.

While waiting to hear if her brother would be allowed to come to her, Bess received a devastating letter from her husband. He can no longer bear to live and instructs his wife how to continue once he is dead, 'for his sake who will be cruel to himself to preserve thee'. Ralegh was not going to wait for trial and execution. Suicide was the only way to escape the dishonour he had brought on himself and his family, the only decent thing he could do. He justifies himself knowing full well that 'it is forbidden to destroy ourselves' but arguing that he did not despair of God's mercy: 'Be not dismayed that I died in despair of God's mercies, strive not to dispute it but assure thy self that God hath not left me nor Satan tempted me'. The implication is that he did, in contrast, despair of any mercy from the King: 'Oh God I cannot resist these thoughts'. He hopes that death will bring 'dark forgetfulness' and longs to be released from torment: 'O death destroy my memory which is my tormentor: my thoughts and my life cannot dwell in one body'.

What he does not ask of himself, he asks of his wife. She must go on living, she must learn to forget, she must endure the dishonour and she must marry again, if only to pay the bills.

Biographers and historians have been stern about this letter, no doubt partly because of the continuing taboos and unease surrounding suicide and depression but partly because of what has been viewed as its crass, even 'effeminate', emotionalism. It has been seen as essentially a fake, a performance designed to draw attention to Ralegh's predicament, 'nauseating and meaningless'.

The letter was not an empty threat: Sir Walter stabbed himself in the heart with a table knife. His contemporaries were as harsh on him as later historians. It was all for show. It was only a flesh wound. Ralegh's attempted suicide was merely another sign of his guilt and of his weakness as a man. Interrogation and torture had succeeded in its purpose: 'the property of the rack is not only to stretch the joints, but reach the conscience, and make it give', wrote one observer, while the King suggested that Ralegh needed to be forcefully reminded that it was the state that would decide what happened to his body, not the traitor.

Ralegh did not die. By early August, he was recovering in mind and body, having worked out that his only problem was Cobham's retracted statement. Others knew this already. Robert Cecil wrote to the English ambassador in France that Cobham 'seems now to clear Sir Walter in most things and to take all the burden to himself'. Cecil knew that, in legal terms, a single witness could not bring about the conviction of a suspected traitor. The Crown therefore redoubled their efforts to get more dirt on Ralegh, examining suspect after suspect.

That summer of 1603, thousands were dying of plague each week in London. Thirty thousand would die in this epidemic, mainly from the poorer classes, as the disease did its deadly work in the over-crowded parishes just outside the city gates. As one of Shakespeare's rivals, Thomas Dekker, expressed it: 'Death (like a Spanish Leaguer or rather like stalking Tamberlane) hath pitched his tent in the sinfully polluted suburbs'. Unable to understand the indiscriminate disease, contemporaries could only view plague as a sign of God's displeasure. It was an apocalyptic backdrop to Ralegh's fall.

Plague would not stop the Crown's quest. It did, however, ensure the postponement of James VI and I's ceremonial entry into London, the withdrawal of the political elite from London, the delay of the start of the law term and the relocation of the law courts to Winchester, some seventy miles south-west of the capital. King James and his court settled at Wilton, near Salisbury.

September. The outlook was brighter for the prisoner. The judges met to discuss the case and acknowledged that Ralegh might escape punishment because the proofs 'are not so pregnant' in his case. Nevertheless, the political will remained: there was 'a strong purpose to proceed severely in the matter, against the principal persons'.

By October, Ralegh's opponents were again confident. Robert Cecil was sure that the accusation was 'well founded' and the 'retraction so blemished' that the outcome was a formality. Even more tellingly, Lady Ralegh was making plans for the inevitable death of her husband (attempting to obtain 'a gift of all his goods', even though it would not even begin to cover his debts). Nevertheless, she continued to seek a last chance for Sir Walter: 'my Lady Ralegh hath offered £5,000 to bring her husband's business to a Star Chamber'. This step revealed both her knowledge of the legal system and her willingness to pursue extreme courses of action. The court of the Star Chamber was even then an anomaly in the justice system; a jury-less court that did not obey English common law and that was presided over by the Privy Council and two judges appointed by the King. Crucially, however, although to be tried in Star Chamber was to acknowledge the guilt of the offender even before the trial started, the court could not impose a death sentence.

By the end of the month, it is not worth counting the dead in London; plague was doing its work. Ralegh writes to Cecil, begging for mercy. He knows who really matters now. All he can do is to make a passing appeal to the past ('To speak of former times it were needless' but, oh, how he needs Cecil to remember those past times) and to beg. He writes to Queen Anne. He writes to King James.

All to no avail. The decision was made to bring all the prisoners south to Winchester, partly because of the plague, partly because the King was already in Hampshire, suitably close to what would be the first show trials of his reign and partly because tensions were running high in London. Traitor Ralegh, 'the best hated man in England', a 'viper of hell', was so unpopular it was believed his trial might incite mob violence. It was 'hob or nob' (touch and go) whether the authorities would be able to bring the prisoner alive 'through such multitudes of unruly people'. And indeed, on 13 November, there was a riot in London directed against Ralegh.

It was time to move him. As the prisoners travelled to Winchester, crossing Hounslow Heath, south-west of London, Sir Walter saw an old man and recognised him as someone to whom he owed money. He asked for the coach to be halted, announced his debt and asked, formally, for the King to 'be good to this worthy gentleman'.

This small but powerful gesture is just as significant to an understanding of the man as the waves of hatred directed towards him. Every ounce of Ralegh's charm, every ounce of his ability to use language, to perform on the grandest of stages, the qualities on show on Hounslow Heath in a small way, would be needed when on trial for his life. It would literally be a performance, because trials were public, theatrical spectacles, with seats going for high prices. It did not matter that there was no clear-cut case and that the prosecution was far from straightforward. What mattered was that it was Ralegh.

The setting was the thirteenth-century Great Hall, or Arthur's Hall, of Winchester Castle. It is an imposing, profoundly atmospheric space that survives intact (complete with its Round Table) although the rest of the castle, the casualty first of civil war then urban development, has almost entirely disappeared.

Proceedings began on 17 November. The charge against Ralegh was based on Cobham's (retracted) testimony from 20 July. The court was told that Sir Walter had conspired 'to deprive the king of his government…to raise up sedition within the Realm, to alter Religion… to bring in the Romish superstition, and to procure foreign enemies to invade the kingdoms'. Furthermore, he had sought to place Arbella Stuart on the throne, for which he would receive £600,000, before retreating to safety in Jersey.

No one could question his fortitude now. Ralegh was in his element. He 'sat upon a stool within a place made of purpose for the prisoner to be in, and expected the coming of the Lords, during which time he saluted divers of his acquaintance with a very steadfast and cheerful countenance'. Exuding confidence, he refused to challenge the composition of the jury: 'I know my own innocency and therefore will challenge none. All are indifferent to me'. Behind the scenes, Lady Ralegh was less indifferent. She had worked tirelessly to find a sympathetic jury and succeeded in putting in two of her connections. Then, overnight, the jury was changed: her attempt had failed. Her husband remained master of the situation and of himself: 'humble, yet not prostrate; dutiful, yet not dejected [to the Lords], towards the jury affable, but not fawning; not in despair nor believing, but hoping in them, carefully persuading them with reasons, not distemperately importuning them with conjurations; rather showing love of life, than fear of death'. If he lost his temper, it was always strategic. If this were a show trial, a way of establishing the power of the new regime, Ralegh was taking over the show.

It became obvious that the prosecutor Edward Coke was being forced into attacking Ralegh's character because of the legal weaknesses in the Crown's case. Coke behaved 'violently and bitterly', attempting to provoke Ralegh by calling him a 'monster', 'viper', 'odious fellow', 'the rankest traitor in all England', a 'spider of Hell'. The more Coke ranted, the more the 'standers by' questioned his authority. Ralegh countered with common sense and relentless denials. He had never said he would make away with the 'king and his cubs'. The charges made little economic or political sense, since Spain was bankrupt and would not waste money attempting to destabilise England. Ralegh was also winning the personality contest. He was no peasant traitor; was he 'a Cade? A Kett? A Jack Straw?' Of course not.

Ralegh's priority was to discredit Cobham's statement of 20 July. He made it clear that Cobham had 'passions of such violence that his best friends could never temper them'. But he also knew that there was a serious fault line in the prosecution's case, because two witnesses were required to make a charge of treason stick. Ralegh had done his legal, not to mention his theological, homework, aided by his friend Thomas Harriot. If the court accepted (and they could hardly not) that 'the law of God liveth for ever', then Ralegh could prove that 'by the whole consent of the Scripture', a conviction on the word on one person was insufficient. An alternative interpretation placed the treason legislation enacted by parliament over the previous 250 years above scripture. The Crown's case was that, if a statute had lapsed, as it had done, then common law and common sense prevailed: one witness was enough.

Ralegh's command of the occasion meant that only his voice was heard. 'You tell me of one witness, let me have him' he cried. He threw English precedent, Daniel and Deuteronomy at his audience. He demanded that his accuser be brought into the court. If they did not bring Cobham, then his trial would be by 'not law but by the Spanish inquisition'. He cast himself, expertly, as the underdog, 'weak of memory and feeble as you see', a man without legal training. Would anyone present want to be tried on the basis of 'suspicion and inferences'? No one would be safe.

His *coup de grâce* was to produce a letter of exoneration from Cobham, which had been smuggled to him. Coke met fire with fire: he brought out a second statement from Cobham, confirming his damning, deadly accusations. Ralegh had been the ringleader, he had negotiated with foreign powers (not 600,000 crowns but a less spectacular, although still welcome, annual pension of £1,500, in return for foreign intelligence) and Ralegh had told Cobham, 'coming from Greenwich one night' that he had already passed on information. A statute of 1351 demonstrated that it was treason 'to compass or imagine' the death of a King. Ralegh's imaginings damned him.

It was all over very quickly. The jury voted unanimously that the prisoner was guilty of treason. Sir Walter Ralegh was attaindered: condemned to death as a traitor, with all his civil rights and capacities extinguished. His entire estate, both real and personal, was forfeited to the Crown and his blood decreed to be corrupted. His son Walter would not, could not, inherit anything.

Sir Walter was told he would be hung, drawn and quartered. Lord Chief Justice Popham lectured the prisoner on the Christian faith and warned him to disregard the dangerous ideas of Thomas Harriot. Ralegh was dismissed as a 'revenger' and a man who had climbed too high.

He fought back as best he could. He asked that the proofs be shown to the King and insisted that the jury would live to regret their verdict. Then he 'talked a while with the Lords in private'. As he was taken back to prison by the Sheriff, he walked 'with admirable erection, yet in such as sort, as a condemned man should do'. His performance, even in defeat, had been impeccable. As the commentator Dudley Carleton observed, Ralegh:

> served for a whole act, and played all the parts himself…He answered with that temper, wit, learning, courage, and judgment, that, save it went with the hazard of his life, it was the happiest day that ever he spent.

Carleton believes that if Ralegh's name had not already been so tarnished, he would have been acquitted and concludes by reporting a bystander's comment:

> he was so led by the common hatred that he would have gone a hundred miles to see him hanged, he would, ere he parted, have

gone a thousand to save his life. In one word, never was a man so
hated and so popular in so short a time.

Ralegh remained convinced that he had been 'strongly practiced
against'. Did he have a point? In public, Robert Cecil spoke of Ralegh's
fall as a 'tragedy'. Some have argued that, in private, the entire
conspiracy was manufactured by Cecil to consolidate James's power
and bolster his own position, even at the expense of his brother-in-
law, Lord Cobham. Certainly, the discovery of the plot led to a new,
hard-line policy, with an edict drafted in July 1603 (although enacted
only some seven months later) expelling all Roman Catholic clergy,
'Jesuits, Seminaries and other Priests', from James's kingdom. Was this
a new regime consolidating its power, manufacturing a threat, needing
and thus finding scapegoats? Other historians are dismissive: it 'would
have been the height of daring, or folly, to have manufactured complex
conspiracies, even had time, imagination and resources permitted such
creativity', writes Mark Nicholls. Most likely, Ralegh was fool enough
to give the new monarchy all it needed; a few words spoken in anger
'coming from Greenwich one night'.

Although Cecil almost certainly did not actively engineer Ralegh's
fall but he was not the man to prevent the final elimination of a potential political rival for the sake of a past friendship. And Lady Ralegh
was not the woman to allow that final elimination to go unchallenged.
Her letter to Cecil might be hard for a modern reader to follow in its
original spelling, but to read it as it was written allows some of its
terrible urgency to come through:

> To the most honnerabell me Lord Cissell
> If the greved Teares of an unfortunat woman may resevef ani
> fafor, or the unspekeabell sorros of my ded hart may resevef ani
> cumfort, then let my sorros cum before you wich if you trewly
> knew, I asur my selfe you wold pitti me, but most espescially your
> poour unfortunate frind ich relyeth holy on you honnorable and
> wontid fafor: I knoo in my owne soule wich sumthing knooeth his

mind that he douth, and ever hath doon, noy unlly honered the king, but naturally loveth him, and god knooeth far: from him to wish him harme, but to have spent his life as soune for him, as ani cretuer leveng.

I most humly beseich your Honnar – even for god sake – to be good unto him; to onns more make him your cretur, your relifed frind; and dell with the Keng for him – for onn that is more worti of fafo than mani eles; having worthe, and onnesti, and wisdom to be a frind. pitti the name of your ancient frind on his poour littell cretuer wich may leve to honnor you. That wee all may life up ouer handes and hartes in prayer for you and youres, bind this ouer pooure famlies to prayes your honnar and wonted good natur let the hole world prayes your love to my my pour unfortunat hosban, for cristis sake, wich rewardeth [at this point, Lady Ralegh runs out of space on her sheet, so she moves to writing vertically in the margin] all mercies, pitti his just case; and god for his infeni marci bles you for ever, and worke in the king merci: I am not abell I protest befor god to stand on my trembling leges otherwies I wold have watted now on you: or be derectid holy by you: chee that will trewly honnar you in all misfortun

E Ralegh

Lady Ralegh can only beg 'me lord' Cecil in the name of God to make her husband live again. At the same time, the letter is thoroughly, and problematically, defiant. Nowhere does she acknowledge her husband's guilt. Instead, she offers a litany of his virtues: worth, honesty, wisdom.

Cecil did not listen. He did not need to, because with Ralegh condemned to death, Cobham was willing to talk, putting the nails in Sir Walter's coffin. Cobham recalled that some recent exchanges with Robert Cecil had left Ralegh 'full of discontent' on that night when he came from the court at Greenwich. Pushed to his limit (and that never took much), Ralegh had encouraged Cobham to negotiate with Arenberg that he should 'advertise and advise the King of Spain to send an army against England to Milford Haven'. As Ralegh expressed it, 'many more had been hanged for words than for deeds', therefore he had nothing to lose by acting.

If, at Ralegh's trial, Coke had known about the Milford Haven discussion he would have used it. This was new evidence but it changed very little. The rest was familiar: the Spanish pension of £1,500 a year, the *quid pro quo* of providing information if England were to threaten either Spain or the Low Countries.

Cobham clearly felt he had nothing to lose in the run-up to his own trial, which took place on 25 November. As a peer of the realm, he was tried by his fellow noblemen in the Court of the Lord Steward. There was no abuse from Coke but there was also no eloquent defiance from Cobham. Indeed, 'never was seen so poor and abject a spirit', who 'heard his indictment with much fear and trembling'. Cobham attacked George Brooke, his own 'viper' brother, much to one onlooker's disapproval: he 'accused all his friends and so little excused himself'. A day later, it was the turn of another noble conspirator to be tried at Winchester: Thomas Grey, 15th Baron Grey of Wilton Grey, one of the evangelical Protestants drawn into the Bye Plot. This was different again; the devout Grey making 'a long and eloquent speech' that 'held them the whole day, from eight in the morning until eight at night, in subtle traverses and escapes'. Grey was rebuked: he should not challenge the court. Only a week earlier, 'the master of shifts', Sir Walter Ralegh, had shown this to be futile.

Ralegh's supporters were doing their best. It was open knowledge (a 'pretty secret') that the 'lady of Pembroke hath written to her son Philip and charged him of all her blessings to employ his own credit and his friends and all he can do for Ralegh's pardon', but it was also open knowledge that 'she does little good'. Ralegh himself made one last effort. On 27 November, he wrote to five Privy Counsellors, including Robert Cecil, pointing out that he was condemned by the 'first accusation' that has now disappeared. Therefore, if he were to be killed, he would be one who 'perished innocent'. Ralegh throws everything into this letter, peppering his case with quotations from the Bible and even a mention of Christ (noticeably absent from the vast majority of his writings): 'I do beseech you for his sake that shed his blood for us to think of this one argument'. He attacks Cobham, who has always 'had a cruel desire to destroy me, hoping thereby to extenuate his own offences' but also attempts to be magnanimous. It is a moment for charity, so Ralegh 'will only for this time accuse his memory or mistaking'. And he restates his innocence, in both senses of the word. His only crime is 'giving ear to some things and in taking on me to harken to the offer of money'. He ends by begging:

> And if I may not beg a pardon, or a life, yet let me beg a time at the king's merciful hands. Let me have one year to give to God in a prison and to serve him. I trust his pitiful nature will have compassion on my soul, and it is my soul that beggeth a time of the king.

The reality was that the only possible escape from the scaffold was a personal intervention by James. Ralegh had one more letter in him, to write to the King in a final attempt to save his life. Two versions of this letter survive, the one that reached James and an unsigned draft in Ralegh's less neat hand. It begins superbly: 'This being the first letter which ever your Majesty received from a dead man'. Did Ralegh really believe that he would be dead by the time James read the letter or did he hope that this final plea would prompt the King to an act of mercy?

James was not the only audience that Ralegh had in mind. The letter was copied and recopied, the scribes working from a third version that someone had made available for public consumption. Ralegh would not go quietly. The world would know of his innocence.

James read 'every word' of it (Cecil wrote to Ralegh's keeper to let him know). And did nothing.

The scaffold: Winchester

THE WEATHER IS TERRIBLE: 'A fouler day could hardly have been picked out, or fitter for such a tragedy', writes Dudley Carleton to his fellow news-gatherer, John Chamberlain.

Sir Griffin Markham is the first conspirator to be brought to the scaffold, walking past the slowly rotting quarters and severed heads of the priests who had received the Crown's justice days earlier. There is a commotion in the crowd. John Gib, a Groom of the King's Bedchamber, is struggling to get the Sheriff's attention. At last he succeeds, the Sheriff stepping down to 'secretly' confer with Gib while Markham awaits his death. The Sheriff climbs back up on to the scaffold but only to tell Markham that he is 'so ill prepared' in a spiritual sense that it has been decided by the King that he can have 'two hours' respite'. Markham is taken away and 'locked' into 'the great hall to walk with Prince Arthur'.

Now it is the turn of Thomas Grey, 15th Baron Grey de Wilton. He approaches the scaffold surrounded by his friends, with 'such gaiety and cheer in his countenance' that he seems like a 'dapper young bridegroom'. His hot Protestant faith sustains Grey to the last but his fervent, zealous prayers test the patience of the crowd, keeping them standing in the rain for half an hour. Too long on such a filthy day. They are here for an execution, not a prayer meeting.

Grey is hardly spiritually 'ill prepared' but the Sheriff again intervenes, saying he has 'received orders from the king to change the order of execution and that the Lord Cobham was to go before' Grey. The crowd becomes restless, as a second conspirator is led away to Prince Arthur's Hall.

Lord Cobham is then brought to the scaffold, only to be joined by the other two men. What was happening? All three men together 'looked strange one upon the other, like men beheaded, and met again in the other world'. Dudley Carleton views the day as theatre, every move 'part of the same play'. If it is theatre, this is a drama written and directed by King James, and he has given his Sheriff the script. A 'short speech' is read to the three men, informing them just how appalling their offences have been, how lawful their condemnation was and spelling out what is to happen: their imminent deaths. The three men, broken, assent to every word.

James delivers his final plot twist. The Sheriff pronounces: 'see the mercy of your prince, who of himself hath sent a countermand and given you your lives'. The King has changed his mind. The three men will live. The crowd go wild, 'such hues and cries that it went down from the castle into the town and there began afresh, as if there had been some such like accident'.

What of Sir Walter? He was watching every moment of the drama unfold, because he 'had a window opened that way'. He had (Carleton again) 'hammers working in his head to beat out the meaning of this stratagem', knowing that his 'turn was to come on Monday next'.

His turn did not come, for he finds, after an agonising interval, that 'the king had pardoned him with the rest, and confined him with the two lords to the Tower of London, there to remain during his pleasure'. His body would be spared but he remained attaindered. He was, and remained, a traitor. Sir Walter Ralegh, the man, was declared legally dead.

PART TWO

Defeat

KING JAMES WON THE BATTLE on the day, the crowd shouting 'God save the King' at his suitably regal, if belated, display of mercy. But would he win the war? Ralegh's reputation had begun a remarkable turnaround in Winchester. His words and actions at the trial had established him as a powerful voice in direct contest with the authority of Stuart justice. As the new century unfolded, this oppositional voice, born of the occasion – he did not want to die – would be picked up, exploited and transformed, by reformists and radicals alike. At the time, more powerful still, scribes copied and recopied the transcripts of the proceedings, feeding the appetite of readers hungry to know of the events at Winchester. Ralegh was swiftly transformed from the 'best hated man in England' into a popular hero.

He was also good box office. The winter of 1603 saw William Shakespeare and Ben Jonson battling it out for theatre audiences on the south bank of the Thames and they knew a good story when they heard it. In *Sejanus His Fall*, Jonson reimagined Ralegh as Silius, a tormented, Hamlet-like figure, yet a noble man of action, facing the tyrannical pederast Emperor Tiberius. Unlike Shakespeare's vacillating hero, who puts down his 'bare bodkin' from fear of 'the undiscovered country' of death, Silius escapes 'the slings and arrows of outrageous fortune' and succeeds in killing himself in Act Three. Jonson's play, following Roman rather than Christian doctrine, seems to applaud Silius's death: 'Look upon Silius, and so learn to die'.

The 'clotted style, lack of irony, and grinding moral emphasis' (in the words of one critic) of *Sejanus* means it is rarely revived, but it was performed at court in the winter of 1603 by the King's Men, including William Shakespeare, who may have played Tiberius. Jonson referred to a 'second pen', although his co-writer was probably not Shakespeare, since the Bard was busy with his own response, *Measure for Measure*. Shakespeare's company first performed this new play for the King in the banqueting hall at Whitehall on St Stephen's Night, 26 December 1604, a year after the events that the play echoes. Shakespeare, meanwhile, is at his most topical in *Measure for Measure*, alluding to the plague (which was still widespread, leading to the closure of the theatres in spring 1604), to the making of a peace (brokered with Spain in August 1604) and to the Main and Bye Plots that had dominated the previous winter. As Mistress Overdone the brothel madam complains, 'what with the war, what with the sweat, what with the gallows, and what with poverty, I am custom shrunk'. Shakespeare's Duke of Vienna dispenses justice at the end of the play in a theatrical manner, echoing James's tactics with Ralegh and his fellow conspirators the year before.

Opinion is divided on whether Silius represents Ralegh or the Duke represents King James, but Rome and Vienna are certainly London. Both playwrights show a city at breaking point and a society struggling with sleaze, corruption and disease. The dramatic solutions offered by Jonson and Shakespeare, whether honourable suicide or ostentatious displays of princely mercy, leave the underlying social and political problems raised by their plays unsolved. As with the execution of Essex just a few years earlier, it appeared the blood-letting had not cleansed the sickly body politic. That didn't stop people being interested in the fallen Ralegh in his new home, the Bloody Tower in the Tower of London. The Tower was very much on the capital's tourist circuit. Visitors marvelled at traitors past ('look there, where Anne Boleyn was executed', 'those are the very cannons the Earl of Essex brought back from Cadiz', 'that's the exact place where the brave Earl was beheaded', 'here's the chapel he's buried in') and sought glimpses of celebrated traitors present.

Was it any consolation to the traitor himself that he had lived a life less ordinary in the years leading to his imprisonment? For, by any measure, then or now, Ralegh was exceptional in the scope of his abilities, the flagrancy of his flaws, the range of his achievements and the spectacular nature of his failures. It seems not. Ralegh could barely lift his pen. From his rooms in the Tower, he managed the most formulaic of gestures of gratitude. He wrote to Robert Cecil, acknowledging he had 'failed both in friendship and in judgement' and asking if he should write to the King. There is a subtext that Cecil has betrayed him but it is never made explicit. Cecil doesn't reply until 20 December and then only indirectly, asking the Lieutenant of the Tower to tell Ralegh he wished him well and suggesting he should write to the King to thank him for being his sole deliverer. By then, Ralegh had already done so, in a tired reiteration of his loyalty.

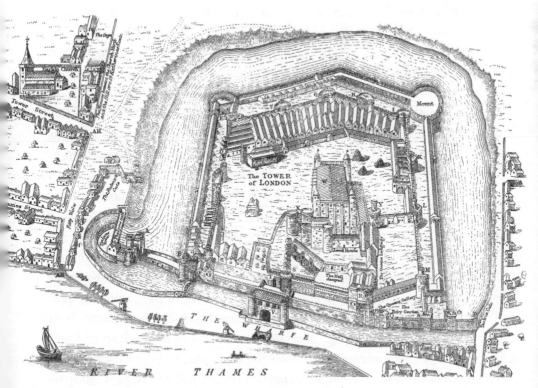

The Tower of London in 1597

Psychologically, he was struggling. Being legally dead, all his powers had been transferred to others, including Lady Ralegh: 'My tenants refuse to pay my wife her rent'. Bess, being Bess, was taking on more and more of her husband's responsibilities, despite living in a world in which, as her correspondents reminded her, women were barred to 'discourse of matters' and 'judge of questions'. She simply had to do it.

In these darks days there are glimmers of Ralegh at his best, especially as a friend. Lawrence Keymis, who had been close to Ralegh for years, remained in the Tower until 31 December 1603, collateral damage from his patron's fall. Keymis had lost his annuity and his vision of a plantation in the Indies and was so 'examined', so 'pressed', about his connection with Ralegh, that his 'staff is now broken'. Ralegh for his part attempted to offer support ('be good to Keymis for he is a perfect honest man who has suffered much for my sake') and refused to accept Keymis would have given away anything, even under torture: he was a friend.

There were also faint splutterings of Sir Walter's old pride. A year into his imprisonment, he seemed perplexed he was no longer receiving money from wine licences, the patent for which he had been granted by Elizabeth and which had not been transferred to anyone else. A few months earlier, in June 1604, he had refused to give up the seal of the Duchy of Cornwall to a messenger. Ralegh was stalling, just because he could, but he also had a point to make. He would send the seal to Cecil, and Cecil could deliver it to the King, because Ralegh had received it 'from her Majesty'. More and more he looked back to the Elizabethan years, clinging to the idea that James might look past his misdemeanours, as Elizabeth had. He so wanted to 'perish not here [in] misery only'. He begs: 'Do not forget me, nor doubt me, for as God liveth I shall never forget your true honour and remorce of me'. Only James can lift him 'out of the grave'. James, on his part, had no intention of doing anything to help a man he both despised and feared.

James Stuart's negativity towards Ralegh was a product of the whispering campaign of the final years of Queen Elizabeth's reign. But the degree to which James disliked and distrusted Ralegh remains hard to explain, the more so since fear was something familiar to James Stuart, part of his make-up and, ironically, one of the sources of his success as a ruler. In 1584, the French agent at the Scottish court offered a detailed analysis (here summarised by the historian Pauline Croft) of the young King, then only eighteen. James was:

> timid from being brought up in fear, but also intellectually able. He grasped and understood quickly. He judged carefully and with sensible discourse, he retained much and for a considerable time. He was learned in many languages, sciences and affairs of state, not only those of his own realm. In appearance, James was unimpressive, and as a result of lacking good instruction, very rude and uncivil in speaking, eating, manners, games and entertainment in the company of women. He hated music and dancing but was restless, never standing in one place and taking particular pleasure In moving around. His carriage was bad, with erratic and vagabond steps. Grave in speech, he was '*un vieux jeune homme*', old in a young man's body, but on the other hand he was lazy, too devoted to his pleasures, especially hunting which he loved above all.

As Croft points out, 'the curious combination of ability and complacency, idleness and shrewd government, warm emotions and lack of discretion' remained typical of James throughout his life. What is striking about the description of James at eighteen is that he has many of Ralegh's qualities – intellectual ability, wide-ranging knowledge, and a certain restlessness – without any of Ralegh's flair and energy, without his charisma and, to be blunt, without his good looks. Could this explain some of James's hatred towards him?

Autumn 1604 found Ralegh still in the Tower. On 20 September, he experienced some form of stroke or paralysis. A doctor visited and diagnosed 'palsy'. The timing was terrible, because Lady Ralegh had a surprise for her husband. At thirty-nine, she was pregnant again. The couple's third son would be born in February 1605, a baby of the Tower, christened Carew (a family name) in its parish church, St

Peter ad Vincula. Carew had been conceived in the summer of 1604, when Ralegh still clung to his hopes of early release and Bess was still working tirelessly towards that end: 'My wife told me that she spake with your lordship yesterday about my poor estate and hers'. Sir Walter and Bess both believed his lordship, Robert Cecil, would ensure the Sherborne trust was honoured, which was why Ralegh could write that he hoped he might not have to remain in the Tower but could be confined 'within the hundred of Sherborne'. Or maybe not Sherborne. Casting around, he offers to live in Holland ('where I shall perchance get some employment upon the Indies') or, most astonishingly, offers to manage one of Cecil's estates: he will 'keep but a park of yours'. The desperation is obvious.

The prospective father struggled through the autumn and winter but the worst was still to come. Plague reached the Tower of London, even to the very next room to Ralegh who, 'withered in body and mind' is:

> Daily in danger of death by the palsy, nightly of suffocation by wasted and obstructed lungs, and now the plague being come at the next door unto me, only the narrow passage of the way between, my poor child having lain this 14 days next to a woman with a running plague sore and but a paper wall between, and whose child is also this Thursday dead of the plague.

There is more. Ralegh's 'wife and child and others in whom I had comfort have abandoned me'. The pregnant Bess, and young Walter, aged eleven in November 1604, were able to flee the plague (if only to a house on Tower Hill, near All Hallows Barking). Ralegh had to stay.

His depression deepened. He wrote more and more about death as a release, while still making half-hearted attempts to provide for his family, his 'wife and a child and a wife with child', for whom he could do little or nothing.

Summer 1605. The world is even darker for Ralegh, despite Bess being safely delivered of Carew. A new, more authoritarian governor takes charge of the Tower and Lady Ralegh is instructed to 'resort to her house on Tower Hill or elsewhere with her women and her sons'. She cannot visit her husband and is forbidden to drive into the Tower in her coach, as she has been wont to do. Ralegh writes that he is:

> Every second or third night in danger either of sudden death, or of the loss of my limbs and sense, being sometime two hours without feeling or motion of my hand and whole arm. I complain not of it: I know it vain for there is none that hath compassion thereof.

'I complain not'? Hardly. Lady Ralegh's 'crying and bewailing' is all he receives: 'she hath already brought her eldest son in one hand and her sucking child in another, crying out of her and their destruction, charging me with unnatural negligence and that, having provided for my own life, I am without sense and compassion of theirs'. All Ralegh wants is compassion; all he gets is his wife's bitterness. He curses the time 'that ever I was born into the world and had a being'. Ralegh may not have been quite as low as this letter suggests; one must take into account his rhetorical talents and his sense of audience. He was writing to Robert Cecil, who he hoped might help in supporting Bess and his two sons, even if not Ralegh himself.

But he was certainly in no condition to withstand the next crisis: the Gunpowder Plot. Catholic rebels, led by Guy Fawkes and backed, allegedly, by Spain, sought to blow up the King and his parliament. Lady Ralegh was suspected of involvement on two counts. The first, plain and simple, was her family origins: she was a Throckmorton. Although her Protestant father, Nicholas, was an exception to the Catholic Throckmorton observance, Bess had had treacherous cousins who had paid the price of it, and now she had cousins who were at the heart of the plot. It was to Coughton, the Throckmorton family's main estate, that Robert Catesby's servant, Bates, rode to tell of the conspiracy's failure. Even though the Throckmorton name did not feature markedly in the cast of conspirators, a quick glance at the matrilineal family tree reveals a network of Throckmorton women at the conspiracy's heart. Robert Catesby's mother was Anne Throckmorton. Francis Tresham's mother was Muriel Throckmorton. The historian Pauline Croft identifies an interlinked group of four crypto-Catholic families who provided the foundations for the attempted assault on James and his parliament. The group comprised Catholic women with conforming husbands and fathers, bonded by intermarriage, creating 'striking networks of closely related wives, sisters and mothers'.

This was precisely the kind of network from which Bess was excluded, because of her father's rejection of his family's faith. Her brother Arthur was quick to distance himself from his 'unkind kindred'; unkind in its older meaning of unnatural, as well as its more modern sense of cruel. Lady Ralegh's impeccably Protestant and loyal background should have protected her from any suspicion. It didn't. The reason was, of course, her marriage to Ralegh, convicted for his treacherous conspiracy with Spain just two years before.

Bess was specifically charged with having gone down to Sherborne to prepare for the imminent Spanish invasion that would follow swiftly on the act of terrorism against the King and parliament. She had even been seen cleaning the armour there, by a spy who had been placed in her household by Robert Cecil.

Yet again, Ralegh underestimated, or misunderstood, the King's chief minister. (A small minority of historians has suggested the Gunpowder Plot was actually devised and engineered by Robert Cecil and his network of spies to further discredit the English Catholics, a similar conspiracy theory to the one of 1603. It's a familiar cry when atrocities are committed or discovered, and one that's hard to prove or disprove.) While Ralegh was busy writing to Cecil in the hope he would make some effort to help Lady Ralegh, Cecil had insinuated his spy Edward Cotterell into her household under the name of Captain Sampson. Lady Ralegh paid him five shillings a week while he reported back to his real master, Cecil. Sampson had much to report. He noted that at the Tower Sir Walter 'did speak at a window in the wall of the garden' with 'any person that he desired to speak withal'. The command quickly went out to block up the window and by that means prevent the prisoner's communication with the outside world. At Sherborne, Sampson reported that all the talk had been 'that Sir Walter Ralegh should be set at liberty at the parliament'. Lady Ralegh's activities at Sherborne were deeply suspicious:

> [She was] twice there that summer, and about September she did cause all the armour to be scoured as he thinketh because it was rusty. And then she caused also two walks to be made in the garden the furnishing whereof was a great charge unto her, and the house to be dressed up, where before all things lay in disorder.

What could this mean? Was Bess gleefully preparing for a Spanish invasion or was she merely being a good housekeeper? Cotterell/Sampson was not sure, but hoped to find out more when he travelled back to London with Lady Ralegh later in the year. By this stage, however, she was deeply suspicious of him and when he arrived, with two of her real friends and kinsmen, he was left, literally, out in the cold, during which time 'he walked upon the Tower Hill'. Cotterell/Sampson paced the streets until 'the Lady Ralegh returned him answer that she would have nothing to do with him, and presently on her coming forth, the Lady Ralegh went to the Tower'.

Lady Ralegh's caution meant Cecil had no hard evidence against her but he kept probing, insisting on a further examination of people in Sherborne. All he could come up with was rumour: a witness reported he had met some unnamed person at the local fair and that this unnamed person had said that on 6 November Ralegh would be in danger of his life but would 'escape, and come to greater matters'. Flimsy though it was, it was enough to get Ralegh into trouble; he was questioned on 9 November. He acknowledged he had been visited by Captain Whitlock, formerly an associate of the Earl of Essex but now in the household of the Earl of Northumberland and, more immediately relevant, one of the conspirators in the Gunpowder Plot.

Ralegh insisted there was nothing in the visit. He had merely 'familiar and ordinary discourse' with Whitlock, who only came to visit the prisoner because he, Whitlock, was bored. Ralegh had hoped Whitlock could describe the Earl of Northumberland's attitude towards him but had only received a 'dry and friendless answer'. There had been no correspondence with the Earl.

Henry Percy, Ninth Earl of Northumberland, born in April 1564, the same month and year as William Shakespeare, had successfully kept out of trouble during his youth at Elizabeth's court. He put some religious distance between himself and his father and uncle, both committed Catholics and was made a Knight of the Garter in 1593. He successfully walked the tightrope of courtly politics; marrying the Earl of Essex's sister in 1594 while at the same time becoming close to the Earl's rival, Sir Walter Ralegh. As Ralegh's fortunes waned in the later 1590s, Northumberland became the patron of Thomas Harriot, who flourished in the Earl's household and took full advantage of his remarkable library. The Harriot connection fanned the flames of suspicion surrounding Percy's intellectual interests, which had gained him the nickname of the 'wizard earl'. He was, they said, a man 'who troubled not much himself' about religion.

The accession of King James did not interrupt Henry Percy's quiet but the Gunpowder Plot did. Thomas Percy, a second cousin once removed and, more pertinently, the constable of Northumberland's Alnwick Castle, was one of the ringleaders. And Thomas had dined with his noble kinsman on 4 November. Henry Percy insisted their discussions had touched only on estate business but he would hardly say anything else. It was both good and bad news for the Earl when his treacherous cousin was killed soon after in open rebellion; Thomas Percy could neither accuse nor clear him. As the Earl put it, 'noen but he can shew me clere as the day, or darke as the night'.

Whitlock was an equally dangerous link that tied Ralegh and Northumberland to the Plot. But, as with Thomas Percy, there was nothing to see. Pressed once more, Sir Walter insisted that his only other contact with the man was over some trivial business with the French ambassador's wife. She had requested 'a little balsam of Guiana' and Ralegh had sent it to her via Whitlock.

Despite Cecil and his colleagues' best efforts, it seemed the Raleghs were telling the truth: he was not involved and she was a good house-wife. There was no fire. There wasn't even any smoke. Their loyal friend Thomas Harriot was, however, caught up in the crossfire, more by virtue of his position in the Earl of Northumberland's household than any specific link to the Raleghs. King James moved against Earl and scientist, imprisoning both in the Tower. Harriot was interrogated on the charge he had cast King James's horoscope in an attempt to use his magical powers to influence the King's future. He was lucky and did not remain long imprisoned in the Tower's Gatehouse. His patron the Earl, more of a threat, was held without any prospect of release.

So it was also with the legally dead Ralegh. Worse still, the Plot justified the imposition of a stricter prison regime. Cecil's spy had noted that 'Owen a waterman brought him diverse times beer and ale in bottles'. It would not do. Not content with stopping up a window to the outside world, the Crown stopped another small pleasure for the prisoner.

In the aftermath of the Gunpowder Plot, Ralegh was under constant watch, denied access to his garden and his family, and ill in mind and body. A doctor's report said:

> All his left side is extremely cold, out of sense and motion or numb. His fingers on the same side beginning to be contracted. And his tongue taken in some part, in so much that he speaks weakly and it is to be feared he may utterly lose the use of it.

The doctor recommended, in March 1606, that Ralegh be moved to warmer quarters, to a 'little room which he hath built in the garden adjoining to his still house [laboratory]'. The modern editor of Sir Walter's letters sternly warns readers to remember that 'Ralegh was an accomplished actor' and may have exaggerated his paralysis to make his daily life more comfortable in those early spring days of 1606. But perhaps it was not exaggeration: in his early fifties, Ralegh was, it seems, broken in mind and body. The rest might indeed be silence.

Revival

THIS WAS RALEGH, HOWEVER. In his quarters in the Tower of London he might, with all his trademark melancholy, write that he has played his 'part in this world and now must give place to fresh gamesters. Farewell. All is vanity and weariness, yet such a weariness and vanity that we shall ever complain of it and love it for all that'. But it was a disingenuous farewell. Ralegh, always good at complaining, was even better at restlessness. Only a few months after the doctor's stark warning of imminent collapse, it appears Sir Walter had decided he had not quite finished with 'this world'. He still had a part to play.

The first sign of the old Ralegh re-emerging was that he was reported to be walking on the wall of the garden of the Tower of London 'in view of the people'. What is more, 'he stares at them'. 'Indiscreet' they said. But would the qualities that had fuelled both his meteoric rise and equally spectacular fall serve him well in the new England of King James? And what use were they for a legally dead man as, month after month, year after year, he remained a prisoner in the Tower?

Ralegh's years at Elizabeth's court meant he understood only too well that, in a personal monarchy, favour relied primarily on access. Ralegh, as Captain of the Guard, had been used to intimate access to Queen Elizabeth, while his wife Bess had, until the crisis of 1592, been even closer, as a Gentlewoman of the Privy Chamber. But now there was a King, not a Queen, on the throne. Now Gentlemen of the

Privy Chamber controlled the physical and symbolic divide between public and private. What is more, James had made sure his immediate entourage was almost exclusively Scots. In part this indicates a desire to have familiar faces around him but it was also both a reminder he was King of the Scots as much as of England and a sensible way to ensure Scottish nobles and lairds could retain access to their monarch. Captain Ralegh's success in achieving intimacy with the private Queen in the 1580s had relied on his exceptional powers of persuasion, his physical attractions (however defined) and his being useful in various ways to Elizabeth. Even were Ralegh not a prisoner, this level of success would have been a challenge to achieve under James.

It was not that James hid himself away. Historians agree that, for all its seediness, promiscuity and corruption (no change there, then) the court was an open, accessible and diverse political arena. The politician and writer, Francis Bacon, observed James 'giveth easy audience'. James himself emphasised the importance of being available to one's subjects in his book of advice, *Basilikon Doron*, addressed to his eldest son, Prince Henry. James was intellectually self-assured, a King who never minded disagreement or debate. Surely this court of tolerant pluralism and easy communication would, in the words of the historian David L. Smith, be open to a plea from the rhetorically-astute Ralegh.

It was not to be. The most obvious reason was James's preference for intimate male favourites. While the King functioned on one level as a heterosexual husband (he had fathered two sons, Henry and Charles, as well as a marriageable daughter, Elizabeth), his contemporaries accepted and understood that socially, sexually, and most significantly politically, James preferred the company of young men.

This provided an opportunity for the great families of England to get their men into the literal and metaphorical heart of the monarchy. The Howards had their protégé ready early: Robert Carr, 'straight-limbed, well-favoured, strong-shouldered and smooth-faced'. James found him irresistible. Carr, people grumbled, 'hath all favours'; his rewards were as significant and lucrative, more significant and lucrative than those bestowed on the equally irresistible Ralegh by his Queen twenty years before. Groom and Gentleman of the Bedchamber, Knight of the Garter, Viscount Rochester; Carr, they said, 'hath so great a power of prevailing with the king as never any man had the like'. Carr most definitely prevailed in 1613 when he became involved with the married Frances Howard, Countess of Essex. James sat back as a special commission demonstrated, conveniently, that her marriage had never been consummated, due to her husband's impotence, and certified Howard to be a virgin. Contemporaries were sceptical but by the end of 1613, the Countess and Carr were married. James generously made her new husband an earl, to ensure Frances would not lose her status by the marriage. Less fortunate was Carr's political adviser, Thomas Overbury who, suspicious of and hostile towards Frances Howard, ended up in the Tower of London in April 1613 because, when his King offered him an ambassadorial role in a faraway land, Overbury refused to be sidelined. His death in the Tower, just five months later, would come back to haunt Carr and Howard.

On paper, sodomy was a capital offence. Religious authorities might thunder that the sodomite was a 'monster' but being an absolute monarch has its advantages. No one was going to call James on his sexual preferences, just as they appeared to accept the late Queen's preference for chastity over a woman's natural roles of wife and mother. Needless to say, Elizabeth's virginity was more politically rewarding for Ralegh than James's preference for, and preferment of, young men.

The King was unapologetic about his love for men. Later, in 1617, he defended to the Privy Council his love for Carr's successor in his affections, George Villiers, Duke of Buckingham. The King was 'not God, nor an angel, but a man, a man like any other' and he loved Buckingham 'more than all other men and more than all who were there present'. This was far from being a 'defect', because James was like Jesus: 'Christ had his John' and James 'has his George'. The King referred to Buckingham as both his son and his wife; writing to 'my sweet child and wife' from 'your dear dad and husband'. He understood himself to be married to his 'sweet heart'. Without him, the King was a widow. Ralegh didn't stand a chance.

Fortunately for him, and in another major change from the Elizabethan era, Sir Walter had more than one monarch to attempt to seduce politically, and more than one court in which to pursue his ambitions. King James had a Queen, Anne of Denmark, and an heir, Prince Henry, invested as Prince of Wales in 1610. Both Anne and Henry had potential for Ralegh. King and Queen, husband and wife, made little pretence of amity. The French ambassador rather enjoyed the fact James was a King 'whom the comedians of the metropolis bring upon the stage' and, even better, Queen Anne 'attends these representations in order to enjoy the laugh against her husband'. She is 'an able woman', he goes on, who is aware 'that her husband cannot exist without a minion'. Ralegh, and just as significantly Lady Ralegh, did their best to gain her favour, although even if Anne were completely committed to securing the prisoner's release, she remained dependent on the political will of her husband even as she laughed at him.

More promising, because he was potentially more powerful, was Henry, Prince of Wales. Courtiers fell over themselves in their admiration for the vigorous, manly, young Prince. He was tall, strong and well-proportioned, 'his eyes quick and pleasant, his forehead broad, his nose big, his chin broad and cloven, his hair inclining to black', his 'whole face and visage comely and beautiful...with a sweet, smiling, and amiable countenance...full of gravity'. A precocious teenager, 'none of his pleasures savour the least of a child. He is a particular lover of horses...He studies two hours a day, and employs the rest of his time in tossing the pike, or leaping, or shooting with the bow, or throwing the bar, or vaulting.' Henry was not just an athlete. He collected paintings and bronzes, coins and curiosities; he actively sponsored musicians and scientists at his court of St James's. No wonder it was said that Henry's court was full of 'gold, the learned and the militant [a] courtly college...or collegiate court'. Almost five hundred men were attached to it and to him, among them close friends and kinsmen of Ralegh; men such as Arthur Gorges, who presented Henry with a plan for making money and in return gained a place in the Prince's newly-established household.

It looked particularly good for Ralegh that Henry was determined to reject almost everything his father stood for, being an enthusiast for all things military and chivalric and with a strong interest in ships and shipping. Knowing this, Arthur Gorges prepared an account of the 1597 Azores voyage, to which was attached Ralegh's *Observations on the Navy*, and presented it to Henry. Politically, the existence of a *dauphin*, whose portraits showed him in full armour or with sword ready to be unsheathed, was a gift to the English war party, which was increasingly at odds with James, *rex pacificus*. Henry was a hawk to his father's dove. And he had money to burn. When he was invested as Prince of Wales in June 1610, Henry wore an ermine-lined gown that cost more than £1,300. An entire year of celebrations was packed with masques, tilts and pageants. The Prince was Ralegh's kind of man. Sir Walter was missing out and he knew it.

The negotiations for Henry's marriage, and that of his sister Elizabeth, provided an opportunity for Ralegh to join the conversation, even from the Tower. The Spanish Infanta (one of the contenders for the English throne in the closing years of Elizabeth's reign) was a possible bride until it was discovered, in 1610, that her father, King Philip III of Spain, had secretly arranged for her to marry the French heir apparent. In the aftermath of this revelation Philip III, to placate King James, encouraged the Duke of Savoy to consider a double wedding between his children and Henry and Elizabeth. Both marriages were opposed by the committed Protestant Prince Henry, who allegedly said that 'two religions should never lie in [my] bed'. Ralegh was of a similar mind but for different reasons.

He picked up his pen to share them. *Concerning a Match propounded by the Savoyan between the Lady Elizabeth and the Prince of Piedmont* and *A Discourse Touching a Marriage between Prince Henry of England and a Daughter of Savoy* are both ostensibly addressed to King James but Ralegh claims to be writing in obedience to the 'commandment of my lord the prince' Henry, who has asked him to send the King his 'opinion of the match'. His opinion was it would be madness for Elizabeth to marry a 'poor popish prince'. As for Henry, he should marry 'but not yet' and certainly not to a mere Savoyan princess. Some seven years into his imprisonment, Ralegh had clearly not learned political tact. Indeed, he took the opportunity to launch a sustained attack on the Spanish, which has embedded within it one of his most famous critiques of Elizabeth:

> If the late queen had believed her men of war as she did her scribes, we had in her time beaten that great empire in pieces, and made their kings kings of figs and oranges, as in old times. But her majesty did all by halves, and by petty invasions taught the Spaniard how to defend himself.

Ralegh is writing as a man who knows the world, knows the Spanish and has served his country. He looks back to the mistakes of the 1580s, making a casual, if inflammatory, comparison between Spanish and English imperial activities:

> Four thousand men would have taken from him all the ports of the Indies…He is more hated in that part of the world by the sons of the conquered, than the English are by the Irish. We are too strong for him by sea.

Ralegh may be lifting the lid on his years of frustration with Elizabeth's cautious foreign policy – 'did all by halves' is harsh but fair – but he also reveals himself to be an unreconstructed opponent of Spain: 'It is the Spaniard that is to be feared: the Spaniard who layeth his pretences and practices with a long hand'.

It is hard to understand how Ralegh thought he would gain James's favour in this way and even harder to understand quite how he had got himself imprisoned on a charge of conspiring with the Spanish in 1603. They remained the enemy ('Spain to which England is irreconcilable');

upstarts inflated by, and reliant on, New World gold and vulnerable to any concerted attack.

Ralegh would write several more position papers about or for the Prince, including one 'touching the model of a ship'. In them, attack is often his best form of defence, whether it is his criticisms of Queen Elizabeth or his taking apart of the Prince's chief shipbuilder, Phineas Pett, who had displayed a model of his new ship in November 1607, 'fairly garnished with carving and painting and placed in a frame, arched, covered and curtained with crimson taffeta', designed to tempt Prince Henry to build a new, enormous vessel. For all Ralegh's efforts, his critique remained unheeded and the huge boat, the *Prince Royal*, was duly built.

Because of these tracts, many have seen Ralegh as a 'valued correspondent and adviser on naval, colonial, and matrimonial matters' to Prince Henry. How many of these works were commissioned, let alone attended to and acted on by him, is quite another question. Nevertheless, rumours continued to circulate the Prince was indeed a supporter (much later, an historian would write that Henry said of Ralegh 'no man but his father would keep such a bird in such a cage') working behind the scenes to get him out of the Tower.

A letter from one of Ralegh's old enemies, Henry Howard, the Earl of Northampton, punctures these illusions. Howard, visiting the Earl of Northumberland in the Tower, had 'a bout with Sir Walter Ralegh and found him as bold, proud and passionate as ever'. Howard believes it is the 'lawless liberty of the Tower' that is giving Ralegh confidence, nourishing 'hopes exorbitant'. Howard remains unconcerned: 'And yet your lordship may assure His Majesty that by this publication he hath won little ground' ('publication' was then used to describe any circulated work, whether in manuscript or print). It is unclear which 'publication' Howard refers to, but it was probably one of Ralegh's position papers on the proposed marriages.

In early October 1612, Prince Henry began to experience headaches and uncharacteristic weakness. By the end of the month, he could not move from his bed. Despite the best efforts of a host of doctors, who bled and cupped the desperately ill Prince, and despite a special delivery of Ralegh's famous cordial (of flowers of borage and rosemary, marigold and red gilly, saffron and juniper berries, sassafras of Virginia, pearl and ambergris and musk, mixed with the syrup of lemons and red roses) the Prince died of typhoid fever on 6 November. The nation went into a paroxysm of mourning, lamenting the loss of England's young lion.

Ralegh found a unique way of honouring Henry. More than eight hundred folio pages long, *The History of the World* is Ralegh's *magnum opus* and, on the surface, a response to the failure of the prisoner's hopes of release through the mediation of the young Prince. Looking more deeply, Ralegh's fascination with history has a profoundly personal dimension. While imprisoned in the Tower, he became preoccupied with the past; being Ralegh, that preoccupation found its expression in writing. Just as in the 1580s he had asked Harriot to teach him science and mathematics, so Ralegh taught himself history in the 1610s. It was part of his quest to understand the world and to engage with it. In prison, he built up a rich personal library of five hundred books, vital tools for the writing of a universal history. In prison, he drew maps of lands he would never visit, studied battles on land and sea that had taken place millennia before and brought to vivid life ancient civilisations that had crashed and burned. In prison, he questioned where, how and why events had unfolded as they had, always hinting at, but rarely spelling out, their relevance to contemporary life.

No wonder Howard felt the Tower was a place of 'lawless liberty', of the mind if not of the body. In Ralegh's time, as Howard knew, to study, let alone to write and, God forbid, to publish, a history, any history, was a political act. The accepted aim of all history was to look back and to apply that knowledge to current circumstances for political ends. This was why history mattered and also why it was rigorously censored, with strict prohibitions on explorations of recent English history. Playwrights who were seen to use historical events to comment on contemporary matters found themselves imprisoned and their plays banned. Prose writers were equally vulnerable. John Hayward's best-selling history of *Henry IV* may have been a two-hundred-year-old story but, crucially, its author was accused of 'intending the application of it to this time'. The work was scrutinised for treasonous passages, the more so because of its dedication to the Earl of Essex, who was being carefully watched in 1599. Its author, having previously written eloquently about the relevance of history to contemporary 'affairs of state' was – with good reason – unwilling to repeat those claims when under investigation. Hayward's new-found caution did not stop him being sent to prison, where he remained for the remainder of Elizabeth's reign. Ralegh himself had acted as a censor in the 1590s, so he knew very well he was playing with fire with his *History of the World*.

The writing and publication of *The History of the World* was the bold (and, as it turned out, beautiful) action of a man who had been politician and soldier, courtier and colonist. A man who, denied an opportunity to participate in the active world because of his imprisonment, turned to reading histories and then to writing one. All to contribute to the common weal. Ralegh's work is self-consciously indebted to Cicero's understanding of history as not simply another kind of literature, not simply a review of the past, but a source of correct action and human wisdom, here and now.

Ralegh's is the long view of history. And it is a dark view, at least for those in power. He has 'set down' the 'beginning and end of the three first monarchies of the world: whereof the founders and erectors thought that they could never have ended'. Ralegh could not, and would not, spell out what this meant for the monarchy in the early years of the seventeenth century, because that would have been both dangerous and foolish; he had learned some lessons from his past. Instead, he neatly places all responsibility for political interpretation on others. He cannot help it if they, with their guilty consciences, perceive themselves in his historical text. He himself is entirely innocent and free from malice. Ralegh's *History* is anything but innocent and free from malice but his sleight of pen is admirable.

Admirable too is its author's use of Prince Henry. Ralegh writes that his *History* was begun in the service of the Prince, who had read parts of it. Many have taken Ralegh at his word and seen the Prince as the inspiration, editor and ideal reader both for the *History* and for the series of political and naval tracts which culminated in this *magnum opus*. If that is the case, it follows that the Prince's death was disastrous for Ralegh's fortunes and explains why the work breaks off suddenly (if a work of more than eight hundred folio pages can be said to end suddenly). But Henry was more useful to Ralegh dead than alive, since it remains uncertain whether the Prince was ever in a position to enable the release of his father's most celebrated prisoner.

By 1614, it was downright convenient that the work had been 'left without a master', since no one could prove Ralegh was at best exaggerating the Prince's support or at worst asserting an outright lie. With Henry dead, Ralegh could use *The History of the World* to rewrite their relationship. Prince Henry would provide a buffer between Ralegh and his critics, a ghostly master of what was a master-less text, a justification for the publication of an unfinished work.

The invocation of Henry is a cover. It is not the Prince but a public readership that Ralegh addresses directly in his remarkable, powerfully-written 'Preface'. His audience and his subject for his *History* are the boldest possible. He is writing for 'the world' and his plan is simple but grandiose: 'For, beginning with the Creation: I have proceeded with the history of the World'. And he has some very powerful things to say to the world about Kings and Princes. The final paragraphs of the *History* are worth quoting almost in full, partly because of their sheer political bravura – Ralegh is writing of the death of Kings – partly because of their almost-blasphemous diminishment of God and elevation of Death (with his earlier line of poetry 'Only we die in earnest, That's no jest' now highly politicised) but above all because of their eloquence:

> The kings and princes of the world have always laid before them
> the actions, but not the ends, of those great ones which preceded

them. They are always transported with the glory of the one, but they never mind the misery of the other, till they find the experience in themselves. They neglect the advice of God, while they enjoy life, or hope it; but they follow the counsel of Death, upon his first approach. It is he that puts into man all the wisdom of the world, without speaking a word; which God with all the words of his Law, promises, or threats, doth not infuse. Death which hateth and destroyeth man, is believed; God which hath made him and loves him, is always deferred. 'I have considered (saith Solomon) all the works that are under the sun, and behold, all is vanity and vexation of spirit' but who believes it, till Death tells it us. [...] It is Death alone that can suddenly make man to know himself. He tells the proud and insolent that they are but abjects, and humbles them at the instant: makes them cry, complain, and repent, yea, even to hate their forepassed happiness. He takes the account of the rich, and proves him to be a beggar; a naked beggar, which hath interest in nothing, but in the gravel that fills his mouth. He holds a glass before the most beautiful and makes them see therein their deformity and rotteness; and they acknowledge it.

O eloquent, just and mighty Death! Whom none could advise, though hast persuaded; what none hath dared, thou hast done; and whom all the world hath flattered, thou only hast cast out of the world and despised: thou hast drawn together all the far stretched greatness, all the pride, cruelty, and ambition of man, and covered it all over with these two narrow words, *Hic jacet* [Here lies].

Ralegh is one of the great prose stylists of his era. Of any era. His writing stands shoulder to shoulder with that most remarkably rich and enduring of contemporary works, the 1611 King James Bible. Many of Ralegh's phrases from the *History* also have the power to endure but unlike the Bible, Ralegh's work is not embedded in the modern world. Ralegh was not looking for twenty-first-century readers, however. He needed someone – anyone – to hear him in 1614. His *History* may be one of the most striking results of Ralegh's Tower experiences and his connections and intellectual life but in the end, Ralegh's concern with 'the world', with a readership beyond the court, the no-holds-barred assault on the rich and the powerful, clearly indicate that he was looking beyond the King for a way out of the Tower.

The irony was that it was his fellow prisoners in the Tower and their networks that had educated Ralegh in the potential of print,

The frontispiece to Ralegh's The History of the World, *1614*

if the author of *The Last Fight of the Revenge* (state-sponsored print propaganda) and *The Discovery of Guiana* (self-promoting print propaganda) needed educating. They even helped him find a printer and a publisher, Walter Burre and William Stansby, willing to take a risk on a book that would take three years to print and which had only just squeaked past the censors.

The Crown had reluctantly agreed to the publication of the *History* providing it remained anonymous. Its author was, after all, legally dead. Ralegh's name appears nowhere but nevertheless, the work reeks of him. The very frontispiece provides a key to his biography: the Caribbean, South American rivers, sea battles in the North Atlantic, Cadiz, Dublin, even perhaps Winchester (a church and a building are marked in the south of England); each screams Ralegh's achievements.

The poem accompanying the image insists on the triumph of history over death and oblivion, explaining the iconographical representation of history trampling death under her feet. Just as truth will emerge from death or dark oblivion, so Ralegh will speak from the Tower. Just as providence will eventually reward and publish individuals, so Ralegh and his persecutors will be judged. This is a history of the world offered to the world, a sustained act of personal display and vindication.

The *History* also stands as the culmination of Ralegh's thinking about the connection between language and power. As he puts it, when considering the invasions of Turks and Tartars, they consumed 'the very names, language and memory of former times'. The powerful destroy not just the physical bodies but also the mind and language of the conquered. This, of course, increases the value of history, that preserver of memory and identity, a concept written into Ralegh's work. It also enhances the value of someone who can use words wisely: 'I ever found that men's fortunes are oftener made by their tongues than by their virtues and more men's fortunes overthrown thereby also than by their vices', he wrote in another work from this time. Writing and reading become a metaphor for Ralegh's whole life and for his misfortune. As he puts it, in his straight-talking 'Preface':

For conclusion: all the hope I have lies in this, that I have already found more ungentle and uncourteous readers of my love towards them, and well-deserving of them, than ever I shall do again. For had it been otherwise, I should hardly have had this leisure, to have made myself a fool in print.

He makes a direct connection between his imprisonment and his *History*, with correct reading becoming a metaphor for political life and communication. In the past, his 'love' has been read incorrectly, thus he has been imprisoned. Now, because of that imprisonment, he exposes himself and his policy to the reading of the world, which will interpret it as it will.

There were those who applauded him for what they saw as his new seriousness, his rejection of his previous life as a foppish courtier. From the crucible of sickness, imprisonment and his fall from power had come the true, religious man:

> In greatness thou art lost, as in a wood;
> Treading the paths of flattery, falsehood, blood,
> The way to Heaven neglected, thou didst stray
> As others do now in thy Politic way.
> But now thou'st find thyself; and we have found
> That sickness taught thee Art to make men sound.
> For had'st thou never fall'n, th'hadst never writ:
> Nor had'st thou clear'd, but clouded us with wit.

Whether Ralegh was seeking a way to 'Heaven' or simply out of the bloody Tower he had, in the genre of history that acts to preserve memory and to convey political advice to leaders, found a way to make his voice heard and remind the world of his existence, despite being a legally dead man. The very publication of this history of the world, offered to the world for lack of a master, stands as Ralegh's most significant political act since his imprisonment in 1603.

It did not gain him his freedom. Perhaps the only person to be unsurprised, then or now, by the suppression of the *History* by royal command, within weeks of its publication in December 1614, was Ralegh. It seems he had (astonishingly) attempted not to antagonise King James. The scholar John Racin showed many years ago that Ralegh's edits of his work not only demonstrate he carefully supervised its printing, a sign of his commitment to the project, but also that he made late editorial changes designed to flatter the King. The gossip of John Chamberlain adds further weight to the argument: Ralegh took the calling-in of all the copies of the *History* 'much to heart, for he thought that he had won his spurs and pleased the king extraordinarily'. Once again, Ralegh had utterly failed to understand James. How could the King approve of a work which condemned individual monarchs with a ferocity rarely seen in the writing of the period? James was outraged by Ralegh's 'description of the kings that he hates, whomof he speaketh nothing but evil'.

Ralegh remained undaunted, returning to his writing only slightly chastened. And he continued to talk to his fellow prisoners in the Tower. As many regimes have found to their cost, if you put political prisoners in the same place, they start talking to each other. In 1597–8, Ralegh had known a John Hoskins; they had performed together in the Christmas season at the Inns of Court. The Inns were not merely places for the study and practice of law (and the putting on of shows); they were part of what have been called 'textual communities', 'communities of exchange' or 'active transcriptional cultures', which functioned via scribal publication. They were also a breeding ground for a new kind of political actor: the parliamentarian. As a member of parliament during the 1580s and 1590s, Ralegh himself had been extremely active, indeed vocal, by the standards of his time, but men such as Hoskins were taking things to a new level. This was why Hoskins found himself in the Tower in 1614, having spoken out against the King in the parliament of that year. The online *History of Parliament* takes up the story.

On 3 June Hoskins delivered the most notorious speech of the Parliament, during the debate concerning the king's message threatening dissolution unless the Commons voted supply [voted for money to be raised]. He began by stating he at least was prepared to see the Parliament dissolved rather than submit to the king's demand, for just as he had been the last to speak in the previous assembly, so he was prepared to be the last to speak in this. He then reminded the House of the king's opening speech, in which James had declared this Parliament would be 'the Parliament of love', for it was now clear 'the arguments that are made are rather of fear'. It was no way for the government to obtain supply for it to say it would not hear the Commons' complaints against impositions. The king should be urged to suppress impositions and to prevent the sale of Crown lands, for 'if the wealth of the kingdom be carried away without consent of Parliament we shall not be able to supply His Majesty'. Hoskins further insisted that all strangers should be sent home, as they were both riotous and dissolute. Here, as in his speech of 23 Nov. 1610, he was implicitly attacking the Scots, of whom the most influential and most hated was the royal favourite, Robert Carr, Earl of Somerset. According to one newsletter writer, Hoskins added 'he could wish His Majesty would be more reserved of his honours and favours to strangers, and more communicative to those of our native country, especially in weighty affairs of state'. In the most sensational part of his speech, Hoskins referred openly to the Sicilian Vespers and also (according to one report) the more recent St Bartholomew's Day massacre. Although one diarist failed to understand the implications of this statement, better-informed listeners could hardly have failed to interpret it as a threat that unless the Scots went home they would be massacred.

The Sicilian Vespers was a violent, and successful, rebellion against French rule in 1282. The St Bartholomew's Day massacre of Huguenots by their countrymen in France's civil wars in 1572 was more recent, and in the living memory of some. They were both inflammatory topics, but to mention the Sicilian Vespers was asking for particular trouble. Hoskins was arrested on the final day of the parliament. Asked

218 • PATRIOT OR TRAITOR

'whether he well understood the consequence of that Sicilian Vesper', he answered 'that he had no more than a general information thereof, being but little conversant in those histories that lay out of the way of his profession'.

It was a familiar defence and almost entirely unbelievable of a well-educated, politically active man. Hoskins remained in the Tower, and talked with Ralegh, who then wrote *A Dialogue between a Counsellor of State and a Justice of Peace* (to give the work its full title); his response to the proceedings of what came to be known as the 'Addled Parliament' of 1614. Ralegh's very first words in his prefatory address to James are 'Those that are suppressed and hopeless, are commonly silent'. Ralegh, never content with the common, will not be silent and instead develops a powerful discussion of the place of free speech in an absolute monarchy. This foray into the history and practice of parliamentary politics also stands as his most clear articulation of his political beliefs, constituting a passionate defence of the need for a public sphere characterised by freedom of speech. And, inspired by Hoskins's experiences in the 1614 parliament, Ralegh mounts a full-scale assault on the 'great ones' who were destroying the kingdom and who could and should be delivered up to the new political force, the 'people' and their representatives, the Commons. In an earlier dialogue (between a Jesuit and a Recusant) these issues are tacked on to the end of a work that is predominantly concerned with typical Raleghan themes such as foreign policy, the art of war and the Roman Catholic/Spanish threat, but the later *Dialogue* focuses exclusively on internal politics, national history and secular arguments. It is an astonishing work from a political prisoner of nearly twelve years.

Since James is in desperate financial trouble and since the people are armed and at the height of their power, a solution is needed, and quickly. But one of the characters in the *Dialogue*, the cowardly 'Counsellor', dare not call a parliament because it will be personally dangerous. He knows full well that evil counsellors tend to be removed as part of the bargain in return for taxation. Ralegh causes his other character, a Justice of the Peace, to predict that James will 'cast himself

upon the general love of the people' and duly deliver up his evil counsellors. If he doesn't, then the people will force his hand:

> My good Lord, the people have not stayed for the king's delivery
> neither in England nor in France: your Lordship knows how the
> Chancellor, Treasurer and Chief Justice with many other at several
> times have been used by the Rebels: And the Marshals, Constables,
> Treasurers, and Bishops in France have been cut in pieces in
> Charles the 6th time.

Deeply inflammatory, Ralegh raises the spectre of the mob. What is
even more incendiary is that at no point does Ralegh assure James of
the 'love of the people'. At best he suggests it is precariously held. Even
at his most eloquent, there is a certain tactlessness in the suggestion
that James might need his prisoner's prayers:

> It is therefore Love (most Renowned Sovereign) that must prepare
> the way for your Majesty's following desires: It is Love which obeys,
> which suffers, which gives, which sticks at nothing: which Love, as
> well of your Majesty's people, as the Love of God, that your Majesty
> may always hold, shall be the continual prayer of
>> Your Majesty's most
>>> humble vassal
>>>> W: Rawleigh.

Did Ralegh know full well his political analysis was not going to please
James? It's quite possible. There's a hint in his continued preoccupation with 'ungentle and uncourteous' readers, as he had described
his enemies in the *History*. But now they had become the vicious and
dangerous readers of the *Dialogue*. To start with, it is only the evil
(and of course entirely fictional) Privy Counsellor who intentionally
misunderstands the worthy Justice of the Peace. It's obvious which
character is the surrogate for Ralegh. However, at the very end of
the work, the King himself is pictured reading, or rather misreading,

every word of Ralegh's. The Justice hopes against hope the truth will be seen by the King. The Counsellor disabuses him: 'the misliking, or but the misconceiving of any one word, phrase or sentence, will give Argument unto the king, either to condemn or reject the whole discourse'.

James did, predictably, condemn and reject the whole discourse. But the *Dialogue* had done, and would do, other work. It was widely circulated in manuscript, a reminder of the relative freedom in which the Tower prisoners lived with easy access to friends on the outside, but also a reminder that manuscripts were a good way to circumvent the Crown's censorship. Not content with the hard-hitting *Dialogue*, Ralegh followed up with *A Discourse of the Original and Fundamental Cause of Natural War*, his harshest critique of political and social corruption to date. He compares a thief and a judge (as part of a digression on the nature of justice and the possible responses to oppression and injustice). The judge gives wealth and position to his friends or his favourite and he:

> Says that the rule of justice will have it so, that it is the voice of the law and ordinance of God himself: and what else herein doth he, than, by a kind of circumlocution, tell his humble suppliants that he holds them idiots or base wretches, not able to get relief?

Ralegh goes further: there is no more difference between the thief and the judge 'than in the manner of performing their exploits, as if the whole being of justice consisted in point of formality'. Worse and worse, God and justice are mere words, 'points of formality', deployed to validate social control.

Ralegh was shouting dangerously against the wind. He remained in the Tower. Writing to a friend, he knows everything he has is in the hands of his wife and young sons. He even imagines himself being under the wardship of his own children. All he has now is the power of 'persuasion': 'who am but a dead husband to the one and a dead father to the other (your suit in law against us having made them known much of their own strength)'. Again and again his words, his 'persuasion', had proved useless.

Ralegh's topic for this letter was Sherborne. The King had decided to reclaim the estate from his legally dead prisoner, something the prisoner understandably saw as 'against the law of nature and the honour of mankind'. But Robert Carr wanted Sherborne and Robert Carr got it. Ralegh believed that having conveyed Sherborne to trustees in 1603, it could not be confiscated. He had planned for this moment. Unfortunately for him, on 27 October 1608, the Sherborne deed was declared invalid due to a scribal error. Ralegh wrote directly to Carr, unable to resist an opportunity to state his own innocence: 'His Majesty, whom I never offended (for I ever held it unnatural and unmanly to hate goodness) stayed me at the grave's brink'. As if this would make Carr give up Sherborne. By the summer of 1609, the estate was being conveyed to the King. It had been 'lost in the law for want of a word'.

For Lady Ralegh the real fight had only just begun; if not for Sherborne, then for adequate compensation. Her husband had a different perspective. He hinted he would be willing to sacrifice Sherborne for one thing, and one thing only: a pardon. There was more. If he were granted a pardon, he would be able to voyage to Guiana and bring back gold for his King.

13

Gold

THE EMPIRE OF EL DORADO: Ralegh had been (almost) silent on the subject for a decade. In the intervening years, others had made the same journey, benefiting from Ralegh's expeditions of the mid-1590s, from his translators and from his reputation. The Dutch went as early as 1598, the Swedes founded a 'West Indies company' and in 1604, Captain Charles Leigh led a small fleet, to attempt to establish an English outpost in the region.

Spain had kept tabs on Guiana since Ralegh's expedition of 1595. Francis Sparrey, captured by the Spanish during that expedition, talked; a sensible decision when facing service in the galleys. Sparrey told the Spanish that Ralegh persuaded the locals to show him the gold, that he saw it himself and took it back to England 'to make assay'. Sparrey convinced his interrogators he could reveal a cache of gold hidden on the banks of the lower Orinico. No wonder, therefore, there are so many documents in the Spanish archives on the subject of 'the said guaterrale' (the most common spelling of Walter Ralegh's name, although he appears in many guises, including 'Watawales'). Sparrey was back in England by 1602, having negotiated his freedom. He took care not to mention his betrayal of Ralegh to the Spanish but he did report gold six miles upstream from San Thome, although the water so 'overflowed' it was impossible to get to. What is more, he told his English masters, the Spanish were not able to go there 'on account of the war with the Caribs'.

Two years later, Leigh's 1604 expedition revealed the situation in Guiana to be constantly changing. There was only so much cachet to be accrued by being an Englishman who was not Ralegh. Leigh's men fell ill and 'divers of them died of the Flux: which the Indians...know right well for to cure, yet concealed it from our general'. Four years later, Leonard Ragapo met an English adventurer and colonialist, who reported that Ragapo still had 'great affection' for Sir Walter.

Others had clearly been busy. Ralegh had been silent until 1607. Why the rekindling of interest? The economy was one reason: Ralegh was wise enough to know King James's financial difficulties might make him more willing to consider supporting a voyage. Politically, that year saw a temporary crisis in Anglo-Spanish relations, which would make an incursion into Spanish territory less problematic. Personally, Ralegh had, for the moment, given up the idea that James would use his royal prerogative and show mercy to his prisoner. Lady Ralegh saw the summer of 1606 as a watershed, having hoped the visiting King Christian IV of Denmark, brother of Queen Anne, would intercede on behalf of her husband. No one interceded. No one was going to intercede. It was up to Ralegh to make his case. He had bought his way out of prison in 1592. It might work again.

His first target was Robert Cecil. Ralegh's rival of the 1590s was now dominant, the King's right-hand man, the man who lifted the burdens of administration from the shoulders of his monarch. 'My little beagle', writes James, both grateful and patronising, 'now that I have seen your abstract, wherein no material point is omitted' he can relax, sure in the knowledge that Robert Cecil will 'add in divers particular points, wherewith I need not to be troubled'. James wrote this to his 'little beagle' in December 1607. Six months earlier, Ralegh, far less intimate, was attempting to convince Cecil that the gold of Guiana was not merely 'an invention of mine to procure unto my self my former liberty, suspicions which might rightly fall into the cogitation of a wise man'. There is gold and Ralegh can prove it. He acknowledges, slightly grudgingly, that he had promised the expert refiner ('a man very skillful but poor') 'twenty pounds if he could find gold or silver' in the ore samples he has kept back for this very moment. One can almost see Cecil raising his eyebrows.

Typically, Ralegh immediately raises the stakes. He's 'content to be hanged' if the ore proves worthless. Equally typically, he plays devil's advocate, showing he is well aware of Cecil's scepticism. Who would not think that, with 'a ship two or three', Ralegh would 'turn my course some other way'? All he can say is why on earth would he, in his 'old years', become 'a runnegate [renegade?] and live from my wife, children and friends in a strange country'? One final raising of the stakes and Ralegh is done. He will make the voyage as a private man, giving the captaincy of the ship to someone else; if he, Ralegh, suggested a change of course, he should be cast 'into the sea'.

There is the small matter of Spain and the continuing, if currently precarious, peace to consider. Ralegh suggests the 'journey may go on under the colour [pretence] of Virginia' and only then swerve south to Guiana. 'We will break no peace, invade none of the Spanish towns. We will only trade with the Indians and see none of that nation except they assail us.'

Then he gets to the money: the expedition will cost £5,000. Ralegh is hoping Queen Anne and Cecil will each pay a third, with Ralegh and his friends providing the rest. If it comes to it, he will pay for it all and give Anne and Cecil half the proceeds, as long as he can keep the rest. The expedition will be expensive because they will need to 'ride at anchor 3 or 4 months in the river and, carrying with us six pair of great bellows and brick in ballast, we would melt down the mineral into ingots as fast as we gather it, for to bring all in ore would be more notorious [conspicuous]'.

Ralegh closes with a killer blow: 'Your lordship may have good gold cheap'. Cecil had been dubious about the gold of Guiana in 1595, and remained dubious. But, in November 1609, as the Sherborne negotiations continued, the Spanish ambassador reported:

Watawales who is in the Tower has left his fortune so that the king may give it to a Scotchman, who thereupon will give him 1,200 ducats. Thus he expects to regain his liberty and that the king will banish him to Guiana, where he left some people and wishes to send more.

By 31 December 1609, the ambassador is quite sure Ralegh will be out of the Tower:

> In like manner there will sail for Guiana two small vessels with small crews, but I hear that if any of the people which Watawales left there, should be found, they will send more, because they praise that country very much and say that Gold and Silver are found there, and it is thought they will take Watawales out of the Tower, that he might go there.

The Spanish ambassador was too optimistic. King James and Robert Cecil remained unmoved. Ralegh remained in the Tower. Over the coming months and years, Ralegh would make his case to anyone who would listen. His key phrases are repeated over and over: the expedition would assure the 'attaining of honour and riches', it would be a 'journey of honour and riches', an enterprise 'feasible and certain' and – invariably – he should be cast into the sea if he deviates from his course. Even that wasn't enough: 'if I bring them not to a mountain near a navigable river covered with gold and silver ore, let the commanders have commission to cut off my head there'.

A report received in February 1611 was promising. San Thome could be easily taken; some of the inhabitants were already in open rebellion and all were in daily expectation of the arrival of a judge to investigate their illegal trade with foreigners. The Spanish are 'equally proud, insolent, yet needy and weak: their force is reputation, and their safety opinion'. 'All the Spanish news here is of the king's purpose to plant Orenoque and it is a matter of great consequence, for the River runs into the heart of the main and hath much wealth upon it.'

This was music to Ralegh's ears. Cecil was more cautious. He feared precipitating war with Spain and wanted more evidence of gold. Perhaps, suggested Ralegh, the English tobacco traders, who knew San Thome, could reconnoitre discreetly? He turned to Queen Anne, in a beautifully written letter, full of his own troubles, from his 'extreme shortness of breath' (he is not allowed to walk with his keeper 'up the hill within the Tower') to his being, after eight years of imprisonment, 'as straightly locked up as I was the first day' and beseeching her Majesty that 'I may rather die in serving the King and my country than to perish here'. Cast into the sea? Beheaded aboard ship? Still not enough but 'my wife shall yield herself to death if I perform not my duty to the King'. The Queen ignored the self-pity, the potential sacrifice of Lady Ralegh and the request for support for Ralegh's trip in search of Guiana's gold.

All the heady rhetoric in the world could not conceal the crucial, troubling question: was there gold to be found? For Ralegh, the gold was real, not least because otherwise the Spaniards would not have 'tormented above an hundred of the natural people to death to find the place'. It would be a tragedy if they were to find it first. Now, 1611, was the moment to act (1607 and 1609 had also been the moment): 'it may now be brought away by two ships, the next year hardly with twenty' and for the 'hazard of a reed, for the adventuring of an old and sorrow-worn man for whom death' is near, Cecil – or any other man – could gain a fortune. Ralegh was not going to 'outlive another winter'. It is a thoroughly mixed message: now is the moment, and Ralegh is necessary, but he also is old and close to death. Hardly heroic adventurer material.

Hidden behind the mixed message was something even more troubling: a hint of a threat to James. As Ralegh wrote to Queen Anne, the King lacked 'treasure, by which (after God) all states are defended'. Without treasure, the treasure that only Ralegh could unlock, the King was vulnerable both to his 'malicious enemies' and his 'grunting subjects at home'. It was a theme Ralegh was increasingly, and tactlessly, drawn to, as is evident in his political writings from this period: 'what can a Prince do that is poor, and hath not the love of his people?'.

I did lately presume to send unto your Maiestie the coppie of a letter written to
my Lord Treasorer touthing Guiana, that ther is nothing done therin I could
not but wounder with the world, did not the mallice of the world exceede the
wisedome therof. In mine owne respect the euerliuing God doth witness
that I neuer sought such an imployment, for all the gold in the earth could
not invite me to trauell after miserie and death, bothwkith I had bine
likeler to haue ouertaken in that voyage, than to haue returned from it
but the desire that ledd me, was the approving of my fayth to his Maiestie,
and to haue done him such a seruice as hath seildome bine pformed for
any king. But most excellent Princes although his Maiestie do not so
with loue him self for the present as to accept of that ritches, which God hath
offred him, therby to take all presumption from his enemies, arising from the
want of treasor, or which (after God) all states are defended: yet it may be that
his Maiestie will consider more deiply therof hereafter, if not to late, and that
the dissolution of his humble vassall do not preceede his Maiesties resolution
therin; for my extreeme shortnes of breath doth grow so fast on me, with the
dispaire of obtayning so much grace to walke with my keeper vp the hill
within the towers, as it makes me resolue that God hath otherwise disposed of
that busenes and of me; who after eyght yeers imprisonment am as straygsly
ly lockt vp as I was the first day, and the punistment dew to othermens
extreame negligence layd altogether vppon my patience a disobedience.
In which respect (most worthy Princes) it were a sute farr more fitting the
hardnes of my destinie (who euery day suffer and am subiect euery day
to suffer for othermens offentes) rather to desire to die oure for all, and
therby to giue end to the miseries of this life, than to striue agaynst the
ordinance of God, who is a trew iudge of my innocentce towards the
king, and doth know me.

for your Maiesties most

humble and most

bound.
vassall.

Ralegh's letter to Queen Anne, written from the Tower in July 1611

Promises and threats did nothing to impress either Robert Cecil or King James. It seemed the only people taking seriously Ralegh's ambitions in the Guiana region were the Spanish. They kept a spy on him throughout his years in the Tower and reported on the various trials of ore that took place. The spy reported the trials came out well but regrets he does not have any precise information about the location of the mine, knowing only it is near 'a mountain' and had been shown to Ralegh by a local leader, a *cacique*, who is now dead. In a follow-up report the Spanish mention the 'great courtesy and gentleness' with which Ralegh treated the *cacique* and observe that his being shown the mine was to 'requit the courtesy which he had received':

Thus conducting him some 5 or 6 miles from his dwelling carrying two spades and a hammer or iron pickaxe he told him that he did not wish to take any other with him from that point because if what he showed him should get out and reach the ears of the Spaniards he would not escape with less than his life and thus he did not trust even his own son in this matter. In view of this, Ralegh ordered twelve of his own musketeers to wait for him there to guard against any surprise attack accompanied by another captain who has since died and by Captain Keymis who is still living and is a member of the said Ralegh's household, his servant and henchman, the four arrived at a certain mountain which was not very high, three French leagues in circumference and a league and a half across. The aforementioned cacique having seized a pickaxe dug out a clod of turf exposing some sand underneath, yellow like gold, assuring him that he would forfeit his life if it were not possible to separate a quantity of very fine gold. Further on they made the same test in another place and presently in another with the same results, the cacique taking great care to replay the clod and turf which they had taken out so it could not be noticed. Having done this they descended the mountain approaching the place where they had left the musketeers about one mile back who knew nothing of what had happened.

The Spanish knew only too well the precarious nature of their own position in the region. One reported, on 11 February 1612, from San Thome, that 'it is more needful here to go with musket on shoulder than with pen in hand, for there are so few men, and so many enemies, and I must say, it is necessary to sleep like a heron, on one foot'.

By the time of this letter, Robert Cecil was in no position to respond to Ralegh's Guiana visions. In the spring of 1612 he suffered an 'ague, a deflation of rheum upon his stomach' and had difficulty breathing. He was understandably 'melancholy and heavy-spirited' but made one last effort to take the waters in Bath. In April, they seemed to 'promise a cure' but it was a false hope. Cecil relapsed and decided to leave. He left the city on 21 May to return to London but only reached Marlborough in Wiltshire, where he died three days later. Cecil was tormented by weeping, probably cancerous, tumours but his death, attended by Dr Poe (Ralegh's erstwhile doctor in the Tower) was in the end peaceful. Although sinking rapidly:

> He insisted on standing erect with the aid of crutches, while prayers were being offered…then lying with his head on two pillows and his body in a swing, he called for Dr Poe's hand, which he gripped hard, when his eyes began to settle, and he sank down without a groan, sigh or struggle.

His long struggle was over.

With Cecil gone and with Prince Henry dead, Robert Carr, the new owner of Sherborne, was in the ascendant, preparing for his controversial marriage to Frances Howard, due to take place as part of the Christmas festivities of 1613. Yet again, Ralegh renewed his push for Guiana, creating, in the words of Joyce Lorimer, already noted as a Ralegh-sceptic, an 'imaginative reconfiguration' of the situation because it was 'the only story which would sell'.

But it didn't. Even Ralegh knew he was flogging a dead voyage. It is no coincidence that in these years he turned more and more to other activities, writing about politics and history, and to supporters and audiences beyond the court. Nevertheless, the court was still on his mind and some of his writings aimed at some very specific courtly targets. Robert Carr, for example, was the very image of the corrupt favourite of Ralegh's *Dialogue* who could and should be removed. Coincidence? Probably not. September 1615 was absolutely the right moment to target Carr; early in the year, James had become attracted to the twenty-two-year-old George Villiers. It did not help that Carr had displayed much 'insolent pride' towards his King and, James complained, seemed more interested in Frances Howard as a bedfellow than in him. James wrote, astonishingly frankly, to Carr, complaining of his 'long creeping back and withdrawing…from lying in my chamber, notwithstanding my many hundred times soliciting you to the contrary'. Just as James became involved with Villiers (another coincidence?) the truth emerged about the death of Thomas Overbury, Ralegh's fellow prisoner in the Tower from April 1613 until his death five months later. Frances Howard, shortly before her marriage, had arranged for him to be poisoned, not satisfied with the mere imprisonment of her enemy. Carr's fall was swift. Ironically, he and his wife became Ralegh's fellow prisoners in the Tower, their death sentences commuted to imprisonment thanks to their merciful King.

Villiers rose, if anything, even more rapidly than Carr had: 'This is now the man by whom all things do & must pass, & far exceeds the former in favour and affection'. George and James's bedrooms were even linked by a secret passage (discovered only in 2004), which suggests those who see only a 'powerful and tempestuous intimacy', a close – but platonic – friendship between James and his favourite might be de-sexing the dossier.

For Ralegh it was a golden opportunity, because Villiers was backed by the old-style Protestant war party. Suddenly, his hawkish message was relevant again. Cecil's replacement, Ralph Winwood, was ready to listen. Ralegh quickly set about presenting a revised version of the Guiana negotiations of the last eight years. Unstinting in his criticism of Robert Cecil, who would always, wrote Ralegh, retreat into his *arrière boutique* (back room), the prisoner had the nerve to suggest Cecil was unable to raise money for James and therefore came to Sir Walter to persuade him to renew his former offers.

Ralegh sends Winwood all the letters from 1611 and 1612, including those to Queen Anne, making clear James could have anything he wanted from the proposed voyage but also hinting the King would need to fund the expedition. Ralegh was in his element, at least rhetorically:

> What I know of the riches of that place not by hearsay, but which mine eyes have seen, I have said it often, but it was then to no end, because those that had greatest trust, were resolved not to believe it, not because they doubted the truth, but because they doubted my disposition towards themselves.

Once again, he appeals to the language of personal monarchy, of a personal relationship with James that has broken down, but keeping very quiet about any crime he may, or may not, have committed: 'had his Majesty known me, I had never been here where I now am [...] his Majesty not knowing of me hath been my ruin...'. Ralegh allowed himself to hope again and by the end of the year he was bribing a Spanish informant to get information about a third mine. This one was not on the Caroni River, nor on the mountain downriver from Putijma's territories – both put forward in earlier documents as the locations of the mine – but lay five to eight miles inland from San Thome, the town having moved from its original site. Ralegh had underestimated the sand samples he had taken, using them as 'blotting sand when he wrote for the space of three years or more it having a high lustre'. It was all getting very real.

And still the Spanish watched, anxiously. By mid-December 1615, they had sent five hundred more men into the Orinoco region. They knew its vulnerability.

In London, Lady Ralegh continued to work tirelessly behind the scenes, as she had done since 1603. She made sure that two well-connected courtiers each received £1,500, with the promise of a further £700 if her husband's release were effected. But in the end one man, and one man only, counted: the war-hungry George Villiers. Ralegh's basic proposals for the Guiana voyage had remained unchanged since 1607. It had taken nine years of campaigning to get the commission he craved, but at last, someone was listening. Someone who was happy to consider taking on Spain. Someone who had influence over the King. It was Villiers to whom Ralegh wrote, thanking him for getting him back 'again into the world'.

14

Ralegh released

ON 19 MARCH 1616, SIR Walter Ralegh was 'enlarged out of the Tower, and to go his journey to Guiana, but remains unpardoned until his return'. He was a dead man sailing. Any potential pardon relied on finding the gold of El Dorado.

What were the chances? It was more than twenty years since he had voyaged to the 'large, rich and beautiful empire' of Guiana. In the intervening decades, profound changes had occurred in its indigenous communities and Ralegh had little chance of reconnecting with those who had supported him in 1595. Nor had the Spanish stood still; they were now there in increasing numbers. But Ralegh knew his name lived on, that 'Waterali' remained an honorific, and that his return was expected. As the anthropologist Neil Whitehead writes, the practice of the Indians in keeping 'Guatteral' alive by giving their children the name, adds to a 'mythic-like quality to his existence – which no doubt would have pleased him well'. But it was not merely a matter of Ralegh's ego. The exchange and use of personal names was a way of indicating marital, commercial and political alliances, both among the indigenous communities and between them and the European incomers. Guatteral, Gualtero, Waterali: all were significant signs of Ralegh's enmeshment in the indigenous cultures, for good or for bad.

Ralegh hoped it would be for good. He believed England had a right to Guiana, because he himself had staked his monarch's claim in 1595, using the language of the people of the Orinoco delta: 'EZRABETA

CASSIPUNA AQUEREWANA, which is as much as "Elizabeth, the Great Princess, or Greatest Commander". But the question remained: was there gold for the finding?

In 1595, Ralegh had written eloquently, if not always truthfully – *The Discovery of the Large, Rich and Beautiful Empire of Guiana* was an exercise in marketing – of two sources of gold: the fantastical kingdom of El Dorado (with descriptions taken straight from Spanish sources) and the more prosaic gold mines on the banks of the Orinoco (which, he said, he himself had seen). Both visions seduced readers and, according to some, possibly also the *Discovery*'s author. Since 1607, and intensifying after the death of Robert Cecil in 1612, Ralegh's belief in the riches of Guiana, perhaps his need to believe in the riches of Guiana, induced what has been described by Lorimer, sceptical as ever, as 'a fatal amnesia' of the reality of South America. Sir Walter insisted he had seen a seam of gold in the sandy rock close to the Spanish settlement of San Thome. No matter that, if the gold were there and easy to get at, it seemed somewhat strange that the Spanish had not found the mine and worked it.

Perhaps Ralegh was not self-deluding but playing a sophisticated political and military game. He knew the situation on the ground in Guiana. Did he hope, by his incursion into Spanish territory, to precipitate a confrontation, war even, between England and Spain? If this was his secret aim (and it is consistent with his anti-Spanish views throughout Elizabeth's reign), he was – again – playing with fire.

Ralegh's hostile contemporaries believed they had the measure of the man: once a pirate always a pirate. A leading naval historian of the twentieth century agrees: K.R. Andrews insists Sir Walter's rhetoric, whether of empire or gold, is simply a blind. When Ralegh writes 'it became not the former fortune in which I once lived, to go journeys of picory…to run from cape to cape and from place to place, for the pillage of ordinary prizes', Andrews is aghast. Ralegh, his captains and his associates 'committed illicit spoil of neutrals, embezzlement of prize-goods, bribery, fraud and outright piracy'. How can Sir Walter say he is no pirate? At the time, it did not help Ralegh's case that it was said he had (there is no hard evidence) spoken at length with the new Lord Keeper of the Great Seal, Sir Francis Bacon. In conversation, he admitted his true aim was to seize Spain's silver fleet. Bacon suggested this was piracy. 'Tush, my Lord, did you ever hear of any that was counted a pirate for taking millions? They are poor mychars [petty thieves] that are called in question for piracy, that are not able to make their peace with that they get.' Ralegh allegedly went on: 'If I can catch the fleet, I can give this man ten thousand and that man ten thousand, and six hundred thousand to the king, and yet keep enough for myself and all my company'.

There's a strong flavour of Ralegh in this swagger: the idea if you are going to go, go large. That anyone, even monarchs, could be bought. How had he got out of the Tower in 1592 if not through the capture of the *Madre de Dios* and a timely gift of £80,000 to the Queen? If Ralegh did indeed say this (and he may well have; discretion was never his strong suit) then it was more than foolish to tell it to Bacon, the King's trusted servant.

More straightforwardly, thirteen long years of imprisonment might have induced neither self-delusion, antipathy to Spain, nor piratical tendencies but merely the desire to get out and get away. As soon as he had a boat, he would be gone, a guest of a friendly nation, a free man, but forever in exile.

The only certainty in the summer of 1616 was his commission. James had 'given and granted unto me the said Sir Walter Ralegh full power and authority and free licence and liberty of this realm of England or any other of his Majesty's Dominions to have take carry and lead for and towards my intended voyage into the South parts of America'. He would have sufficient:

> Shipping, Armour, Weapons, Ordinance, Munition, Powder, Shot, habiliments, victuals, and such other wares and merchandises as are esteemed by the wild people in those parts, clothing, implements, furniture, cattle, horses, mares and all other such things as I shall think most necessary for my Voyage and for the use and

defence of me and my company and trade with the people there and in passing and returning to and fro in those parts to give away, sell, barter, exchange and otherwise dispose of the same, merchandises and promises to them of benefits.

On paper, it looked like just another trading voyage, an opportunity to 'sell, barter, exchange' with the 'wild people in those parts'. There is no mention of gold but also no mention of a pardon, no granting of the King's great seal to the voyage's commander. James took care to omit the usual phrase – 'trusty and well-beloved' – when conferring command on prisoner Ralegh.

Ralegh knew that his commission was half-hearted and almost immediately attempted to drum up the support of the Dutch. It was an early indication that he was wary of his chances of success without international backing or indeed an international escape route. He wrote asking for money, ships, men from the wars and, stretching the truth, told the Dutch that 'his Majesty doth assure all Sir Walter's partners by the great seal of England', that the voyage was guaranteed success by the King himself. There was no seal, there was no pardon. But it was worth a try.

Looking at events through hindsight, it is easy to see that Ralegh was, once again, a small cog in the very large machine of international power politics. It is harder to tell who was pulling the levers. Was the voyage itself part of a Spanish powerplay? For all their public antipathy, it would suit Spain very well if the expedition ran its expected doomed course. There was no gold to be found; at least, no gold to be easily found. There was a Spanish occupation of Guiana. Ralegh would fail. Ralegh would die.

Or was James, an 'expert in hard-nosed and cynical brinkmanship' (according to Lorimer, no supporter of Ralegh) playing both sides? If the mine existed and Ralegh could reach it without open conflict with Spain then James – desperate for money – would be a happy monarch. If Ralegh failed, Ralegh would die. Same outcome, although less money for the King.

In the mean time Sir Walter needed to put together an expedition. His energy was astonishing. Ralegh was in his early sixties and had spent thirteen years as a prisoner, yet threw himself into the business of appointing his captains and commanders and the preparation of '4 ships and 2 barks with their victuals and other necessaries for a voyage to Guiana in the West Indies'. The estimated cost was £10,000 plus £4,000 for victualling. That cost would rise. And rise.

The gentlemen volunteers (among them many younger sons, eager for adventure) contributed £30, £40 or £50 each to expedition funds. Lady Ralegh was the most significant investor, putting in £8,000, the money she had received in compensation for Sherborne. She went even further, selling her own property in Mitcham. Either she believed in the Guianan gold or she had nothing left to lose. Ralegh's son, Wat, now in his mid-twenties, was closely involved and assigned his own ship. Little that is known about Wat suggests that he could be relied on in any way. At Oxford, Ralegh had to write to his son's tutors to warn them of Wat's tastes for 'strange company and violent exercises'. A tutor wrote back about Wat's 'planetary and irregular motions', confirming his father's view but adding a sense of the young man's unpredictability.

Some three years later, in 1612, the Raleghs had hired the poet and playwright Ben Jonson to take their teenaged son around Europe. This was the same Ben Jonson who had written *Sejanus*, just one of the plays that got Jonson into trouble with the authorities during his long and rabble-rousing writing career. *Sejanus* may or may not have featured a character akin to Ralegh but certainly did feature the paedophilic Emperor Tiberius and his serving boy and sexual partner, Sejanus. Ben and Wat's first stop was Paris, capital of a country riven by years of religious wars. There, they heard one of Wat's old tutors from Oxford take part in an academic dispute about the Real Presence. Whether Christ was actually present in the bread and wine of communion was the crux of the continuing conflict between Catholics and Protestants. Wat, who really should have known better, took the idea of the Real Presence and ran with it. His first action was to make his 'governor' Ben Jonson 'to be drunken, and dead drunk, so that he knew not where he was'. This was not a difficult task; Jonson was a notoriously heavy drinker. The many hours that Jonson spent in London pubs are now the stuff of literary legend: The Mermaid Tavern, with Donne, Beaumont, Fletcher and maybe Shakespeare; The Devil Tavern, with Herrick and Carew, the 'tribe of Ben'. An early biographer records that so long as Jonson did not lack wine 'of which he usually took too much before he went to bed, if not oftener and sooner', he didn't care much about the future. Sober theological discussion was never really on the cards for Ben and Wat.

Young Wat laid the drunken Jonson flat on a cart, which was drawn by labourers through the streets of Paris, 'at every corner showing them his governor laid out, and telling them, that was a more lively image of the crucifix than any they had'. After this escapade, deeply offensive to the Catholic majority in Paris, Wat and Ben beat a hasty retreat. Jonson, looking back, remembered Lady Ralegh 'delighted much at the sport' but Sir Walter abhorred his son's behaviour. On their return, things were not much better. Between May 1614 and July 1615, Wat was involved in at least four private quarrels, three of which resulted in drawn weapons and wounds inflicted on his adversary. As for the fourth, only the intervention of the King's officers prevented a duel. He clearly had not grown out of his need for 'violent exercises'. Indeed, in the months after his father's release, Lady Anne Clifford tutted that Wat Ralegh and his 'crew' were up to no good on the south coast, indulging in 'Bowling, Bull baiting, Cards & dice with such sports to Entertain the time'. Some of Wat's crew joined the Guiana voyage; their first chance to show their mettle on a real expedition, not just in sport.

Then came the dinner party from hell. The newly released Sir Walter and his son were dining with 'some great person'. Father warned son to behave: 'thou are such a quarrelsome, affronting [blank], that I am ashamed to have such a bear in my company':

[Wat] humbled himself, and promised to behave very well indeed. Wat sat next to his father and was very demure at least half dinner time. Then said he, 'I, this morning, not having the fear of God before my eyes but by the instigation of the devil went to a whore. I was very eager of her, kissed her and embraced her, and went to enjoy her, but she thrust me from her and vowed I should not 'For your father lay with me but an hour ago'. Sir Walter being so strangely surprised and put out of his countenance at so great a table, gives his son a damned blow over the face. His son, as rude as he was, would not strike his father.

Instead, Wat turned to 'the gentleman on his other side, hit him in the face and instructed him to pass it on, claiming twill come to my father anon'.

It makes a good story, even four hundred years on, and may provide a glimpse of Sir Walter's post-Tower sex life, but it suggests neither a mature head on Wat's young shoulders nor a reliable captain of men.

Slowly, Ralegh brought his fleet together, complete with 'spare shirts, fishing nets, flyboats, surgeon's chests, great barges for river work, canary wine and aqua vita for medicinal purposes'. Its flagship would be the aptly named *Destiny*, a 'goodly ship of 500 tons', designed by Phineas Pett, former target of Ralegh's critiques of shoddy ship design. The *Destiny* was launched in January 1617, just ten months after Ralegh's release. Sir Walter, it was said:

> Purposes to set sail towards his golden mine, whereof he is extremely confident. The alarm of his journey is flown into Spain, and, as he tells me, sea forces are prepared to lie for him, but he is nothing appalled with the report, for he will be a good fleet and well manned.

Ralegh was right about Spain. Every detail of the preparations had gone straight to the Spanish, whose long-standing antipathy to *la pirata* was being raised to new heights by the belief that, once in Guiana, Ralegh would not be able to resist mounting an attack. They knew Ralegh and his supporters felt confident, given their boast that they would have '500 men, which is a competent army to perform any exploit upon the continent of America, the Spaniards (and especially at Orinoque) being so poorly planted as they are'. Spain's concern was what precisely that 'exploit' might turn out to be.

Almost exactly a year after his release from the Tower, Ralegh's 'ship fell down the river unto the Downs'. Already the voyage was invested with something of the mythic: 'He goes for the Orenoquen mine. God grant he may return deep laden with Guianian gold ore!' wrote one. Another feared 'he doth but go (as children are wont to tell their tales) to seek his fortune'. Ralegh was not just seeking his fortune; he sought another chance at life.

Immediately, the fault lines began to show. Recruiting five hundred good men had proved harder than predicted. Ralegh ended up with an unpromising, poorly-trained rabble. Delay after delay occurred. On 19 March 1617 Ralegh wrote from 'Lee' (presumably Leigh-on-Sea in Essex, on the Thames estuary), where he was sorting out supplies and trying to get the *Thunder* away to join the rest of his fleet, waiting at the Isle of Wight. His impatience to be under way is overwhelming, but two months later the expedition was still in Plymouth.

Delays provided an opportunity to reflect on the King's commitment, or lack of it, to the voyage. This prompted Ralegh to open communications with France, seeking a commission from the French King. Sir Walter was aware of what he called a 'happy turn of events' in French politics (the murder of Concini, the French Queen Mother's favourite, on 14 April 1617) and seized the moment to offer his services, together with inside information about his voyage. The Spanish heard all about it from one of their informers, who reported that Ralegh had gained 'esperance and courage' from the events in France, emotions hardly inspired by James's lacklustre support. To the French, Ralegh writes, indeed admits, that if he does not find the mines 'satisfactory and of the quality I want', there is another plan. He will share it with the French, if it can be done securely. He even sends a map.

The map survives in the Simancas archive in Spain. Nothing Ralegh did or wrote was missed by the Spanish, not least that the French took

Ralegh's bait. A commission from Admiral Montmorency, dated 20 April 1617, gave Ralegh leave to trade and use arms in self-defence in South America and permission, on his return, to enter any French port from which, if necessary, to negotiate with King James.

When Ralegh wrote, later, that 'my one design was to go to a gold mine in Guiana, and 'tis not a feigned but a real thing that there is such a mine about three miles from S. Thomas…these things are as sure as that there is a God' it is an interesting lie. Neither the (verifiable) attempt to gain a French commission and the (less reliable) testimony of Bacon on Ralegh's plans to intercept the Spanish fleet if no gold were found undermine his primary goal to bring back gold. But they do indicate that he feared failure, despite his assurance that the mine was a 'real thing' and sought alternatives even before the voyage left English waters.

When the Guiana expedition at last left Plymouth on 12 June it looked well, with '7 good ships of war and 3 pinnaces; he is excellently well manned, munitioned, and victualled, and will be able to land 6 or 700 men, his ships being guarded'. The mayor of Plymouth gave a dinner, costing a generous nine pounds and paid for by the town authorities, while a drummer played 'Sir Walter Ralegh's company aboard ship'.

They only got as far as Falmouth. One of the sailors wrote that the voyage had hitherto been 'very tedious and without comfort to all that are on ventures' and that 'we hear of none, neither French nor Dutch, that mean to accompany us'. The delays provided a chance for frustrated, heavily-armed young men to fight among themselves. The same sailor reported numerous quarrels and fighting 'amongst our own company with many dangerous hurts'. The letter ends with the hope that when 'we get to sea…they will be more quiet'. As he noted, with a hint of bitterness, 'we are still fed with hope'.

If hope was increasingly hard to muster in Falmouth, it disappeared almost entirely when the expedition ran into storms off the southern coast of Ireland. 'Foul weather' had enforced the Falmouth stop but a vicious storm *en route* to Ireland meant that one of Ralegh's 'pinnaces was overset with a sail and lost in his sight'. They were a ship down, four months late and not even in the Atlantic.

The forced stop in Ireland, where Sir Walter stayed with Richard Boyle, later Earl of Cork, who had bought Ralegh's Munster plantation in the final months of Queen Elizabeth's reign, provided Ralegh with a further dangerous chance to reflect on King James's behaviour over the preceding months. His last dregs of optimism disappeared.

The Spanish ambassador, Gondomar (or, to give him his full title, Don Diego Sarmiento de Acuña, Count of Gondomar) was, for his part, extremely content with Ralegh's faltering start, noting that even while in Plymouth the pirate found himself faced 'with a shortage of money and provisions for the voyage' and that this was pushing him into rash decisions. He 'was resolved to set sail with the first wind, and was ready to do so at a moment's notice'. Gondomar remained sceptical of Ralegh's destination (perhaps the Cape of Good Hope, the Red Sea, even the East Indies?) but was certain that 'he will undertake the voyage – as I have told your Majesty – in any form that he may find possible'. While writing, Gondomar received further news. 'Gualtero Rale had set forth with seven ships, indifferently equipped both as regards men and provisions, but with very good guns and munitions of war'. Gondomar was certain that Ralegh's was not an exploratory venture in search of gold but a military force bent on attacking Spanish interests wherever they could find them. Time would tell.

15

Dead man sailing

A T LAST. RALEGH NOTES IN his journal that 'the 19th of August, 1617, at 6 o'clock in the morning, having the wind at N.E. we set sail in the river of Cork, where we had attended a fair wind 7 week'.

There were brief stops in the Canaries. At La Gomera, a present from a countess of 'an English race' of 'oranges, lemons, quinces and pomegranates' was 'better welcome unto me than a 1,000 crowns would have been'. Ralegh carefully preserved the fruit in fresh sand; weeks later they would save his life.

Spain continued to be concerned. The President of the Council wrote to King Philip III in early October about 'Gualtero Reale', 'the Privateer'. The expedition had grown since the last detailed report in June and would grow further, because 'five or six ships of adventurers were being armed in Holland in order to join him'. The President warns that there's another threat looming, further north in Virginia; vessels were being armed for an attack. Spanish outposts need to be alerted. At the same time, no one in Spain is losing sight of the ostensible reason for the expedition: gold. Special care should be taken to prevent Ralegh reaching any mines. The President is waiting for more information but as soon as he has it, then 'the best remedy will be adopted'.

Ralegh didn't stand a chance. Spain was determined to bring down the arch-pirate, while in England his King was surrounded by people with precisely the same goal. As Gondomar wrote to King

Philip: 'many honourable Englishmen will be very glad' if Ralegh were stopped and punished for his efforts. One of those Englishmen was Sir John Digby, recent recipient of the Sherborne estate and therefore a man with his own reasons for wishing Ralegh ill success. As Gondomar notes, Digby 'protested here frequently and vigorously against the evils which would arise to England if Walter Ralegh were allowed to go on this voyage'.

For a time, it seemed as if nature might do the job for James. Ralegh's journal of the voyage makes harrowing reading. Alongside the meticulous recording of leagues covered (or not covered), the politically correct accounts of engagements, violent and non-violent, with the Spanish in the Canaries ('I had no purpose to invade any of the Spanish king's territories, having received from the king my master express commandment to the contrary, only I desired for my money such fresh meat as that island yielded'), the moments of ordinary humanity ('we landed our men to stretch their legs') and the constant quest for food and drink ('wheat, goats, sheep, hens, and wine' at Gomera), Ralegh's journal becomes a record of illness and death. On 24 September, fifty men are ill. Two days later, the number has risen to sixty. Then the dying begins. 'Monday being Michaelmas day, there died our Master Surgeon, Mr. Nubal, to our great loss; the same day also died Barber, one of our quarter-masters, and our sail-maker.' That same night a pinnace, one of the small boats supporting the larger ships, sank, 'having all her men asleep'.

According to the 'Orders to be Observed by the Commanders of the Fleet', Divine Service had to be:

> Read in your ship morning and evening, in the morning before dinner, and at night before supper, or at least (if there be interruption by foul weather) once the day, praising God every night with singing of a psalm at the setting of the watch.

No action could prosper without the 'favour and assistance of Almighty God'. Was the disastrous beginning to the voyage a sign of

God's displeasure? Or was it simply that Ralegh's captains and commanders were inexperienced and ill-disciplined? Ralegh is sure that
human error led to the sinking of the pinnace, which 'having all her
men asleep and not any one at the watch drove under our bowsprit
and sunk, but the men were saved though better worthy to have
been hanged than saved'. Ralegh's faith in his men, never robust, was
reaching rock bottom.

Even during daylight, the skies were dark, making a latitude reading
almost impossible. The expedition had to steer by candlelight. By mid-
October, one Captain Bayley had had enough. He deserted the fleet,
writing that Ralegh had turned pirate. (Bayley would be imprisoned
for 'defamation and desertion' in the Gatehouse in January 1618, but
by then the damage was done.) Things became worse:

> [A] hurricane fell upon us with most violent rain, and broke both
> our cables at the instant, greatly to the damage of the ship and all
> our lives, but it pleased God that her head cast from the shore and
> drove off. I was myself so wet as the water ran in at my neck, and out
> at my knees, as if it had been poured on me with pails. All the rest
> of our fleet lost their cables and anchors; 3 of our small men that
> rode in a cove, close under the land, had like all to have perished.

More deaths.

> This Monday morning died Mr. John Haward, ensign to Captain
> North, and Lieutenant Payton and Mr. Hues fell sick. There also
> died, to our great grief, our principal refiner, Mr. Fowler…This
> Sunday morning died Mr. Hues, a very honest and civil gentleman,
> having laid sick but six days. In this sort it pleased God to visit us
> with great sickness and loss of our ablest men, both land men and
> seamen; and having by reason of the tornado at Bravo failed of
> our watering, we were at this time in miserable estate, not having
> in our ship above seven days water, 60 sick men, and nearly 400
> leagues of the shore, and becalmed.

Sir Walter lost two of his closest associates, 'Captain John Pigott, my Lieutenant General by land' and 'my honest friend Mr. John Talbot, one that had lived with me eleven years in the Tower, an excellent general scholar and a faithful true man as lived'.

There is real pain in that last sentence. Yet Ralegh remains utterly fascinated with the physical phenomena he is witnessing: 'I observed this day, and so I did before, that the morning rainbow doth not give a fair day as in England; but there followed much rain and wind'. He notes rainbows, Magellan's Clouds – two dwarf galaxies only visible in the Southern Hemisphere – and, ruefully, that 'the rules and signs of weather do not hold in this climate', even as he must limit his men to half their water allowance:

[A] double rainbow on Wednesday morning paid us towards the evening with rain and wind, in which gust we made shift to save some three hogsheads of water, besides that, the company having been many days scanted and pressed with drought drank up whole quarter cans of the bitter rain water.

Then Ralegh himself became ill, taking:

A violent cold which cast me into a burning fever, than which never man endured any more violent nor never man suffered a more furious heat and an unquenchable drought. For the first twenty days I never received any sustenance, but now and then a stewed prune, but drank every hour day and night, and sweat so strongly as I changed my shirts thrice every day and thrice every night.

There was no celebration when, at last, on 11 November 1617, they reached their destination.

At home, Ralegh's enemies were mustering. Gondomar recounts a visit from Sir Thomas Lake, who 'came personally to express to me the great sorrow of the king and all good people at what Ralegh has done'. This is a reference to Ralegh's encounters in the Canary Islands, encounters that Ralegh himself believed mostly harmless. Gondomar reports that King James 'promises that he will do whatever we like to remedy and redress it'. Gondomar is sure that James has only one aim: to destroy Ralegh. Meanwhile, 'Ralegh's friends are greatly perturbed, and are trying to find excuses for him'. Those friends were reeling from the death in late October of Sir Ralph Winwood, his chief supporter at court. Winwood was replaced by Robert Naunton, a man who would not even try to find an excuse for Ralegh. The net was tightening. Sir Thomas Lake spelt out James's not-so-secret position to Gondomar. He has been told that:

> His Majesty is very disposed & determined against Ralegh, and will join the king of Spain in ruining him, but he wishes this resolution to be kept secret for some little while, in order that, in the interim, he may keep an eye on the disposition of some of the people here

Not content with bringing Ralegh to his final destruction, James wanted to flush out his supporters.

At the mouth of the Orinoco, Ralegh could not move from his bed but sent his skiff to:

> Inquire for my old servant Leonard the Indian, who had been with me in England 3 or 4 years, the same man that took Mr. Harcourt's brother and 50 of his men when they came upon that coast and were in extreme distress, having neither meat to carry them home nor means to live there but by the help of this Indian, whom they made believe that they were my men; but I could not hear of him by my boat that I sent in, for he was removed 30 miles into the country.

Ralegh decided to head for Caliana, where 'the Cazique was also my servant, and had lived with me in the Tower 2 years'. At least there was food (birds and fruits) and the Indians they met were friendly, 'offering their service and all they had'. Ralegh was desperate to leave his 'unsavoury ship, pestered with many sick men, which, being unable to move, poisoned us with a most filthy stench' and though appallingly weak, managed to make it on to dry land. Things began to improve:

> [His] servant Harry came to me, who had almost forgotten his English, and brought me great store of very good Casavi bread, with which I fed my company some 7 or 8 days, and put up a hogshead full for store; he brought great plenty of roasted mullets, which were very good meat, great store of plantains and piones [the seeds of the peony?], with divers other sorts of fruits and pistachios, but as yet I durst not adventure to eat of the pione, which tempted me exceedingly, but after a day or two, being carried ashore and sitting under a tent, I began to eat of the pione, which greatly refreshed me, and after that I fed on the pork of the country, and of the Armadillos, and began to gather a little strength. […] Here I also set all my sick men ashore, and made clean my ship, and where they all recovered; and here we buried Captain Hastings, who died 10 days or more before, and with him my Sergeant major Hart, and Captain Henry Snedul.

The fruits preserved in sand from distant La Gomera were to his 'great refreshing'. He wrote to Bess, his 'Sweet heart', on 14 November with a touch of his usual confidence:

> To tell you that I might be here King of the Indians were a vanity: but my name hath still lived among them. Here they feed me with fresh meat, and all that the country yields; all offer to obey me.

He could only write in:

> a weak hand, for I have suffered the most violent calenture, for fifteen days, that ever man did, and lived: but God that gave me a strong heart in all my adversities, hath also now strengthened it in the hell-fire of heat.

He had survived the calenture. The ramshackle fleet had made it. His name 'still lived'. Now the real work would begin. The only problem was Ralegh could not do it; he was simply too weak. So was his second-in-command, Sir Warham St Leger. Fortunately, he had two people he could rely on. One was Lawrence Keymis, a veteran of the 1590s voyages and Ralegh's long-standing friend. The other was his son Wat who, as he wrote to Bess, was in 'never so good health, having no distemper, in all the heat under the Line'.

Four hundred men, in five small boats of shallow draft, well-suited to the Orinoco delta, set off on 10 December with a 'month's vittles or somewhat more'. Just over three weeks later, they arrived at San Thome.

And attacked.

They said, of course, that it was self-defence; that the Spaniards had surprised them. They said, of course, that they did not know they were attacking San Thome, because it had moved twenty miles from its previous site. (Not strictly true: it had moved only one mile.) They said, of course, that because it was night, they were in the town before they really knew what was happening.

The attack was led by Wat Ralegh, crying: 'Come on, my hearts, here is the mine that you must expect; they that look for any other mine are fools'. How could he? In one shout of bravado he destroyed his father's vision, revealed his disbelief in the mine and exposed the true purpose of the expedition – or rather his foolish, juvenile, selfish vision – to be an attack on hated Spain.

There was little that was heroic about this small incident of military history. Spanish accounts are harsh about the cowardice of their own soldiers, the men who were supposed to protect their Governor. They fled; he was killed. The African and indigenous people who were necessary to the Spaniards' running of their fort were caught in the crossfire. 'Juliana de Mojica, an Indian woman speaking Spanish' (she was married to a soldier) happened to be with 'Ines, an Indian woman in the service of Captain Cardenas', doing their washing, which they 'kept among the stones by the banks of the river Orinoco'. The English conquerors took the two women and made them serve them by grinding maize. The English soldiers turned to plunder: thirty thousand ducats worth of goods, including five hundred quintals of tobacco.

And Wat Ralegh, still only twenty-four, was killed. Wat, christened in an English country church in the hamlet of Lillington, near Sherborne, was buried beneath the high altar in a church in a burnt-out Spanish town far, far from home. His father, waiting at the mouth of Orinoco, remained oblivious of his son's rash and bloody passing.

Keymis had lost control, if he had ever had it, and now he lost the plot. Desperate to find the gold that might, just might, redeem his friend and patron, he set off into the interior, with no idea of where to look. He and a group of men travelled another 180 miles upstream, leaving an occupying force in San Thome. They found no gold, no silver, nothing. Keymis asked his men to sign a document to say they had done their best. Returning, they collected the rest of the men, who in the meantime had been fighting guerrilla attacks from the evicted Spanish, burned San Thome to the ground and returned to the mouth of the Orinoco.

During these weeks, Sir Walter Ralegh was anchored at Puncto Gallo, 'where we stayed, taking water, fish, and some Armadillos, refreshing our men with palmetto, Guiavas, piniorellas, and other fruit of the country, till the last of December'. It was a peaceful existence, with time one day to note '15 rainbows and 2 wind gales, and one of the rainbows brought both ends together at the stern of the ship, making a perfect circle, which I never saw before, nor any man in my ship had seen the like'. Ralegh's sense of wonder had not left him.

It was a fleeting moment of contentment. On the last day of January, he and his fleet returned to the mouth of the Orinoco, hoping to meet the return party. They were desperate for news, struggling to make sense of garbled second-hand reports from Spanish-speaking:

Indians of the drowned lands, inhabited by a nation called Tibitivas, arriving in a canoe at his port, told him that the English in the

Orinoco had taken St. Thome, slain Diego de Palmita, the governor, slain Captain Erenetta and Captain John Rues, and that the rest of the Spaniards, their captains slain, fled into the mountains, and that two English captains were also slain.

Two English captains slain? An attack on San Thome? This was not good, but it was not confirmed. By now, Ralegh was using threats and taking hostages from indigenous communities in his efforts to find the truth. Every time, the Indian being questioned managed to escape. At last, Ralegh sent his own men: 'The same evening I sent Sir W. Sentleger, Captain Chudley, and Captain Giles, with 60 men, to the Indian town to try if I could recover any of them'.

Those are the last words in Ralegh's journal, written on 13 February 1618. He would not, could not, put on paper what had happened at San Thome: the loss of his dream of gold, the breaking of the peace with Spain; above all, the death of Wat, his son.

The following weeks show Ralegh at his worst. He was consumed with anger towards Keymis, who claimed (justifiably) that the English force was expected by the Spaniards and that the search for gold was impossible under these circumstances. Keymis said that 'the disgrace of not bringing our men to this mine will, I know, whilst I live rest heavy upon me in the judgment and opinions of most men'. He chose not to live with his 'disgrace'. His first attempt at suicide failed because the bullet bounced off a rib; he then 'thrust a long knife under his short ribs up to the handle and died'.

Ralegh remained unmoved. His sole aim was to return to San Thome. The man who could not write of his son's death in his journal seemed now to be focusing solely on the quest for gold. His men were having none of it and the expedition sailed north, to Newfoundland. The mission was over.

Eventually, Walter managed to write to Bess, admitting that 'I was loath to write because I know not how to comfort you. And God knows, I never knew what sorrow meant till now'. His 'brains are broken and 'tis a torment to me to write, especially of misery'. He is 'heart-broken'; his enterprise has failed, he is ready to die. 'Comfort your heart (dear Bess): I shall sorrow for us both. I shall sorrow the less because I have not long to sorrow, because not long to live.' The only consolation is that their son, Wat, died a hero. Only by re-imagining the botched raid on San Thome as a valiant venture could Ralegh grieve for his boy.

It is a brief letter from a broken man – he has 'slept so little and tra-vailed [worked] so much' – but then, in a deeply characteristic move, Ralegh gets a second wind. Into a sprawling postscript he pours his anger towards Keymis, his sense that the Spaniards (and their sup-porters at the English court) did not play fair and his confidence that he has documentary proof of his impossible position. Papers found at San Thome will show 'there was never poor man so exposed to the slaughter as I was'. All that is needed is for everyone to have a proper understanding of the events of the voyage.

His next letter, fired off to Ralph Winwood, reveals Ralegh's sus-picions of the King's double-dealing. About time. Ralegh is full of outrage at what he saw as James's betrayal:

> For it pleased His Majesty to value us at so little as to command me upon my allegiance to set down under my hand the country and the very river by which I was to enter it, to set down the number of men and the burden of my ships, with what ordnance every ship carried which being made known to the Spanish ambassador, and by him in post to the King of Spain, a dispatch was made by him and his letters sent from Madrid before my departure out of the Thames, for his first letter, sent by a barque of advice was dated the 19th of March 1617 at Madrid, which letter I have here enclosed [and] sent your honour.

'What shall become of me now I know not', he writes. 'I am unpar-doned in England and my poor estate consumed, and whether any other prince will give me bread I know not'. Ralegh says he does not know what will become of him but surely must have realised, even before he received the news that Winwood was dead, that all the documentary proof in the world was not going to help now. Or did he, yet again, underestimate King James's political will and duplicity? He was certainly beginning to realise that he had been used as a pawn in the negotiations with Spain and that the King had abandoned his cause long before the attack on San Thome.

Towards the end of March, the last remaining ships deserted Ralegh. They had followed him thus far, but no further. Walter Ralegh could have sought other harbours but he turned the *Destiny* towards home.

16

The last days of Ralegh

BACK HOME, THE CAMPAIGN FOR hearts and minds had begun. March 1618 saw the publication of *The Newes of Sir Walter*, an early salvo in what would become a pamphlet war, as both sides attempted to make their case through this new, cheap medium. The *Newes* is dated 17 November; the author, identified only as RM, offers an eyewitness account of Ralegh's great adventure. RM places the voyage in a grand context of English colonial endeavour and revels in Ralegh's personal triumphs as an explorer and naval commander. It is full of echoes of *The Discovery of Guiana*, whether the language of 'honour and riches', the virtue of English sailors, the good treatment of the natives, the plentiful food or the lack of sickness. Guiana is a paradise, a place surpassing 'Art', a place of rebirth, hope, promise and fulfilment.

It was, of course, 'fake newes' but readers in England did not have access – yet – to the petty, violent, hungry reality of the voyage. By the time Ralegh's expedition, or what was left of it (ships disappeared one by one, to safer waters), limped into southern Ireland, the true story had reached London. Gondomar, for one, was delighted to hear about the attack on San Thome. It simply proved what he had said all along ('*Piratas! Piratas!*').

Now the King called for people to come forward with evidence against Ralegh, so that 'we may thereupon proceed in our princely justice to the exemplary punishment and coercion of all such, as shall be convicted and found guilty of so scandalous and enormous outrages'. The Crown's proclamation made sure to name 'Sir Walter Rawleigh' and those who adventured with him. Their crime?

> [The] hostile invasion of the Town of S. Thome (being under the obedience of our said dear Brother the king of Spain) and by killing of divers of the inhabitants thereof, his subjects, and after by sacking and burning the said town (as much as in them for their own parts lay) maliciously broken and infringed the peace and amity, which hath been so happily established, and so long inviolably continued between us and the subjects of both our crowns.

James proclaimed this commitment to 'exemplary punishment' from his 'manor of Greenwich, the ninth day of June'.

As soon as Ralegh's ship reached Plymouth, it was impounded. Just as swiftly, he picked up his pen, writing to George, Lord Carew. The two men had known each other for decades; at court, in Ireland, through war and peace. The only surviving manuscript copy of *The Discovery of Guiana* is addressed to Sir George, as he was then. Carew had done well under James. He had been made a baron in 1606 and appointed to the Privy Council in 1616: he might be Ralegh's last best hope of getting to the King. On Midsummer's Day, Sir Walter offers Carew a powerful, if chaotic, defence of himself and the expedition, packed with bravado but riven by fragility. Ralegh's postscript shows an almost broken man: 'want of sleep for fear of being surprised in my cabin at night has almost deprived me of my sight, and some return of the pleurisy which I had in the Tower has so weakened my hand that I cannot hold the pen'. His pen was never more needed. Nor was it ever more carefully watched. The only reason we know about this letter is because a Spanish agent obtained a copy and promptly sent a translation to his masters, which a British historian discovered in Seville and retranslated.

Ralegh begins by blaming Keymis. His 'obstinacy' meant that he did not find the mine: if he'd talked to a 'cacique of the country, an old acquaintance of mine' or to the 'servant of the Governor [of San Thome] moreover who is now with me' then he would have been led to 'two gold mines, not two leagues distant from the town, as well as to a silver mine, at not more than three harquebus shots distant'. The gold mines were only about six miles from San Thome and, even more astonishingly, the silver mine was only about three hundred metres further. Later, Ralegh increased the number to seven or eight mines close to San Thome, citing the testimony of Christopher, the Spanish Governor's servant. As for the taking of the town:

> Although I gave no authority for it to be done, it was impossible to avoid, because when the English were landed at night to ensure Keymis's passage, the Spaniards attacked them with the intention of destroying them, killing several, and wounding many. Our companies thereupon pursued them, and found themselves inside the town before they knew it. It was at the entrance of the town that my son was killed, and when the men saw him dead, they became so enraged that, if the king of Spain had been there himself in person, they would have him but little respect.

Ralegh is bemused, however, by the burning of the town: it was 'never my intent; neither could they give me any reason why they did it'. The Spanish started it; it all happened quickly; his son is dead.

This is still not enough for Ralegh. He goes on to make the political argument that Guiana was not a Spanish territory, in direct challenge to the Crown's proclamation, which insisted that San Thome at least was 'under the obedience' of James's 'dear Brother' the King of Spain. 'I myself took possession of it for the Queen of England, by virtue of a cession of all the native chiefs of the country'. Later in the letter, Ralegh appears surprised to hear that King James could see it any other way: 'Since my arrival in Ireland I have been alarmed not a little, and have been told that I have fallen into the grave displeasure of His Majesty for having taken a town in Guiana which was in the possession of Spaniards'. This is presented as new information, offered as the reason why his men, having found it out, were 'so afraid of being hanged' that they were 'on the point of making me sail away again by force'.

Ralegh is walking a tightrope. He needs to make clear that James was not the secret mastermind behind the attack. Therefore, while admitting that he had 'acquainted his Majesty with my intent to land in Guiana', he makes clear that he did not tell his Majesty that 'the Spaniards had any footing there' and acknowledges that he had no 'authority by my patent' to remove the Spaniards 'from thence'. Ralegh's explicit statement that James had no 'foreknowledge' is then undercut by a characteristic qualification: 'But knowing his Majesty's title to the country to be the best and most Christian, because the natural lords did most willingly acknowledge Queen Elizabeth to be their sovereign, who by me promised to defend them from the Spanish cruelty'. Knowing all this, Ralegh had no doubt that he might enter the land 'by force' since the Spanish had 'no other title but force'. Who needs a patent when you have the historical and moral right to evict the enemy?

Ralegh is well into his self-justificatory stride, rewriting the history books. There would have been five thousand Englishmen in the Orinoco region if only – if only – he had not served his country in Cadiz or the Azores. If only Her Majesty had not been distracted by Tyrone's Rebellion (which made 'her Majesty unwilling that any great number of ships of men should be taken out of England till that rebellion were ended'.) If only 'her Majesty's death, and my long imprisonment' had not given time to the Spanish to set up their forts. Yet, there is still hope: the Spanish do not, and cannot, control the indigenous peoples, 'as by the Governor's letter to the king of Spain may appear'.

Metaphorically waving a piece of paper, Ralegh moves on to give the King, via Carew, a lecture on policy. If James acknowledges any culpability or offence, then it will weaken 'His Majesty's title to the country, or quit it' (and also, more prosaically, damage the lucrative trading possibilities). What is more, the Spanish attacked first: it is lawful to defend oneself. No wise monarch would back down on this point.

Moving from presumption to self-pity, a Ralegh-esque turn in this instance well-deserved, Ralegh ends by reminding Carew (and, he hopes, the King) that he has 'spent my poor estate, lost my son and my health, and endured as many sorts of miseries as ever man did, in hope to do his Majesty service'. He could have quietly disappeared, turned 'corsair' and flown far away. Instead, he is man enough to face his accusers: 'at the manifest peril of my life, I have brought myself and my ship to England'. 'Even death itself shall not make me turn thief or vagabond', signs off 'your poor kinsman, W. Ralegh'.

Ralegh was being economical with the truth. He was in fact making secret plans to escape from Plymouth, before the arrival of Sir Lewis Stukeley, sent from London to carry him back to face his exemplary punishment. With Bess and Samuel King, one of the few captains who had remained loyal, Ralegh left Plymouth on a misty summer night. And failed to find his boat in the Plymouth roads.

Did he change his mind? Or was he becoming aware that there might be a reason why Stukeley was taking so long to reach Plymouth? That escaping was precisely what some people close to the Crown wanted him to do? It might be best if he did just disappear, rather than risk another *coup de theâtre*. Everyone remembered Winchester in 1603.

Whatever his reasons, Ralegh returned to Plymouth. The Crown, meanwhile, reprimanded Stukeley for his 'vain excuses' and threatened that if he did not bring Ralegh swiftly to London: 'you will answer the contrary at your peril'.

The party – Sir Walter and Bess, Captain Samuel King, Stukeley and a French doctor, Monsieur Manourie – left on the long journey east. It was something of a pilgrimage through Ralegh's past life; through Sherborne, via Poyntington Manor (home of one of those acquitted in the 1603 plot), to Salisbury, where the prisoner fell ill.

Once again, all was not as it seems. In a move more redolent of the stage than real life ('this short comedy'), Ralegh had poisoned himself, to buy time to write:

[He] began to use impostures of disguising his body with sores, blisters, botches, and the like, swimming in his head and dazzling of his eyes. Fancied himself mad, and to that purpose looked vomative, fell into a convulsion of his sinews, made men to hold his hands, rubbed his urinal with a medicine to turn his water, to make the world think he was dangerously sick.

The grotesque subterfuge allowed him to write, between 18 and 31 July, a lengthy *Apology*, drawing on earlier letters and the journal of his voyage that stopped abruptly when he heard of Wat's death.

The *Apology* is a long, tortuous and tortured work, which degenerates into confusion of both syntax and ideology. Lurching from humility to aggression (Ralegh's men are 'the very scum of the world, drunkards, blasphemers, and such like'), it nevertheless lands its punches. How could he have controlled this 'scum' when every man knew he had not been pardoned? Guiana was English territory. The Spanish were the aggressors. The peace between the two countries was a sham: the massacres of English traders demonstrated that. 'To break peace where there is no peace is impossible':

> For either the country [Guiana] is the king of Spain's or the king's.
> If it be the king's I have not then offended; if it be not the king's,
> I must have perished if I had but taken gold out of the mines there
> though I had found no Spaniards in the country.

Ralegh goes straight to the fault line in the Crown's position: James had permitted him to mine gold in Guiana, therefore the territory was to some degree in James's power.

So far so good but when he addresses the King, the language becomes almost impenetrable, in part because Ralegh's fundamental premise is entirely misplaced. The *Apology* appeals to a personal relationship between monarch and subject, based on a bond of 'trust', that had never existed and was never going to.

Ralegh presumably chose to feign illness in Salisbury because he knew James was travelling to the city. It was yet another indication that, in his mind, he harked back to a vanished world of personal access, a world he had successfully negotiated in the 1580s and 90s. But not only had James given his word to the Spanish ambassador Gondomar that there would be no 'injury to the vassals or the territories' of Philip III, but the machinery and mechanisms of personal monarchy were simply not open to the traitor Ralegh.

By early August, the uncomfortable party of five had completed the final stage of the journey. They made a brief stop at Brentford, which provided another opportunity to escape, this time courtesy of the French resident agent, a senior diplomat. Ralegh turned the offer down, hopeful that James would yet see the error of his ways. He was ill, genuinely this time, and allowed to stay in Lady Ralegh's house in Broad Street rather than being conveyed directly to the Tower.

Broad Street quickly became the Crown's focus; an inventory was made of every single item in the house. Ralegh, perhaps already realising that his optimism had been misplaced, once again turned his mind to escape. With the help of Samuel King, he arranged for a ship to take him down the Thames and across the Channel. Unfortunately for Ralegh, the ship's captain went straight to the authorities. Stukeley, in a double-cross, offered to help Ralegh in his escape. Thus it was that Sir Walter, Samuel King and Stukeley headed for a ship off Gravesend, where Ralegh, in a cloak and broad-brimmed hat with a green ribbon (why the green ribbon? No one explains) was immediately arrested.

Ralegh was down, if not out, but so was Stukeley. Word went around that Sir Walter had been 'in a sort betrayed by Sir Lewis Stukeley (who had the charge of him)'. Thus began the nickname that would haunt Ralegh's keeper until his death: Judas. But the vitriol did not stop 'Judas' Stukeley confiscating even Ralegh's personal possessions (his 'private bag') before the prisoner was swiftly despatched to the Tower of London.

The story emerging was worlds away from those in the *Newes* and the *Apology* and also more politically complicated. Was there a high-level French conspiracy that King James ought to investigate? The Privy Council sent out instructions that David de Noyon Esquire, Seigneur de la Chesnay (to give him his full title), who was clerk to the French ambassador, should be kept 'safe and close' and refused access to anyone. The Council believed that de la Chesnay was simply lying ('finding many apparent untruths in his answer') when he denied any French involvement.

Ralegh chose this moment to come clean about his dealings with the French. Writing directly to James, he was 'now resolved to make an effort to save myself in the best manner I can by disclosing the truth to your Majesty, seeing that my enemies in this Kingdom have great power to do me harm'. He still, astonishingly, seemed to hope that James would realise Ralegh was more useful alive than dead:

> I pray you humbly, therefore, to pardon me, begging you to have compassion on me, for that, if it may please your Majesty to grant my life even in imprisonment, I will reveal things which will be very useful to the State, and from which there will result great wealth and advantages, at the same time that my death could occasion nothing but gratification to those who seek it with so much vindictiveness and anxiety.

This is desperate stuff, but Ralegh appears to hope that by being honest about his dealings with the French, his word would be accepted about other matters. Perhaps the Crown might even be distracted by an international problem.

He spilt everything. De la Chesnay had not only met him at Brentford and then again at his house in Broad Street but had also brought the 'French agent himself, who there offered Sir Walter Ralegh a French bark that was then ready in the river of Thames to transport him into France'.

The Spanish investigation, as ever, was ahead of the English; they had examined Anthony Belle in March. Belle claimed he had known Ralegh for six or seven years and was adamant that Ralegh had obtained his liberty by promising James treasure, while remaining hazy on whether the treasure existed. It was through Belle and his friend, Captain Faige, that Ralegh had begun his negotiations with Admiral Montmorency in early 1618, the negotiations that had resulted in the King of France's swift offer of a safe harbour on Ralegh's return from Guiana. Belle, now in Madrid, said he left Ralegh's service because he 'did not wish to go with people who were Huguenots' but confirmed that Ralegh expected four French ships to join him and, 'believing this to be true, gave him a chart...in order they they might find him with greater certainty'.

The French ambassador was swiftly hauled in front of the Advocate General but denied everything. De la Chesnay, less stalwart, admitted his involvement, although only after being presented with the evidence of Ralegh's letter. The ambassador continued his denials. The Privy Council accused him of violating the law of nations and commanded him to return to his house and 'forbear henceforward to negotiate any thing or to do any act as a public minister or agent', until James had advised the French King, his master, of his 'foul offence and misdemeanour'.

Even this international storm could not hide the fact Ralegh had returned empty-handed from Guiana. As ever, he kept up a barrage of letters. All he wants is to go back to Guiana, in a French ship, to mine the gold that really, truly, is there. The mine is 'grounded upon a truth'. The existence of the mine is, in one sense, not the point at stake but it becomes the touchstone of Ralegh's truthfulness. His case is simple: 'What madness would have made me undertake this journey, but the assurance of the Mine; thereby to have done his majesty service, to have bettered my country by the trade, and to have restored my wife and children to the estate they had lost'. But now he was back home, without gold, with only one surviving child, with a wife scrabbling to retain anything at all from the carnage.

Ralegh had supporters. Queen Anne, despite being extremely ill with dropsy, wrote to George Villiers and to her husband, James. She was ignored, partly because she and the King were not speaking, partly because Villiers and James were looking to Spain even as they worried about France. Meanwhile, Ralegh recycled poems from the Elizabethan years for Queen Anne: surely he could 'not call for right and call in vain?' The poems were as effective as *Ocean's Love to Cynthia* had been in 1592.

James was under pressure from Spain, which wanted the pirate hanged or, if not hanged, then sent to Madrid for execution. There was talk of extraditing Ralegh but the Privy Council was unhappy about the message that might send: England was Spain's equal, not its servant. But if Spain were not to have Ralegh's body, then England must show its ability to confer the promised 'exemplary punishment'. And until that happened, England would make his life increasingly intolerable.

He was kept a 'safe and close prisoner'; no one was to speak with Sir Walter, except in his keeper's hearing. Only those who 'of necessity must attend him for his diet and such ordinary occasions as close prisoners usually have' were allowed access. Ralegh's servant, Robin, was removed; a stranger now supplied those 'ordinary occasions'. Ralegh's chemical apparatus was taken from him, not only because 'no one can know what all his chemical things are' but also from spite: 'the things that he seems to make most recking of, are his chemical stuffs'. Ralegh's experiments revealed his godlessness: 'there are so many spirits of things, that I think there is none wanting that ever I heard of, unless it be the spirit of God'. To his keeper, Sir Thomas Wilson, Ralegh was an 'arch-hypocrite' and a 'dangerous subject'. Wilson was certain of Ralegh's damnation: 'I have been wholly busied in removing this man to a safer and higher lodging which though it seems nearer heaven, yet there is no means of escape from thence for him to any place but to Hell'.

Wilson reported to his masters in detail, which is why we know so much about these dismal September days, from the direction of Ralegh's window to his need for strong laxatives. He found the prisoner 'lying upon his bed in the Tower where the lord Cobham lay, which hath two windows, one towards the Mint, the other towards the great

[illegible] at either of which I conceive letters may be thrown down'
to his friends and confederates. His man 'dresseth his sores'. Ralegh
is 'sick of a rupture and swollen on his left side and hath not had the
benefit of nature these 22 days, but as it hath been forced by medicine,
and for that cause he hath an apothecary and surgeon comes often to
him'. Wilson had authority to search anything and everything, even
Ralegh's 'lining apparel' (probably his personal linen). Wilson concludes that 'never man was more desirous to die'.

The suffering continued. Wilson attempted to move Ralegh to
another chamber in the Tower, partly because he was not happy with
his own lodgings, 'one poor bare walled prison chamber allowed me
both for my men and my self right over Sir Walter' and partly because
of security issues. Wilson's plan was to base himself under Ralegh's
room, to enable him to hear any movements, but when he went 'to
move Sir W R', Wilson 'found him so much discontented therewith
that he said he would not go up thither unless they would carry him
by force'. Meanwhile Sir Walter wrote to Bess, in a letter that was
confiscated: 'I am sick and weak [...] my swollen side keeps me in
perpetual pain and unrest. God comfort us'.

He was in pain, recalcitrant, even suicidal but there were remarkable glimmers of Ralegh's other qualities. For a time he was allowed
to keep his chemical stills (even as he was denied visits from friends,
family and servants) and, astonishingly, turned his attention to developing a method for the distillation of sea water. While he lived, he
would remain curious. He would also maintain his ability to come
up with pithy, courageous one-liners, making light even of death. The
prisoner 'said he combed his hair an hour daily before he came to the
Tower, but would not take the same pains now, till he knew whether
the hangman should have his head'.

The Crown continued to interrogate expedition members. Did the
landing party know about the settlement at San Thome? Did they plan
to attack it? Ralegh had nothing to do with any of this since he was
nowhere near the scene, one of those questioned valiantly responded.
Another reminded his questioners that Ralegh was 'in great extremity

of sickness' at the time. Their testimony vividly brings to life the frightened, huddled discussions among the English who were attacked 'in the night time'. Witnesses admitted believing – or having discussions 'to the end'– that their commission would support them attacking the town. Who was 'most inward' with Sir Walter? Who could reveal his plans? The answer: Captain Whitney, 'who went to the Newfoundland, and is now (as this examinate understands) gone for the straights'. The absent Captain Whitney knew which way the wind was blowing. Another 'examinate', Roger North, who had deserted Ralegh at Nevis, was sure Ralegh did not believe in the mine. Keymis had been confident about it until the taking of San Thome, said North but, finding 'the Moors' knew nothing of the mine, gave up on the idea. North's testimony was crucial. If no mine existed, the men's only reward would be the ransacking of the town.

Another man, Chudleigh, added a further twist of the knife. Ralegh acknowledged that he could not command his men to do anything with regard to the mine in the name of the English Crown, since he could not assign his commission to anyone else. However, Chudleigh reported that Ralegh 'added that he had a French Commission whereby they might do themselves most good upon the Spaniard'. If that wasn't a hint, nothing was. His men would indeed do themselves 'most good' in San Thome.

Even the hostile witness, North, is clear that Spanish aggression precipitated events. The English party:

> Landed by the commandment of the Sergeant Major and the forwardness of young Walter Ralegh, five miles short of the Town, about four o'clock in the afternoon, and they had guides of the Indians who directed them [along] the track to the Town. And so they marched towards the Town: and the ships also went further up the river towards the same: and that this was before any shot or assault made from the Town, or before they could perceive that the Town had any knowledge of them. And that the first shot upon them that landed was from the wood at eleven o'clock at night.

On the outside, Lady Ralegh continued her battles to salvage something from the wreckage. She had her small successes. The Sheriffs of London were instructed to make restitution of 'such stuff and goods as were found in Sir Walter Ralegh's house in Broad Street after his late flight' because Lady Ralegh reminded them of a grant from his Majesty that showed the 'stuff and goods' belonged to her. Ironically, the Crown recognised that Ralegh had been, since 1603, legally dead and thus his property had become his wife's. Bess also made one last effort to reach James through Queen Anne: 'It is reported in London that the queen hath begged his life by means of his lady who is great with her'. None of it did any good.

Arthur Throckmorton emerges from the shadows, offering his assessment of his complex, dangerous brother-in-law. He sends a friend Ralegh's 'pleading apology', the work written at Salisbury to justify himself to his King and his public, writing:

> I am my self glad (who many ways have been no stranger unto him but have long somewhat inwardly known him and those many excellent parts in him meet for a servant of the mightiest monarch upon earth) that I have seen this answer, the more for the satisfaction of others than for my self, whereby his carriage in this his enterprise of Guyana, are so fully opened, and all unfriendly exceptions answered with such sincerity and truth as from his aged advised protestations, I do believe that all is true, it being not possible for him to do more.

Arthur muses that the state 'might in my conceit [opinion] have stayed [stopped] this his esteemed golden journey and returned him to his former prison, if such had been his Majesty's pleasure whereby all chances and cases of violence on both sides which adventure of war must of force bring forth, had been prevented'. The whole thing has got out of hand, yet again, thinks the typically measured Arthur. He hopes Ralegh 'may live by service to make all whole' but he does not sound convinced.

By 3 October, the word was that Ralegh was to be executed but it needed to be handled 'handsomely' and to the 'honour of the state'. Winchester in 1603 cast a long shadow. The following day, Ralegh attended to business that looks very like that of a man who knows the end is near, writing to make sure of the care of the mothers of the men who were killed or died on his voyage. And he wants his tobacco back from 'Judas' Stukeley.

It was now a matter of time. Ralegh was handed back into the custody of the Lieutenant of the Tower and his keeper Thomas Wilson was dismissed. Had he any new information 'to the purpose' from his prisoner? No. Did it matter? No.

Bess's house arrest was lifted and she could write to her husband again. Her letter is banal – she knew it would be scrutinised – but reveals Sir Walter as old, frail and broken, ready for death: 'I am sorry to hear amongst many discomforts that your health is so ill, 'tis merely sorrow and grief that with wind hath gathered into your side. I hope your health and comforts will mend and mend us for God'.

On the same day that Bess comforted her husband's sorrow and grief, the Commissioners sent their report to the King. The lead author was Sir Edward Coke, who had prosecuted Sir Walter at Winchester. The echoes of 1603 were becoming stronger and stronger. The report states the obvious, that Ralegh is attainted of high treason 'which is the highest and last work of law', but also its implication, a much more problematic matter for the Crown. Since he is legally dead, he cannot be charged with crimes he has committed, since he cannot be tried for new offences. On the one hand, this means he can be taken straight to execution. On the other, the Commissioners feel that Ralegh's 'late crimes and offences are not yet publicly known'. Much time (a 'great effluxion' of time) has passed since his attainder, the moment when his civil rights and capacities had been extinguished, when his estate had been forfeited to the Crown and when his blood had been decreed to be 'corrupted'. To make it clear to James's loving subjects precisely why, fifteen years later, Ralegh was to be executed, a public exposition of his lies and crimes against the state ought to be made, even though, legally speaking, they had no bearing on the granting of execution.

Having tentatively suggested one course of action, the Commissioners then put forward another, preferable, way to proceed: call Ralegh before the Council and principal judges in the Council chamber and bring in other 'nobility and gentlemen of quality' to hear 'the whole proceeding'. Thereafter (the legal process is gently glossed over), the King's counsel could proceed against Ralegh for 'his acts of hostility, depredation, abuse, as well of your Majesty's commission as of your subjects under his charge, impostures, attempt of escape, and other his misdemeanors'. All the interrogations would thus at least have had some purpose, working to reveal the true extent of Ralegh's perfidy, 'the true state of the case'. The Commissioners also offered a note of caution: any mention of France should be quietly dropped. There was no need for a diplomatic crisis. No matter that Ralegh had a French commission, that French ships should have joined him but didn't, that Ralegh always planned to escape to France 'for that he knew not how things would be interpreted in England' and that the French encouraged him in this. James, never eager for war, was certainly not looking for a fight with France. His Majesty, reported a French observer, 'with his customary mildness, said…he asked for nothing from France except they did not approve of what had been done by their minister, which, as your Serenity well knows, was a somewhat ill-advised negotiation'. The French were not going to admit their dealings with Ralegh and he was left to face his punishment alone.

For the Crown, it was all about due process being seen to be done. Ralegh should be heard, and face witnesses, but then he should be 'sent back; for that no sentence is, or can be, given against him'. The King did not need a new sentence, merely a public judgment, a nudge of advice to put into action the verdict and punishment handed down in 1603. The result: Sir Walter's 'execution upon his attainder'.

Ralegh himself, it appeared, had no desire to live. On 4 October he wrote to Bess, in essence handing her his accounts and his paperwork. Wat is remembered in passing: 'My son whom I have lost has also signed that note, inventory and agreement between me and Master Herbert'. He signs himself 'your desolate husband, WR'. As ever, there are a series of postscripts. The first, which would later be significant, instructs Bess to deal with his papers: 'There is in the bottom of the cedar chest some paper books of mine. I pray make them up altogether and send them me. The title of one of them is *The Art of War by Sea*. The rest are notes belonging unto it'. The second is the now-familiar complaint of physical illness: he has 'grievous looseness' (diarrhoea or dysentery) and wants the 'powder of steel' (that is, iron) and pumice sent to him. Finally, he asks Bess to look after John Talbot's mother. This was Ralegh's servant and friend, John Talbot, 'as excellent general scholar and a faithful true man as lived': words from Sir Walter's *Journal* at the time of Talbot's death on the Guiana voyage. He fears that, her son being dead, Talbot's mother will soon perish. Something needs to be done.

Yet, even as the Commissioners reported to James, rumours flew around London that Ralegh would escape with a 'censure'. James considered his options. He did not want any kind of public, or even semi-public, hearing, since it would make Ralegh 'too popular, as was found by experiment at the arraignment at Winchester, where by his wit he turned the hatred of men into compassion for him'. But to authorise execution of the original attainder of 1603 was problematic, in that Ralegh had been convicted of conspiring with Spain, while now he was being condemned for attacking and plundering a Spanish settlement.

James's solution was simple. Ralegh would appear before the Commissioners ('those who have been the examiners of him hitherto') and there would be no audience. France would be kept well out of it. 'And then, after the sentence for his execution which hath been thus long suspended, a declaration [should] be presently put forth in print, a warrant being sent down for us to sign for his execution.' James could not resist urging his Commissioners, in notes scribbled on the back of these instructions, to emphasise the French doctor's 'confession', Ralegh's boasts about seizing the Spanish silver fleet, 'his son's oration when they came into the town' and – above all – 'his hateful speeches of our person'.

This was on 20 October; two days later, Ralegh was called before the Privy Council.

> His impostures
> He never intended a mine.
> He purposed to set war between the 2 kings of England and Spain.
> He abandoned and put in danger all his company.
> His unfaithful carriage to the King and his company.
> His actions beyond the sea showed his want of love and duty.
> But his actions since at home show his want of fear and duty.
> His vile and dishonourable speeches, full of contumely for the king.

Ralegh is told he is a liar and a coward. That he knew there was no gold. That he had given his King the false 'promise of a golden mine' but truly was intending to engineer war between England and Spain. That he had abandoned his men. That he had betrayed and insulted the King.

Ralegh does not, perhaps cannot, challenge the substantive charges, except to repeat that he did believe in the mine and that he did not abandon his men. He admits he spoke of attacking the Spanish silver fleet if the main attempt to reach the gold failed. He says, foolishly, that he had been 'deceived' in his confidence in James. He had not, however, 'used any other ill speeches against the king'. He might have saved his breath.

On 24 October 1618, Ralegh is told that he was to be executed.

A personal tragedy for Sir Walter is turning into an international crisis. Ralegh has 'confessed spontaneously', notes the Venetian ambassador with some glee, that members of King James's Council had encouraged him to attack Spanish 'fleets' and 'territories', that M. Desmartez, 'the late French ambassador at this court', had promised him he could retreat to Spain and that James has written to the French King and now refuses to acknowledge the French agent. For the Venetian ambassador, tensions will 'doubtless accumulate daily and produce the worst effects'.

They already had for Ralegh. Winwood, his supporter in the Council, was dead. Prince Henry was dead. Queen Anne was dying. There was no one left to plead his case.

Except the man himself.

He made his first attempt on 28 October 1618 when, in his presence, the sentence of death was confirmed at the Court of the King's Bench in Westminster, the highest criminal court in England. Asked why they should not proceed with judgment, Ralegh began to make his case, despite his voice having 'grown weak by reason of my late sickness, and an ague which I now have'. He had his commission, he had tried to bring back gold for his King, and the voyage 'notwithstanding my endeavour, had no other success but what was fatal to me, the loss of my son and the wasting of my whole estate'. He was just getting into his stride when he was interrupted. Sir Henry Montagu, Lord Chief Justice at the Court of the King's Bench, explained that the King had decided 'upon some occasions best known to himself' that the old sentence should now be enforced, and the prisoner could only offer legal arguments. Ralegh changed tack, going for the argument that the commission for the voyage, which conferred upon him powers of life and death over his men, was in effect a pardon. No. The omission of the words 'trusty and well-beloved' from the commission was noted. Ralegh was not trusted, let alone well-beloved. He never had been. What happened in Guiana was now irrelevant. The King was now simply confirming the 1603 sentence.

Ralegh, fifteen years too late, at last begged for mercy but even his begging was tinged with arrogance and a challenge to James. An old man, shivering uncontrollably in a malarial fit, even now he could not summon humility in the face of injustice. The Winchester verdict was flawed ('I had hard measure therein'). The King himself, he felt sure, 'was of opinion' that it was flawed. Montagu sternly reminded Ralegh that the King had been merciful simply by fact of having let him live for fifteen years. Ralegh then had to endure a summary of his life:

Sir Walter Ralegh hath been a statesman, and a man who in regard of his parts and quality is to be pitied. He hath been as a star at which the world hath gazed; but stars may fall, nay they must fall when the trouble the sphere wherein they abide.

Ralegh was patronisingly reassured that he was a good Christian. His *History of the World* was to thank for that.

Execution was granted.

Ralegh was dignified. He requested that he might not be 'cut off suddenly', because 'I have something to do in discharge of my conscience, and something to satisfy his Majesty in, something to satisfy the world in, and I desire I may be heard at the day of my death'.

For the last time, he asked for pen and ink.

17

The last hours of Ralegh

28 October 1618, evening

RALEGH IS TAKEN to the Gatehouse Prison, originally the gatehouse to Westminster Abbey, now a place to keep the most treacherous of the Crown's subjects. A lifetime later, another prisoner incarcerated here would write the famous lines that 'Stone walls do not a prison make, Nor iron bars a cage'. A lifetime earlier, Ralegh, imprisoned in the Tower, had written that it was his mind that suffered when he was confined, rather than his 'body in the walls captived'. In 1592, despair had bolted the doors; he could only speak to dead walls. This time, he is determined to have a voice. He will be heard at the day of his death.

He is visited by the Dean of Westminster, Robert Tounson, who has news for the prisoner. The all-merciful King has issued a royal warrant; Ralegh will be beheaded rather than hung, drawn and quartered. Nobility always received this commutation, gentlemen less often. How lucky he was.

As Dean and prisoner talk, workers are busy providing 'some fit and convenient place or scaffold' at the Palace of Westminster, as per the instructions received earlier in the day from the Court of the King's Bench. Old Palace Yard is chosen for the scaffold, the Yard where Guy Fawkes and his fellow conspirators had rented a house and begun to tunnel from there to the House of Lords, until they realised it would be easier to hire a cellar under the House itself. Fittingly, in the eyes of the Crown, Old Palace Yard was also where Guy Fawkes and his fellow conspirators were hung, drawn and quartered. It is less clear why Old Palace Yard is chosen for Ralegh's execution, although it is just possible that its proximity to St Margaret's Church (the parliamentarians' church) is a factor.

The venue for, and means of, death had been decided but during this night there remained much confusion where Ralegh's body could, or would, be taken once it had been severed from his head. Some believed it would be taken to Exeter Cathedral, to lie with Sir Walter's parents. Lady Ralegh believed she would have charge of her husband's body and be able to take it to her brother's estate in Surrey. Most likely was that Ralegh would be interred in St Margaret's Church, the shortest of journeys, the safest of destinations; there would be little time or opportunity for trouble.

Sir Walter still has one more evening in this world. He is visited by Bess, from whom he has been separated since late summer. He has recovered his poise and his wit: she is the one who is distressed after years of determined struggle on his behalf:

> His Lady had leave to visit him that night, and told him she had obtained the disposing of his body, to which he answered smiling, it is well Bess that thou may dispose of it dead, that had not always the disposing of it when it was alive.

Would she have the disposing of his body? Only time would tell.

Ralegh is determined to speak from the scaffold but knows it is possible this will not be permitted. He knows he has been 'cut off from speaking somewhat he would have said at the king's Bench' earlier in this long, long day. He scribbles a 'remembrance', which he leaves with 'his Lady, written likewise that night, to acquaint the world withal, if perhaps he should not have been suffered to speak at his death'. She finds the 'remembrance' in her pocket the next day.

Would he be allowed to speak from the scaffold? Only time would tell.

Ralegh picks up his Bible, the only book left to him, and writes a poem on its flyleaf. His mind is in another place and at another time. The first six lines he writes are taken directly from the closing verse of a poem of courtship and seduction, written in the 1580s, at the height of his success. Then, the lines were the culmination of an exercise in *carpe diem*-driven wit, celebrating the 'wantonness and wit', the soft belly, the hair, breath and lips of the ideal woman. Perhaps, if we are being sentimental, the woman who is with him, now, as darkness falls in the Gatehouse Prison:

> Nature, that washed her hands in milk,
> And had forgot to dry them,
> Instead of earth took snow and silk,
> At love's request to try them,
> If she a mistress could compose
> To please love's fancy out of those.
>
> Her eyes he would should be of light,
> A violet breath, and lips of jelly;
> Her hair not black, nor overbright,
> And of the softest down her belly;
> As for her inside he'd have it
> Only of wantonness and wit.

Ralegh, always drawn to the dark side, even in his courtier heyday, especially in his courtier heyday, reminds the reader that 'the light, the belly, lips, and breath' will be dimmed, discoloured and destroyed by time; that wantonness will dry and wit will dull. The poem concludes in melancholy, rather than eroticism:

> Oh, cruel time! which takes in trust
> Our youth, our joys, and all we have,
> And pays us but with age and dust;
> Who in the dark and silent grave

When we have wandered all our ways
Shuts up the story of our days.

As time folds in on Ralegh on the night of 28 October 1618, he returns to this closing stanza, written so many years before, changing a word here, a word there but – crucially – rounding it out with a couplet that acknowledges his imminent journey to the grave. His final poem is done:

Even such is time that takes in trust
Our youth, our joys, and all we have
And pays us but with age and dust
Who in the dark and silent grave
When we have wandered all our ways
Shuts up the story of our days.
And from which earth and grave and dust
The Lord shall raise me up I trust.

Are those final two lines an expression, at last, of his private faith, his tentative trust in the Lord God? Are they a veiled critique of the thoroughly legal, but nevertheless cruelly unjust, process that has brought him to this point? Or is Ralegh making a plea that the story of his days will be told, even when he is no longer here to tell it?

He is the poet-courtier to the last. And the explorer and colonialist: even unto death he carries totemic objects from Guiana, a 'stob' of gold (possibly given him by Topiawari), a Guiana idol of gold, a 'plot' (map) of the river Orinoco. 'As if possession of these images were to possess Guiana itself', writes Neil Whitehead, who understands as much as anyone the spell that Ralegh's journeys to South America cast over him.

It is possible that he wrote a further couple of lines, 'on the snuff of a candle':

Cowards fear to die but courage stout
Rather than live in snuff will be put out.

However, as one scholar points out, 'enough poems have been ascribed to Ralegh on the night before he died to have kept him versifying without pause'. Maybe, as John Chamberlain wrote at the time, he wrote 'half a dozen verses [...] to take his farewell of Poetry wherein he had been a piddler even from his youth'. But maybe he did not, because Ralegh is preoccupied with what he will say, if he has the chance to say it, the next morning. He must prepare himself.

Ralegh, the man whose words have both saved and imperilled his life, brought both favour and scorn, spends his final night seeking the right words. Because he hopes he will have one more chance to speak, he picks up his pen. He knows 'dying men's words are ever remarkable, & their last deeds memorable to succeeding posterities, by them to be instructed, what virtues or vices they followed and embraced, and by them to learn to imitate that which was good, and to eschew evil'. So wrote a contemporary, but for Ralegh it was not just a matter of providing a moral lesson, it was his last chance to vindicate himself to the world.

At last, Walter says goodbye to Bess, dismissing her 'after midnight'. He settles himself 'to sleep for three or four hours'.

29 October, 4 of the clock

Ralegh is woken long before the dawn.

He is again visited by Dean Robert Tounson, with whom he celebrates communion. The two men talk, Tounson bringing up the vexed subject of the Earl of Essex and 'how it was generally reported that he [Ralegh] was a great instrument of his death'. Was there no escaping the Earl, even in death? No, for Ralegh had only the day before received 'many reproachful taunts of the vulgar (taxing him with Essex)' as he was taken to his arraignment. Ralegh listens to Tounson, remembers the taunts and gathers his wits for one last response to his great rival.

Ralegh is calm, strangely calm, smoking his pipe, insisting that death is simply another journey to be taken. Tounson remembers Ralegh, after receiving communion, is:

Very cheerful and merry, and hoped to persuade the world that he died an innocent man, as he said. Thereat I told him, that he should do well to advise what he said: men in these days did not die in that sort innocent, and his pleading innocency was an oblique taxing of the Justice of the Realm upon him.

It is the clearest indication that if Ralegh had to go, he would not go quietly. He was innocent, and he would proclaim his innocence, even if it meant challenging the justice of the realm.

He has his final breakfast (a 'dish of fried steaks [and] eggs roasted, and sack burned') and dresses for his final performance:

His attire was: a wrought Night Cap, a ruff band, a hare-coloured satin doublet, with a black wrought waistcoat under it; a pair of black cut taffeta breeches, a pair of ash-coloured silk stockings, and a wrought black velvet gown.

According to most witnesses, the 'wrought black velvet gown' was a nightgown, a fitting garment as Ralegh went to his final rest. Nightgowns could be luxurious, elegant garments: a beauty, a gown of purple silk damask lined with grey silk shag and trimmed with gold braid, survives in the Verney family collection at Claydon House. Ralegh, the man who rode all night to London to make sure he had the black suits to look good for a French delegation, will die wearing the right clothes. Some say he wore a diamond ring given to him by Queen Elizabeth: his loyalty now is to the past.

29 October, past seven of the clock

'They brought him on foot, surrounded by 60 guards, to the square at Westminster, near the palace, where the scaffold had been erected', wrote a Spanish diplomat to his King, pleased that this enemy of Spain was at last being brought to account. Spain's enemy was, however, old, ill and broken by the death of his son. He cannot have needed those sixty armed men to guard him on his last journey, that short walk from the Gatehouse to Old Palace Yard.

It may have been a short walk, but Ralegh nevertheless finds time for one of his characteristic gestures. En route, he gives his nightcap to a bald well-wisher: 'thou has more need of it now than I'. The memorable one-liners, the gestures of largesse to the ordinary man, continue to the last. In his hand he carries his notes.

The crowds are gathered. Among them are Christopher, the Indian servant of the Governor of San Thome, and Ralegh's closest, most loyal, friends. Thomas Harriot will take notes as events unfold: his scribbled memorandum survives to this day. Nobles scramble for the best views, crowding around the windows of surrounding buildings.

This is not the plan. It is Lord Mayor's Day in the City of London; the Crown hopes Ralegh's death will be buried beneath other news, 'that the pageants and fine shows might draw away the people from beholding the tragedy' of the execution. But the execution of Sir Walter Ralegh should not have mattered and should not have been considered a 'tragedy'. Legally dead for fifteen years, the subject of popular vilification after his arrest in 1603, with no faction of his own and no great family behind him. His death should have been unremarkable.

That it was not is due to Ralegh's words and actions in the final hour of his life. His performance is the more remarkable given the failures in communication over the previous months, given that Ralegh's brains were, by his own admission, broken, given that he was desperately ill (suffering shivering fits, probably from malaria) and given that he could barely hold a pen. But he was determined. As he had said the day before: 'I have something to do in discharge of my conscience, and something to satisfy his Majesty in, something to satisfy the world in, and I desire I may be heard at the day of my death'. The question remained: would he be allowed to speak?

29 October, eight of the clock

Ralegh approaches the scaffold smiling, sharing jokes with the crowds. Now is his time. He inclines his 'body with an observant respect' towards the assembled lords and asks them to come closer, to join him on the scaffold. He 'reverently saluted, and embraced them', as 'if he had met them at some feast'. Ralegh would use these lords for his own purposes. But not yet.

He is allowed to speak. He begins by saying (would there have been irony in his tone?) how 'indebted' he was to 'his Majesty who had permitted him to die in this public place, where he might with freedom disburden himself'. In the event, Ralegh disburdens himself for a full forty-five minutes. That too is not the plan: 'they had no thanks that suffered him to talk so long on the scaffold, but the fault was laid on the sheriffs and there it rests'. Forty-five minutes later, his large audience had heard an *apologia pro vita sua* (a defence of his life); a profoundly aggressive, politically charged *apologia*, and witnessed an unprecedented 'play of passion', delivered 'without appearance of fear or distraction'.

Ralegh made utterly sure that all those present saw him, even if they could not hear him, as the hero of his own execution. Did he weep? Some say he did, but passion now elevates rather than diminishes. Did he shiver? If he did, it was because of illness, not fear. Some of the more dramatic features were inherent in the occasion but Ralegh exploits every opportunity to make the moment more visually memorable. He always had known that sometimes a picture is worth a thousand words. In the 1590s, he had shown the indigenous peoples of Guiana images of the cruelties perpetrated by the Spaniards, 'neatly wrought for the better credit of our workmanship, and their easier under-standing'. He would now make it easy for the Westminster crowd to understand his death.

Ralegh uses language both visual and urgent, even, in true dramatic style, drawing attention to the clock's ticking down. He is come from the dark of the Tower into the light to speak to his audience; he will stand before 'the tribunal seat of god within this quarter of this hour'. It is no surprise that the audience recorded the speech as drama and judged it in terms of performance. Public executions were ceremonies designed to generate more than simply terror, but what a performance this was turning out to be. One commentator uses the discriminating tone of the theatre critic: 'His voice and courage never failed him (insomuch that some might think it forced than natural, and some-what overdone)'. Ralegh's 'performance', both at the arraignment and on the scaffold, is such that even the 'severest critic could take no just exception either against his countenance or carriage', argues another. John Chamberlain sums the performance up: 'In conclusion he spake and behaved himself so, without any show of fear or affectation that he moved much commiseration, and all that saw him confess that his end was *omnibus numeris absolutus* [perfect in every detail], and as far as man can discern every way perfect'.

Ralegh's perfect death allows him to acknowledge his sinful life or, more precisely, his immensely rich, active and successful sinful life of service to his country. He asks God to be merciful toward him:

> For I have been a great sinner in all kinds and my course of life hath been such as hath been a great inducement unto it. For I have been a soldier, a captain, a sea-captain, and a courtier which is the course to breed in a man all villainy if by grace he be not prevented.

As another witness puts it, Ralegh admits he has spent his life in 'places of wickedness and vice'; been 'a man full of all Vanity'. How could he not be, given what he has done? It is a high-risk strategy, but it works. Sir Walter 'I'll tell it as it is' Ralegh has done it again.

What is more, Ralegh's behaviour on the scaffold serves to validate his claims of political truth-telling, later ruefully acknowledged by 'Judas' Stukeley: 'they say he died like a Soldier & a Saint, & therefore then to be believed, not only against me, but against the attestation of the State'. Make no mistake, to the very last, Ralegh is making a political point.

His first challenge to the 'attestation' of the state was his insistence that death will free him from being a subject, thus permitting him freedom of speech: 'I come not hither either to fear or flatter kings. I am now the subject of Death, and the great God of Heaven is my sovereign before whose tribunal I am shortly to appear'. He can now 'speak freely and to the discharge of mine own conscience'. It's radical stuff: 'Now what have I to do with kings; I have nothing to do with them, neither do I fear them; I have only now to do with my God, in whose presence I stand, therefore to tell a lie, were it to gain the king's favour, were vain'.

As he had said at his arraignment, he was looking forward to his execution because, on the scaffold, he could speak out 'where I shall not fear the face of any King on earth'. In 1603, he had argued that if the law destroyed him, he would be out of the reach of the King's power and would have 'none to fear, none to reverence, but the king of kings'. These are inflammatory words in a world in which the doctrine of the divine right of Kings was even used to justify tyranny.

Ralegh challenges another 'attestation' of the state: his guilt. Nowhere in his speech does Ralegh admit to having committed the crimes of which he is accused. Even more shockingly, nowhere does he praise the King. The claim of innocence was in itself seditious, flying in the face of the usual form of 'last speeches', which followed the pattern of a confession of crimes (temporal matters), a profession of faith (spiritual matters) and closed with laudatory comments about the monarch. Tounson had warned him earlier that to plead his innocence 'was an oblique taxing of the Justice of the Realm upon him'. As both men knew, Essex had done precisely the opposite, following the accepted format to the letter, acknowledging the justice of his execution, recognising the depth of his sin and begging for forgiveness from his divinely-appointed Queen. The closest Ralegh got to the pattern was forgiving his enemies and traducers but, as Nicholls and Williams say, that was 'common form and he did not necessarily mean what he said'.

Ralegh gives his own account of the Guiana voyage and its aftermath, invoking a vanished era of political honour to endorse his
version of events. He had no ulterior motive in going to Guiana. He
had not plotted with France nor ever considered seeking refuge there.
He was, he admits, duped by Manourie, a 'runnagate Frenchman',
because the runnagate had shown interest in Ralegh's chemical experiments and had a 'merry wit'.

He admits he faked illness at Salisbury, because 'I had advertise-
ment from above that it would go hard with me; I desired to save
my life'. In this, he has the nerve to compare himself to the 'prophet
David' who 'did make himself a fool, and did suffer spittle to fall
upon his beard to escape the hands of his enemies, and it was not
imputed to him as a sin'. The message is simple: Ralegh may have
been foolish, but he is not evil. He is stretching the truth, if not
downright lying, especially about his dealings with France and his
plans for escape. But, on the scaffold, as the minutes pass, he is utterly
convincing.

Ralegh brings in one of the lords that he has called down from the
window to be closer to the scaffold. He recounts a conversation with
the Earl of Arundel, just before he set off for Guiana:

> Then said his Lordship, give me your hand as you are a Gentleman,
> whether you speed well or ill in your voyage, to return again into
> England. I gave his Lordship my hand; and promised to do so, God
> willing, whatsoever fortune befell me.

Ralegh is delighted that Arundel is present and able to corroborate
this anecdote: 'I am very glad that my Lord is here present to satisfy
whether this be true or no'. Arundel did just that, saying, 'It is true'
and 'I do very well remember it', even taking off his hat, for this is a
serious moment. The exchange, orchestrated by Ralegh, fixes in the
crowd's mind that Sir Walter's word was indeed his bond; that he was a
man of honour. Ralegh appeals to Arundel again before the end of his
forty-five minutes, to ask him 'to desire the king, that no scandalous

writing to defame him might be published after his death', and 'that those things I have written be not destroyed when I am gone'. This was wise: the war over his reputation was just beginning. Ralegh was winning this battle.

There were those who believed they saw through the rhetoric, to the real Ralegh. 'Judas' Stukeley was one. Ralegh was truly 'an Angel of darkness', who put on himself 'the shape of an Angel of light at his departure, to perform two Parts most cunningly; First, to poison the hearts of discontented people; Secondly to blemish me in my good name, a poor instrument of the just desires of the State, with false imputations'. No one listened.

Ralegh saves the best until last. All accounts of the speech record that the 'last point' is a statement of his innocence towards the Earl of Essex. He has listened to the heckles from the public, listened to Robert Tounson, knows only too well that he has been accused of desiring 'to feed his eyes with a sight of the earl's sufferings, and to satiate his hatred with his blood'. Now he asks for, and is permitted by the Sheriff, extra time to speak about this matter 'unto the people'. He expresses both outrage ('What barbarism were it in any man to laugh and be merry at the death of any Christian!') and sincere feeling ('I loved the Earl of Essex so well...'), then tackles, with disarming candour (honest Ralegh, yet again) the specific charges: that he grinned at the Earl's execution and, worse, took tobacco. 'There was a report spread, that I should rejoice at the death of my Lord of Essex, and that I should take Tobacco in his presence, when I protest I shed Tears at his Death, though I was of the contrary faction.'

The truth of the matter, or the truth that Ralegh reveals in his final minutes on earth, was that Essex had wanted to be reconciled with Sir Walter at the last. Unfortunately (and in a strategic reminder of just how important Sir Walter had once been), he had his duties as Captain of the Guard; he had to remain in the armoury at the Tower of London. He may have been Essex's rival 'but I wished not his death, for I knew when he was gone, I should not be so much accounted of'. He knew that 'it would be worse with me when he was gone, for those that set up me against him, did afterwards set themselves against me'. Ralegh cannot resist a final swipe against Robert Cecil. It is a striking example of Ralegh's straight-talking wit, his understanding that his very rivalry with Essex at least made him visible at court. The popular impression of a bitter antagonism between the two men is replaced by an impression of a cynical, but not vicious, political relationship. All talk of filthy water, cuckoos and parrots is forgotten. The way is cleared for the popular linking of Essex and Ralegh as twin symbols of the greatness that was Elizabeth's reign.

Ralegh has made his last point.

29 October, approaching nine of the clock

The Sheriff, kindly, thinks Ralegh might be cold, for he has talked for so long. He asks him to come to warm himself by the fire since he would be 'more able to endure what you are going about'. Ralegh rejects the offer: his 'fit' will come upon him in a few minutes and they had better get on with it.

First, he must pray. For a full fifteen minutes. Ralegh has taken God as his witness again and again in his speech but now he embraces the gathered lords and friends, moves from one side of the scaffold to the other to request the public to pray with him and for him, 'to assist him and strengthen him' and finally, kneels on the platform with his friends, in prayer. It goes without saying that he prays in 'an audible voice'.

These fifteen minutes do their work. In the final act of leading the crowd in prayer 'the hated atheist became their priest', writes Chamberlain, while others were astonished, but utterly convinced, that Ralegh 'died a true Christian and a protestant'. And this, even though to the last Ralegh 'spake not one word of Christ' but only of 'the great and uncomprehensible God, with much zeal and adoration'. One observer concluded he 'was an a-christ, not an atheist'. People had always wondered about Ralegh's religious beliefs, been disturbed by his dangerously questioning mind. So it was this chilly morning in Old Palace Yard.

29 October, nine of the clock

The Sheriff clears the scaffold but not before the condemned man uses 'courtly compliments of discourse' with the lords and his friends, not before he throws his hat to an acquaintance, gives his stitched cap (how many hats is he wearing?) to 'Mr Smith' (probably Robert Smith, his servant in the Tower) and hands his purse to an old man who stands by him on the scaffold.

Ralegh takes off his hare-coloured satin doublet and wrought black velvet nightgown. He asks to see the axe. He 'feels the edge, and finding it sharp for his purpose, this is that, saith he, that will cure all sorrows, and so kissing it, laid it down again'. Or, as another remembers, he tests the edge of the blade and says: 'here was a sharp medicine…a physician for all diseases'. The precise words don't matter. What matters is the effect of such wit and insouciance in the face of death.

The executioner, the very embodiment of state justice, struggles: 'the fellow was much daunted (as it seemed to me) at his resolution and courage, in so much that Sir Walter Ralegh clapped him on his back diverse times; and cheered him up'. To comfort your executioner suggests an extraordinary degree of self-control but reveals the extent to which Ralegh was master of his final performance.

He refuses a blindfold. He will look death in the eye. He has no fear of the axe and will not tremble at its shadow:

> Then he began to fit himself for the block, without permitting any help and first laid himself down to try how the block fitted him. After rising up, the executioner kneeled down, and desired him to forgive him, which, with an embrace, he professed he did; but intreated him not to strike till he gave a token, by lifting up

his hand; and then fear not, saith he, but strike home. So he laid himself down to receive the stroke, and the hangman directed him to lay his face towards the east. No matter how the head lie, answered he, so the heart be right. After he had lain a little while upon the block, conceiving some prayers to himself, he gave the watchword.

The aphorism 'no matter how the head lie, so the heart be right', is the stuff of heroic legend, and echoes through almost all the accounts of Ralegh's last moments. Just as significant was the control he was able to exercise over the timing of his death. This mattered in popular belief, as opposed to orthodox theology, which insisted that even the most perfect death should not redeem a sinful life. For many people, however, this conclusion was too pessimistic. A person's behaviour in their 'final moment' mattered and might be the difference between salvation and damnation: 'the end sheweth the life' and 'the last act carryeth away the applause'. Ironically, therefore, execution was preferable to sudden death by other causes, since the victim could determine the moment of death. The executioner waits for a sign, 'a token', before striking. Ralegh is in control to the last.

One manuscript tells a different story. It makes painful reading, painting a far less heroic, a far less controlled, picture. It shows an old man wilfully shutting out the sight of his impending death, crawling around on his knees, his clothes ripped from his back by an oblivious executioner. This witness records Ralegh holding up his hands in devotion, with his eyes to heaven. He then 'kneeled down upon the Executioner's block, being spread of purpose, and, grovelling along on his arms and hands', he attempted 'to reach his neck to the block'. At the last, he pulled his nightcap over his eyes and tugged at the executioner's breeches in an effort to communicate, to give the crucial signal. The executioner was 'busied a-ripping the shirt and waistcoat with a knife, that he might more conveniently bring the axe to his neck' and did not even notice the tug, bringing the axe 'conveniently' to the neck twice, in his own time.

It is easier to read the far more widespread account of Ralegh's final seconds. Unflinching, he lies himself on the block and waits for the strike. It does not come. Has the executioner not heard? Ralegh takes command:

> 'What do you fear?'
> 'Strike, man.'

Two blows of the axe.

Ralegh did not shrink or move. It was over.

Epilogue

*His head was showed on each side, and then put
into a red leather bag; and his wrought velvet
gown cast over his body, which was after conveyed
away in a mourning coach of his Lady's.*

MUTTERING went through the multitude that a braver
spirit never died:

Every man that saw Sir Walter Ralegh die said it was impossible
for any man to show more decorum, courage, or piety; and that
his death will do more hurt to the faction that sought it, then ever
his life could have done.

The ballad writers went to work:

> My head on block is laid,
> And my last part is played
> Fortune hath me betrayed
> Sweet Jesus grant mercy.

Insiders such as Robert Tounson rushed to share their exclusive insights
into the man and their personal memories of his final moments:

I hope you had the relation of Sir Walter Ralegh's death... There be
other reports of it, but that which you have from me is true: one

Craford, who was sometimes Mr Rodeknight's pupil, hath penned it prettily, and means to put it to the press; and came to me about it, but I hear not that it is come forth.

Seasoned news gatherers such as John Chamberlain recognised this was a story that would run and run:

Your Lordship shall from diverse of your friends be advertised of the manner of Sir Walter Ralegh's death; yet being a matter of so much mark and renown, it is fit, that all tongues and pens, both good and bad should be employed about it.

Even those who had never loved Ralegh 'loved him in the catastrophe of his life'. Even the Spanish admitted he 'never faltered' on the scaffold. Those who had been so confident in September ('whatever measures your Majesty may adopt to punish him will be fully justified, and many honourable Englishmen will be very glad of it') were now worried:

The death of this man has produced great commotion and fear here, and it is looked upon as a matter of highest importance, owing to his being a person of great parts and experience, subtle, crafty, ingenious and brave enough for anything. His supporters had declared that he could never be executed.

On the scaffold at just past nine in the morning, Ralegh's 'perfect death' had ensured there was silence where one might have expected 'God Save the King'. This silence became an emblem of the trouble ahead for the Stuart monarchy; the next generation turned Sir Walter into a champion of parliamentary power, even a republican. It is no coincidence, although it is ironic given the facts of Ralegh's life in service of Queen Elizabeth, that the only secular work Oliver Cromwell recommended to his son Richard was *The History of the World.*

The Crown hit back as best it could in that winter of 1618, but it was fighting a losing battle. It sponsored the publication of a petition defending 'Judas' Stukeley on 28 November, and followed with a more substantial refutation of Ralegh's speech from the scaffold and the *Declaration of the demeanour and carriage of Sir Walter Ralegh, Knight, as well as in his voyage, as in, and since his return: and of the true motives and inducements which occasioned his Majesty to proceed in doing justice upon him as hath been done.* These publications insisted Ralegh was only ever an actor. He may have performed his parts 'most cunningly', but the fact he perceived his own death as performance was part of his innate wickedness. He invited people to his death and he lied to invite applause; his whole life was a 'mere sophistication'.

A person of great parts and experience, subtle, crafty, ingenious and brave enough for anything. A man of 'overweening wit', led 'by ambition's humour'. An example to James's subjects of 'terror...not to abuse his gracious meanings'. Surely, the *Declaration* asked, readers could see Sir Walter Ralegh was an angel of darkness, rather than an angel of light?

The jury is still undecided. Ralegh was certainly no angel but a man for whom light and dark co-existed. A man who achieved so much but never as much as he might have done. A man who lived a life less ordinary. Sir Walter Ralegh demands a response: love him or hate him, you must reckon with him.

It remains hard to be certain of anything about Ralegh, except that his contemporaries were sure they would never see his like again. Even now he is a man who, as Isaac D'Israeli wrote many years ago, continues to fill 'a space in our imagination'. That, four hundred years on, he fills a space is due, in part, to his efforts and to the efforts of those who admired, even loved, him in his time.

The tide of imperial history was also on his side for a good three hundred years or more. Even in our post-colonial era, Ralegh's name is linked with that of Virginia, with its iconic lost colony of Roanoke, the first doomed outpost of what would become the British Empire and with potatoes and tobacco, those innovations from the New World. For generations of imperialist historians until the 1920s, Ralegh's 'prophetic imagination called up a vision of England overseas which was translated by his successors into glorious reality'.

The irony, the reality, is that Ralegh never set foot in North America, that John Hawkins introduced tobacco (although Ralegh helped to popularise it) and that potatoes were already grown in Europe when Walter was a teenager. Ralegh's place in the British national memory is due to the tireless work of the propogandists of his time; men such as Richard Hakluyt, who did more than most to establish the powerful myths that would underpin the legitimacy of the British Empire in future centuries and who called Sir Walter his 'chief light into the western navigations'. Yes, Ralegh contributed more than most, in money, in will, in expertise, in propaganda, in sheer effort, to the establishment of English colonies and not only those in the new world. His experiences as soldier, sailor and courtier fed into the colonial project that would shape his nation's destiny to this day. In the end, however, every initiative with which he was involved stuttered and died.

Apologists for British colonialism in the early twentieth century were confused by these failures. On the one hand, they could be explained as Ralegh being a 'man of ideas' rather than a 'man of action'. V.T. Harlow argues that Ralegh deserves his fame because of his vision of empire, which would be taken up by others, rather than because of his achievements. David Beers Quinn is also ambivalent, admiring Ralegh's attempts to work with the native population in the Orinoco but seeing what he calls 'the Guiana episode' as a 'hastily conceived attempt to rerun the Virginia episode'. The act of rerunning is symptomatic of Ralegh's approach to life, writes Beers Quinn, perceptively. But neither historian questions the ethics or morality of the colonial project itself.

For many, the unfinished nature of so many of his endeavours tells us all we need to know about the man: he spread himself too thinly. But those who study naval exploits don't tend to analyse his parliamentary activity; those who consider his life as a courtier don't consider developments in scientific research; those who focus on the failure of the Virginia colony don't consider Ralegh's historical and political writings. A little bit of Ralegh goes a long way.

Sir Walter Ralegh lived more lives than most people of his time, of any time. Prone to periods of extreme melancholy alternating with periods of equally extreme activity, always driven, he was a liar who sometimes, it seems, believed his lies. A cultural relativist, a humanist and a deist in an era of absolutism and fundamentalism. A man who was consumed with wonder as he paddled a canoe up the Orinoco. A man who loved maps, words and silk stockings. Ralegh had a hunger for life, a longing for death, a despair for truth and a passion for words.

For me, his poetry is where the tensions in the life of the man are most visible and most enthralling. When he was young, poetry was a means by which to be recognised; having made it to court, it was one of his weapons in the struggle for dominance. Throughout, poetry was also a way for Ralegh to expose the underbelly of court life, a way to reveal – dangerously – his frustration and anger. His passion.

The (typically unfinished, fractured and beautiful) Hatfield manuscript was not a one-off. Passionate critiques of society's values and laments for what had been lost were Ralegh's trademarks as a writer; as is a strangely modern intensity and complexity, whether unconscious or conscious, that can startle even now. It is most obvious in 'Ocean's Love to Cynthia', but in all his writing there are glimpses of something unprocessed and raw, a sense of something waiting to be unleashed, something (almost) out of control.

Ralegh expresses a powerful sense of conflict in response to the world around him in *The Discovery*, a profound, searching relativism in *The History* and a barely suppressed rage against the establishment in his political tracts. For all his rhetorical sophistication, Ralegh's screaming need, thoughtfulness, intelligence, anger, wonder and vanity seep through into almost every phrase. His writing offers a conundrum. There is so much passion and energy (haste, post haste) but there is also a deep melancholy, a profound scepticism and cynicism, an abiding frustration – and yet a fascination – with the façades of life.

Ralegh puts it better than I can. Life is theatre, a 'short comedy' played after we emerge from the dressing-room ('tiring house') of the womb. The only reality is death; the 'setting sun', the grave:

> What is our life? A play of passion,
> Our mirth the music of division,
> Our mother's wombs the tiring-houses be,
> Where we are dressed for this short comedy.
> Heaven the judicious sharp spectator is,
> That sits and marks still who doth act amiss.
> Our graves that hide us from the setting sun
> Are like drawn curtains when the play is done.
> Thus march we, playing, to our latest rest,
> Only we die in earnest, that's no jest.

Ralegh was not alone in understanding that all the world's a stage, and men and women merely players. For centuries, until our own time, commentators have viewed his life through the lens of theatre. The emphasis on performance can make us lose sight of the lived reality for him and for those who loved him, not to mention the social and political legacy of his actions and beliefs, for good and for bad.

The last word goes to Bess, Lady Ralegh, in a letter written on 29 October 1618, within hours of her husband's execution. The simplicity of her words, the rawness of her emotion, is a reminder that Sir Walter Ralegh, soldier and courtier, coloniser and sailor, explorer and writer, perhaps patriot or traitor, was also a friend, father and husband. From his final, intensely public, hour on the scaffold emerged a national hero. But on the night of 29 October, there was private grief of a wife and the hope (dashed within hours) that she would be able to lay her husband to rest:

To my best brother, Sir Nicholas Carew October 29 1618. I desiar good brother that you will pleased to let my beari the worthi boddi of my nobill hosban Sur Walter Ralegh. The Lordes have geven me his ded boddi, thought they denied me his life. This nit hee shall be brought you with two or three of my men. Let me here presently. God hold me in my wites. E.R.

Sir Walter Ralegh in his own words

Sir Walter Ralegh's Discoverie of Guiana, ed. Joyce Lorimer, Ashgate
    Publishing Company for The Hakluyt Society, 2006.
The Letters of Sir Walter Ralegh, eds. Agnes Latham and Joyce Youings,
    University of Exeter Press, 1999.
The Poems of Sir Walter Ralegh: A Historical Edition, ed. Michael
    Rudick, Arizona Center for Medieval and Renaissance Studies
    in conjunction with the Renaissance English Text Society, 1999.
Ralegh's Last Voyage, ed. V.T. Harlow, Argonaut Press, 1932 (contains
    many of the documents concerning the second expedition to
    Guiana and Ralegh's execution.)

There are no modern editions of most of Ralegh's prose works, not least
the monumental *History of the World*. There is a very fine academic
study of the *History* by Nicholas Popper: *Walter Ralegh's History of the
World and the Historical Culture of the Late Renaissance*, University
of Chicago Press, 2012. In the British Library is Ralegh's notebook
for the *History of the World*, complete with beautiful hand-drawn
maps, some of which you can see here: www.bl.uk/collection-items/
sir-walter-raleighs-notebook-for-his-history-of-the-world

There is also no easily accessible-but-scholarly edition of Ralegh's
poetry, although many of his poems can be found online. The poet
Ruth Padel offers a selection, together with some poems by Ralegh's
contemporaries, including Queen Elizabeth and the Earl of Essex, in
Sir Walter Ralegh (Poet to Poet), Faber & Faber, 2010.

Works consulted

Andrews, K. *Trade, Plunder and Settlement: Maritime Enterprise and the Genesis of the British Empire*, 1480–1630, Cambridge University Press, 1984.

Armitage, C. (ed). *Literary and Visual Ralegh*, Manchester University Press, 2013.

Beer, A. *Bess: The Life of Lady Ralegh, Wife to Sir Walter*, Constable, 2004.

Beer, A. *Sir Walter Ralegh and His Readers in the Seventeenth Century: Speaking to the People*, Macmillan, 1997.

Brigden, S. *New Worlds, Lost Worlds: The Rule of the Tudors, 1485–1603*, Allen Lane, 2000.

Canny, N. *Making Ireland British: 1580–1650*, Oxford University Press, 2001.

Cooper, J. *Propaganda and the Tudor State: Political Culture in the Westcountry*, Clarendon Press, 2003.

Coward, B. (ed.) *A Companion to Stuart Britain*, Blackwell Publishing, 2002.

Croft, P. *King James*, Palgrave Macmillan, 2002.

Doran, S., and Kewes, P. (eds.) *Doubtful and Dangerous: the Question of Succession in Late Elizabethan England*, Manchester University Press, 2014.

Doran, S. *Monarchy and Matrimony: The Courtships of Elizabeth I*, Routledge, 1995.

Fischlin, D. 'Political Allegory, Absolutist Ideology, and the "Rainbow Portrait" of Queen Elizabeth I', *Renaissance Quarterly*, Vol. 50, No. 1 (Spring, 1997), pp. 175–206.

Fuller, M. *Voyages in Print: English Narratives of Travel to America 1576–1624*, Cambridge University Press, 1995.

Gajda, A. *The Earl of Essex and Late Elizabethan Political Culture*, Oxford University Press, 2012.

Greenblatt, S. *Sir Walter Ralegh: The Renaissance Man and His Roles*, Yale University Press, 1973.

Hackett, H. *Virgin Mother, Maiden Queen: Elizabeth I and the Cult of the Virgin Mary*, Macmillan, 1995.

Hammer, P. *Elizabeth's Wars: War, Government and Society in Tudor England, 1544–1604*, Palgrave Macmillan, 2003.

Hammer, P. *The Polarisation of Elizabethan Politics: The Political Career of Robert Devereux, 2nd Earl of Essex, 1585–1597*, Cambridge University Press, 1999.

Lorimer, J. 'The Location of Ralegh's Guiana Gold Mine', *Terrae Incognitae*, 14 (1982) pp.77–95.

Lorimer, J. *Untruth and Consequences: Ralegh's Discoverie of Guiana and the 'Salting' of the Gold Mine*, The Hakluyt Society, 2007.

Montrose, L. 'The Work of Gender in the Discourse of Discovery', *Representations*, 1991, pp.1–41.

Nicholls, M. 'Percy, Henry, Ninth Earl of Northumberland (1564–1632)', *Oxford Dictionary of National Biography*, Oxford University Press, 2004.

Nicholls, M., and Williams, P. *Sir Walter Raleigh: In Life and Legend*, Bloomsbury, 2011.

Oberg, M. *The Head in Edward Nugent's Hand: Roanoke's Forgotten Indians*, University of Pennsylvania Press, 2013.

Racin, J. *Sir Walter Ralegh as Historian: An Analysis of 'The History of the World'*, Salzburg: Institut für Englische Sprache und Literatur, Universität Salzburg, 1974

Reynolds, A. *In Fine Style: The Art of Tudor and Stuart Fashion*, Royal Collection Trust, 2013.

Schneider, G. *The Culture of Epistolarity: Vernacular Letters and Letter Writing in Early Modern England 1500–1700*, University of Delaware Press, 2005.

Smith, D. 'Politics in Early Stuart Britain, 1603–1640', in *A Companion to Stuart Britain*, Coward, B. (ed.), Blackwell Publishing, 2002. Blackwell Reference Online. 31 August 2017 http://www.blackwellreference.com/subscriber/tocnode.html? id=g9780631218746_chunk_g978063121874615

Strong, R. *Henry, Prince of Wales and England's Lost Renaissance*, Pimlico, 2000.

Tromly, F. 'Masks of Impersonality in Burghley's "Ten Precepts" and Ralegh's "Instructions to his Son"', *The Review of English Studies*, 66, 2015, pp.480–500.

Vaughan, A. 'Sir Walter Ralegh's Indian Interpreters, 1584–1618', *The William and Mary Quarterly*, 2002, pp.341–76.

Young, M. *King James and the History of Homosexuality*, Fonthill, 2016 (revised edition).

Younger, N. *War and Politics in the Elizabethan Counties*, Oxford University Press and Manchester Scholarship Online, 2013.

Zaller, R. *The Discourse of Legitimacy in Early Modern England*, Stanford University Press, 2007.

http://www.historyireland.com/early-modern-history-1500-1700/ some-days-two-heads-and-some-days-four/

http://www-history.mcs.st-andrews.ac.uk/Biographies/Harriot.html

Acknowledgements

Sir Walter and I go back a long way, and over the years I have incurred many debts of gratitude. The archival research upon which this book is built could not have been done without the help of numerous librarians and archivists, the insights of historians and literary critics, or the passing conversations with churchwardens, Beefeaters and dowager duchesses. I thank them all.

While it is frustrating not to be able to thank every individual who has helped me understand Ralegh's life, work and time, it is downright painful not to be able to thank Roger Harvey for his love and support over the years. That he knew, before his untimely death, I was going to write this book and that he believed that I would complete it, come what may, is small consolation. *Requiescat in pace.*

I can, however, thank my friends old and new for keeping the faith and bringing comfort and joy into my life. It is invidious to name names, but here's to you: Kathryn Basson, Sam Berman, Antonia Bruce, Gina Cowan, Katrina Crossley, Karen Elliott, Matt Harvey, Martha Maguire, Doris McAndrew, Paul Schwartfeger, Ian and Margaret Slack, Hugh Weldon and Liz Woolley.

Sam Carter has been an exemplary editor and Kirsty McLachlan a truly supportive agent. Thank you both for your expertise and kindness. I am lucky to have you. Colleagues and students on the Creative Writing MSt at Oxford University have provided proper challenge and inspiration and community in equal measure.

I dedicate this book to my big-hearted daughters Rebecca and Elise using, in this year of love and loss, words that may or may not have been written by Ralegh. I'd like to think they are his.

> But true love is a durable fire,
> In the mind ever burning,
> Never sick, never old, never dead,
> From itself never turning.

Chronology

1562	French Wars of Religion start
1564	Birth of William Shakespeare and Christopher Marlowe
	Robert Dudley is created Earl of Leicester
1565	Birth of Bess Throckmorton, future Lady Ralegh
1566	Birth of King James VI of Scotland (later James I of England)
1569	WR in France as soldier
1570	Queen Elizabeth excommunicated by the Pope
1570	Peace of St Germain
1572	St Bartholomew Massacre of Huguenots in Paris
	Birth of John Donne and Ben Jonson
	(?) WR matriculates at Oriel College, Oxford
1576	WR's first published poem
1577	WR living in Islington, Middlesex
1579	Queen Elizabeth I considering marriage to Duke of Anjou
	Rebellion in Ireland
1580	WR to Ireland (Smerwick)
1581	WR's father dies
	WR appointed to a court position
1583	WR joins Humphrey Gilbert's expedition to Newfoundland
	WR granted Durham House by Queen Elizabeth I
1584	WR receives patent for exploration of New World
1585	WR knighted
	First Roanoke settlement in Virginia
	Earl of Leicester (with step-son the Earl of Essex) leads military expedition to the Low Countries
	English intervention in Low Countries leads to conflict with Spain for rest of Elizabeth's reign
	WR appointed vice-admiral of the west, lord lieutenant of Cornwall, and Lord Warden of the Stannaries
	Earl of Essex comes to court
1586	Battle of Zutphen in Low Countries
	Death of Sir Philip Sidney
	WR receives grants of lands in England and Ireland from Queen Elizabeth

1587	Second Roanoke settlement: Virginia Dare born there
	WR nominated as future Captain of the Guard
	Earl of Essex appointed Master of the Horse
	Execution of Mary Queen of Scots
1588	Earl of Leicester dies
	Spanish Armada defeated
1589	Earl of Essex joins Drake and Hawkins expedition to Portugal, in defiance of Queen Elizabeth
	WR to Ireland. Returns to England with Edmund Spenser
	Azores ('Islands') expedition
1590	Spenser's *The Faerie Queene (Books I–III)* published
1591	WR takes up duties as Captain of the Guard
	The loss of the English ship, the *Revenge*
	WR writes *The Last Fight of the Revenge*
1592	WR called back from Panama expedition
	WR imprisoned in Tower and banished from court
	WR writes 'Ocean's Love to Cynthia'
	Birth – and death – of WR's first son, Damerei
	WR granted Sherborne by Queen Elizabeth
1593	Death of Christopher Marlowe
	Birth of WR's second son, Walter (Wat)
	WR writes tract *On the Succession*
1594	Atheism enquiry into WR
	WR's mother (born Katherine Champernowne) dies
1595	WR to Guiana
	WR writes manuscript version of *The Discovery of Guiana*
1596	Edmund Spenser writes *A View of the Present State of Ireland*
	WR publishes *The Discovery of Guiana*
	English forces attack Cadiz
	WR sends small second expedition to Guiana
	Robert Cecil becomes Secretary of State
1597	WR returns to court
1598	End of Wars of Religion in France
	Death of William Cecil, Lord Burghley

1599   Earl of Essex in Ireland
           Globe Theatre opens

1600   WR appointed Governor of Jersey
           WR becomes close to Henry Brooke, Lord Cobham

1601   Rebellion and execution of Earl of Essex

1602   WR sends Samuel Mace to Roanoke to seek lost colonists

1603   Death of Queen Elizabeth I
           Accession of King James I
           WR found guilty of treason

Index